"For many years, Christians have felt that way of life was the presumption t..... we knew what we meant when we said 'God.' Drawing on often-ignored passages in the Bible, Kandiah helps us recover how odd the God we worship as Christians turns out to be. It seems God shows up even as a Jewish peasant. Such a God can scare the hell out of us, but I guess that's the point. So read this book as a challenge to our domesticated imaginations."

Stanley Hauerwas

"Has God become as familiar and forgettable as a fridge magnet? That's the danger Krish Kandiah faces up to in this wonderfully readable and very challenging book. Bible stories come to life as Krish tells them afresh, richly illustrated with personal experience and social relevance, and in each case the living God turns up—strange, dangerous, and, like Aslan, not safe but good. Read it and be prepared, as he says, to 'replace a simplistic, domesticated, anemic, fridge-magnet understanding of God with a more fierce, awe-inspiring, and majestic God that is true to the Bible and big enough for the whole of our lives.'"

Christopher J. H. Wright, Langham Partnership

"Drawing us into a faithful and original encounter with biblical passages we usually avoid, Kandiah challenges us to recognize opportunities to meet God in unlikely places and through people we often overlook. His concern for the strangers and refugees among us is combined with his convictions about the life-changing character of Christian hospitality and the richness of the biblical witness. I strongly recommend this engaging and important book!"

Christine D. Pohl, professor of Christian ethics, Asbury Theological Seminary, author of *Making Room*

"You have no accidental people in your life. Whether family, friends, or total strangers, everyone in your story is there by the providence of God. Christians, then, should be the last people crippled by fear of unexpected people or places. This book will help equip you to love the strangers around you as Jesus does."

Russell Moore, Ethics and Religious Liberty Commission of the Southern Baptist Convention

"*God Is Stranger* will help readers better know a gospel that is truly good news. Krish Kandiah is someone with theological depth and experience living out his faith in the real world. Krish has been an encouragement to me as a friend and exemplar, and I believe he will inspire a generation of Christians to serve a God who loves each person—including the stranger."
Michael Wear, author of *Reclaiming Hope*

"*God Is Stranger* is one of those books that stays with you. Each chapter is filled with the knowledge of who our God is but also contains reminders that to know God is to learn the importance of embracing and loving who our God loves. I have found *God Is Stranger* a refreshing read of biblical reminders, but also a challenge to walk these reminders out in everyday life."
Christy Wimber, author, speaker, pastor, church planter

"In *God Is Stranger*, Krish Kandiah asks us to lean in to the passages of Scripture that challenge our perception of what it looks like when God shows up. As the global refugee crisis marches on, it is imperative for the church to embrace God's heart for the aliens, outcasts, and exiles. This is a profoundly important book for such a time as this."
Brian Fikkert, coauthor of *When Helping Hurts*

"In this xenophobic age of open vilification toward outsiders, Krish Kandiah presents us with the provocative idea that God often comes to us as a stranger. This is such an important book, reminding us that xenophobia is not only irrational, it is sinful. God's concern is for the least, the lost, and the left out, and so should ours."
Michael Frost, Morling College, Sydney

"If there's ever such a thing as a timely book, *God Is Stranger* is it. In a world and culture today where fear is the dominant currency, Krish Kandiah invites us back to the Scriptures to tell us about a God who invites his people to choose faith, hope, and love over fear. Because of who God is, the church is called to seek justice, love kindness, walk humbly, feed the poor, cloth the naked, speak up for the voiceless, welcome the refugee, embrace the orphans, fight for the rights of vulnerable, and welcome the stranger. This is an important discipleship book!"
Eugene Cho, author of *Overrated*

"My friend Krish Kandiah's new book is not only needed 'for such a time as this,' it's one that will help reshape some of our thoughts and feelings toward others and allow us to see strangers more with the eyes of God. Many thanks to Krish for this encouraging book!"

Mac Powell, singer and songwriter

"At a time when many throughout our world are increasingly fearful of refugees and others arriving as 'strangers' in their lands, this brilliant book reminds us that God himself often appears to us—as he did to many of the heroes of the Bible—in unexpected and strange ways. I highly recommend it."

Matthew Soerens, US director of church mobilization, World Relief, coauthor of *Welcoming the Stranger* and *Seeking Refuge*

"In this profound and challenging book, Krish Kandiah calls us to think again about how we view strangers, reminding us of the many times that God appears in the Bible as a stranger in such a way that turns the world upside down. Be warned, this book could seriously affect your view of yourself, the world, and God—and I highly recommend it to you!"

Paula R. Gooder, theologian in residence, Bible Society

"The God of Scripture is not always as familiar as we think. In this lively and fresh book, Krish Kandiah helps us see the strangeness of God and how this transforms how we see the strangers God has put into our lives."

Sam Allberry, Ravi Zacharias International Ministries and the Gospel Coalition

"You know those parts of the Bible you haven't highlighted? It turns out that it's those parts that can point you to a truer depiction of God that is especially helpful in complex and troubled times like today. Krish is a trustworthy and gifted expositor of those Scriptures, a travel guide pointing out both comforting and disturbing truths in these less-traveled lands of our Bibles. Ultimately, Krish points us to the wild and furious love of God, and it's stranger—yet more wonderful—than you've ever imagined."

Brian Mavis, president, America's Kids Belong

"Krish Kandiah reminds us of a simple truth with as many consequences as there are stars in the night sky: God keeps showing up where we least expect him. To know that is to live."

Mark Galli, editor in chief, *Christianity Today*

KRISH KANDIAH

GOD IS STRANGER

FINDING GOD IN UNEXPECTED PLACES

FOREWORD BY ANDY CROUCH

IVP Books

An imprint of InterVarsity Press
Downers Grove, Illinois

InterVarsity Press
P.O. Box 1400, Downers Grove, IL 60515-1426
ivpress.com
email@ivpress.com

InterVarsity Press® is the book-publishing division of InterVarsity Christian Fellowship/USA®, a
movement of students and faculty active on campus at hundreds of universities, colleges, and schools of
nursing in the United States of America, and a member movement of the International Fellowship
of Evangelical Students. For information about local and regional activities, visit intervarsity.org.

While any stories in this book are true, some names and identifying information may have been
changed to protect the privacy of individuals.

Cover design: David Fassett
Interior design: Daniel van Loon

ISBN 978-0-8308-4532-3 (print)
ISBN 978-0-8308-8706-4 (digital)

Printed in the United States of America ♾

InterVarsity Press is committed to ecological stewardship and to the conservation
of natural resources in all our operations. This book was printed using sustainably sourced paper.

Library of Congress Cataloging-in-Publication Data
A catalog record for this book is available from the Library of Congress.

P   25 24 23 22 21 20 19 18 17 16 15 14 13 12 11 10 9 8 7 6 5 4 3 2 1
Y   36 35 34 33 32 31 30 29 28 27 26 25 24 23 22 21 20 19 18 17

To God,

my family,

and other strangers

CONTENTS

FOREWORD

Andy Crouch

There is a funny thing about the Bible from its first page to its last: the more faithfully you read it, the stranger it becomes. All really careful reading of the Bible passes through the shock of *unrecognition*—the sense that things are not at all what we thought they were.

This is as true for believers as unbelievers, and—at least in my experience—as true after decades of study as on our first encounters with the text. Maybe more true. Familiarity with the Bible never leads to the slightest sense that we have fully comprehended it, let alone mastered it. Part of the reason I have become so convinced of the unique authority of Scripture is its endless surprises, its creative resistance to any easy summary, and its ability to speak to us in fresh and frequently uncomfortable ways.

In Scripture, the God who made us and calls us turns out to be so very different from what anyone expects—no matter what we expected. You can be the son rehearsing your abashed plea for servitude on the long road home only to be smothered in the prodigal father's embrace—or you can be the astonished virgins crying out, "Lord, Lord," in front of the locked door and hear the reply, "I never knew you." You can be a widow in the tiny town of Nain regaining her son from death at a word from a passing rabbi named Yeshua—or you can be Job losing his seven sons and three daughters, his questions answered in the end only by more questions flung out of a whirlwind.

This makes me wary of anyone who seems to tidy up God or God's Word too easily—but I am also wary of anyone who turns away too easily from either one. Increasingly, I find myself seeking out teachers and friends who both pursue and are pursued by God with relentless faithfulness.

Krish Kandiah is that kind of person, which is why I go out of my way to be in his presence, and when the ocean between our two countries prevents me from seeing him in person, to read what he writes. Krish has the restless energy of someone who has experienced God's powerful presence but also God's seeming absence, who is totally captivated by the goodness of God and also totally able to face the world's brokenness. Maybe most important for me, he is someone who wants not just to believe but to obey, and over and over has set out on journeys of risk and trust, wherever and to whomever they lead. I want that kind of life.

So I commend this book to you. If you are troubled, it will very likely comfort you; if you are comfortable, it will very likely trouble you. But either way, I believe it will do for you what it did for me: awaken a desire to know God even in his most distressing disguise, to serve him in this world full of strangers, and ultimately to sit down at a table and recognize that he has been walking alongside you and preparing a feast for you all along.

INTRODUCTION

As they fled the only home they had ever known, their fears grew with each step. With only the clothes on their back and little more than a scrap of hope, their world had become a dangerous and strange place. What short-lived happiness they had known as a newly married couple was a distant memory. Now this pair of refugees needed all their energy for survival on the run. Ahead of them lay hostilities they could not imagine.

Like so many migrants, nights spent in makeshift shelters, a daily struggle for food, and potential for disaster at every turn became part of their everyday lives. This went on for years. Their children were born amid violence, fear, and corruption. And although they found safe haven for a number of years, one of their sons would be murdered and another disappeared. This family's experience was far from the only tragedy at that time. There were mass drownings, child abuse, people trafficking, gang rape, attacks that wiped out entire cities. So much devastation and so little reason for it. The world watched on as news of their plight spread—abandoned babies, bereaved women, distraught men, child soldiers, and public executions—and the horror showed no sign of letting up.

At one border crossing some of the family's distant relations fled for their lives, the parents clutching hard to their little boy, while behind them toddlers were killed in their sleep. Though this particular lad would escape death as a child, it would catch up with him as a young adult, and images from his brutal execution at the hands of a barbaric military regime would go viral throughout the world. There was surely no hope left now, as another couple packed up their things to leave the city.

This sounds like another tragic tale emerging from the ashes of modern-day Syria or Afghanistan as civil war and terrorism wreak havoc and misery. But this is not that story. This one could be even more disturbing. It is from a book that has been banned in more countries than any other. A stranger book you will not find. This is the story of the God-initiated global refugee crisis. Perhaps you know it. It is called the Bible.

Perhaps all that does not sound like the Bible you know. It is certainly a bit different from the one I remember being taught about. I was seven years old when I first began reading the Bible. A friend of my mother's generously gave me a copy with a black hardback cover, tiny writing, and red dye along the edges of its pages. It was my prize possession at the time, but I remember feeling more than a little overwhelmed, imagining it would take a lifetime to read. My Sunday school teachers took pity on me and taught and summarized the story of the Bible in terms that I have subsequently heard countless times. The story of God embarking on a rescue operation to put the world he had created right, a story full of people who trusted God and lived happily ever after. It is a story full of heroes and giants and miracles and angels and cities made of gold. It is a beautiful story, full of treasured verses that promise comfort and inspire peace and faith. A story that centers around the amazing life, death, and resurrection of Jesus, who offers to be our personal friend, Savior, and a brother like no other, and whom we look forward to meeting face-to-face in heaven. These two ways of recounting the big story of the Bible couldn't sound more different. Yet that first retelling with all that death and destruction is right there in Scripture. Strange but true. Most of us, probably without even thinking about it, take an either-or approach to these different ways of coming at the Bible. And for the vast majority of Christians I know the simpler, happier, apparently more inspirational story wins hands down. It works better in our songs, and on our fridge magnets and greetings cards. After all, who wants to receive a Christmas card with an infant massacre depicted on the front? Or sing songs about dismembered concubines and young men mauled by bears? The darker, stranger stories of the Bible are awkward at best, and seriously troubling at worst.

Many of us may feel that, frankly, this dark side of the Bible is too embarrassing to be let out in public. And so we sanitize our picture of God with a makeover that depicts him suitably at home among images of doves, rainbows, and laughing children.

But the wholly uplifting version of the Bible is actually pretty hard to pick out. As a seven-year-old, I was given help to spot it in the form of a brand-new chisel-tipped fluorescent orange highlighter pen. Every time I went to church, or in later years when I attended youth group or a conference, the speakers would point out to me the encouraging parts of the Bible worthy of a highlight. Decades went by in which I only really read, studied, preached, and meditated on those oranged-up sections. Less than 10 percent of my Bible qualified for being made fluorescent, but it seemed to be enough to cover most occasions from weddings to funerals, from daily devotions to addressing large conferences. Nobody noticed, or even questioned, the fact that I had never once in my life preached on a psalm where David calls down curses on his enemies, or that chapter in Ezekiel where

God likens himself to a vindictive cuckolded husband. Perhaps nobody noticed because all the other Christians were similarly well versed when it came to highlighting the bright and beautiful story of the Bible we all knew and loved—and ignoring the rest.

Sometimes, though, while flicking through our favorite inspirational passages, we trip over one of those less familiar chapters. Standing there in stark black-and-white script, perhaps it raises a question or two, ignites a worry or three. Once I was so engrossed reading to my family about Daniel getting thrown into the lions' den for praying in public that I forgot to stop at the part when he gets rescued. I accidentally read on and told them how the story continues with the conniving chief ministers being fed to the hungry lions—along with their wives and children.

Once I received a card from a friend who miswrote a Bible reference. Instead of finding the encouragement that God is merciful to me as one of his own (1 Peter 2:10), I came face-to-face with the uncomfortable declaration that God will punish those who follow the corrupt desire of the flesh (2 Peter 2:10). Whether we are just beginning to familiarize ourselves with the Bible, or are intent on reading it through from cover to cover, it takes a superhuman effort to completely avoid the awkward parts.

The issue that highlighted to me the need to rediscover the unhighlighted parts of my Bible was the refugee crisis. Watching the news reports, I was reminded of something I had read somewhere, but I couldn't put my finger on quite where. Then I visited Lebanon.

A refugee family warmly welcomed me into their home. At first sight it was little more than a few wooden posts with plastic sheeting stapled onto them and a threadbare strip of carpet on the cement floor. The family were from Aleppo in Syria, and what few belongings I could see around the home were all they had managed to carry away with them after they were forced to flee. A bomb had exploded in the bakery near their home. They were worse than poor: they were deep in debt, because they'd had to borrow money from loan sharks to pay for a lifesaving operation for their young son. With the mother heavily pregnant, I could not imagine how this family was going to survive the coming winter.

I frantically searched my Bible for some encouraging words to bless them with, but my favorite orange-highlighted verses seemed rather hollow. I flicked past "I have come that they may have life, and have it to the full" (John 10:10), and "My yoke is easy and my burden is light" (Matthew 11:30). Although these promises were no less true, they suddenly seemed insufficient. Where could I find anything in the Bible that could speak to someone in the middle of such a terrible situation?

What I couldn't get out of my head as I stayed with this family as winter approached was the picture of Joseph and pregnant Mary, about to have her first baby in a shack, far from home, with only the belongings they could carry while a corrupt king made plots that would see children die and families become refugees. The words "Merry Christmas" could not have felt less appropriate.

When I returned home to my safe, semidetached, centrally heated, digitally connected house in the UK, I could not shake this idea from my mind. It was not that the treasured Bible verses I had grown up loving so fondly were untrue; it was just that the rest of the Bible suddenly seemed a lot more relevant. Not just for a family in fragile circumstances, fleeing ISIS and the bombing campaign of President Assad, but also for the rest of the world, faced with these strange and terrible times.

It was time for me to rediscover the stranger parts of my Bible. The parts lurking between the highlighted sections. The black-

and-white verses. The angry parts. The eccentric parts. The politically incorrect parts. The forgotten parts. The horrific stories of executions, displacement, genocide, and depression—stories that sadly reflect much of the world today. Although I had always believed them to be just as inspired as the safe, cozy parts of Scripture, I had been inclined to avoid them for the same reason I often turn the television off when I hear the words "Viewers may find some scenes distressing." Some truths had seemed unnecessary to dwell on, just too disturbing for my otherwise peaceful, comfortable life. But now it was time to face up to them.

It was time to look at what I had long considered to be the "lowlights" of the Bible. And as I read those passages, it turned out that I had indeed been missing something—that it was precisely in these places that God turned up, although often unannounced, uninvited, and unrecognized. Suddenly I came across countless passages that talked about God being unpredictable, unfathomable, uncontainable, untameable. He is ineffable, sublime, mysterious, awesome. He is beyond compare and beyond description and beyond analogy. God tells us quite clearly, "My thoughts are not your thoughts, neither are your ways my ways" (Isaiah 55:8). Had I been so keen to know God my Father, Lord, Friend, and Savior that I had missed the Bible's consistent teaching that God is also other, higher, stranger?

As I explored the more difficult passages of Scripture, I discovered an unlikely narrative arc flowing through the whole one that challenged me, that undid some of my most cherished prejudices and made me question the parts of the Bible I thought I knew so well. This narrative that spans the centuries and crosses continents contains a thread of deliberate strangeness. It is full of misery but also full of mystery, packed with the weird but also somehow weirdly wonderful. Through the more perplexing, stranger stories and more difficult incidents related in the Bible, I discovered a God who cannot be fully pinned down, explained, or predicted. Traveling the inhospitable terrain of much of the Old Testament, I discovered there was much to learn about the hospitality of God. In the more fearsome passages, where God turns up as a stranger, I began to hear his offer of an opportunity too good to turn down.

When Adam and Eve hid in fear of the consequences of their disobedience, for example, God turned up not as a friend, but like a stranger they hardly knew, cursing them and banishing them from their home. When Abraham and Sarah feared they would never have a child, God visited them in the form of three strangers and, in a curious postscript, destroyed a city. When Jacob was afraid of his brother, God turned up in disguise to fight him, leaving him permanently injured. When Gideon was in hiding, afraid of his own shadow, God turned up to this anonymous no one to persuade him to lead his people into battle. When Isaiah was fearful for the state of his nation, God turned up in a blaze of glory to give him a message that nobody would listen to. When Ezekiel was afraid he was far away from a place where he could worship God, God turned up with wings and wheels—and followed up with all sorts of weird demands. When bereaved Naomi was fearful for her future, the one thing she could not see was God at work. When Mary was afraid that she would be rejected, God turned up in a way nobody expected. When Cleopas was afraid that all hope was lost, God turned up as a stranger and turned his world upside down.

In all these people's stories, what seemed fearful turned out to be the greatest opportunity of their lives. They didn't get easy victories over their circumstances, but they did get to be part of something bigger that God was doing. Somehow, it was as they encountered God in the form of a stranger that God drew close to these unlikely people, and in the most unexpected ways. It seems that when God turns up unannounced, uninvited, and unrecognized, that is precisely when something truly revolutionary is about to kick off.

What are our biggest fears? Do we fear the future? Do we fear the past? Do we fear failure? Do we fear we will miss out on some important opportunity? Do we fear losing out in life? Do we fear standing out? Or being caught out? Being thrown out? When life hits hard, when the familiar promises of the Bible become hollow, perhaps it is time to step out of our biblical comfort zone and glean some truths from the stranger, less familiar Bible stories— stories that we may find surprisingly relevant.

Or perhaps we are afraid of what we might find. What if we tell everyone we know God, but secretly suspect that we don't or we can't? And what if God is supposed to be mysterious? What if trying to wrestle with who God is, not just blindly accepting what we've been taught, is exactly what our minds were made for? What if it is this pursuit of an unexpected God, a difficult faith, that makes our brain cells fire into life? What if our minds are like a teacup and the knowledge of God is like the unending, unfathomable volume of water roaring over Niagara Falls? What if the very act of wrestling to know an uncontainable God like this is vital for the lives we have to live in a complex, tragic, and mysterious world?

If so, why is it that we are so often discouraged from even admitting there is a gulf or a rift between us and God? We sing, preach, witness, and pray about how amazing it is to have a relationship with God, all the while papering over the cracks of estrangement, fearful to admit our doubts and worries. We try to make life work around the tensions and distance that necessarily come from trying to relate to a God who is above and beyond anything we could even imagine. But, as a couple engaging with marriage counselors may discover, confronting rather than concealing our problems, far from causing new rifts, may bring a richer and stronger relationship. Finding out that God is a stranger does not have to be an admission of defeat, but may rather instigate an attitude of curiosity that could be the start of an adventure. Whoever we are, there is always so much more still to experience of the mystery and enigma of God. This discovery is not an excuse to avoid God. It is an invitation to discover God. As American author and journalist Dennis Covington once said, "Mystery is not the absence of meaning, but the presence of more meaning than we can comprehend."[1]

We may well be afraid of what will happen next, but as finding a maggot in your apple is a lot better than finding half a maggot in your apple, so it may be better to find out that God is a stranger to us now, rather than when it is too late. Jesus did not flinch from challenging his followers whether God might declare himself a perfect stranger to them at the end of time:

> Many will say to me on that day, "Lord, Lord, did we not prophesy in your name and in your name drive out demons and in your name perform many miracles?" Then I will tell them plainly, "I never knew you. Away from me, you evildoers!" (Matthew 7:22-23)

This is surely one of the most frightening verses in our Bible. Is Jesus really suggesting that even those of us who follow him, serve him, and minister for him could end up excluded from heaven? I would love to perform miracles, exorcisms, and prophecy as these devout believers had done. But if they, for all their worship and ministry credentials, end up being told they never knew God at all, what hope is there for the rest of us? Many Christians struggle with an underlying fear that we too may end up excluded from God's kingdom at the end of time. We long for assurance of our salvation, a guarantee of our inheritance, but instead—or as a result, perhaps—our relationship with God is marked with doubt, fear, and insecurity. We will take a closer look at these words in chapter ten, but being aware of this unusual reversal of "stranger danger" will help us. Again, our biggest fear may turn out to be our greatest opportunity.

As we take a look through the Bible, deliberately pausing at some of the places in Scripture where God chooses to turn up unrecognized, we may well need to face our fears. We may need to reboot our idea of who God is and reconnect with his magnificence. We may find that we can replace a simplistic, domesticated, anemic, fridge-magnet understanding of God with a more fierce, awe-inspiring, and majestic God that is true to the Bible and big enough for the whole of our lives. It may not be a comfortable journey, but it should help us to have confidence that the God we follow is the real full-blooded God, powerful, merciful, majestic, and strange.

We may also find that we need to reclaim those forgotten, inhospitable parts of the Bible that are so much more relevant than the church has been able to give them credit for. Too much of the Bible is a no-go area for Christians—the texts are considered too toxic, too hard for us to understand. My aim is not to explain away the difficult bits but to allow us to feel the force of them, to catch the breath of God in them, to have our eyes dazzled and our hearts ignited by these dangerous parts of Scripture.

As we look at these unhighlighted texts, we may discover not just the God we have missed but a whole other exciting but challenging dimension to our lives of faith. As we explore the hidden parts of God's Word, I pray that we will be captivated by God's hidden purposes for us and discover that the opportunity to change our world is not so far removed or out of reach as we might imagine.

We have quite a journey ahead of us. If we are willing, I pray that it will challenge and change us. As we set out, let us be inspired by some of Paul's words. He was the one who simultaneously recognized and didn't recognize God when he turned up on a dusty road in the middle of nowhere. In great fear, Paul blurted out the paradoxical question that is the essence of what we are considering in this book: "Who are you, Lord?" Encountering and recognizing a divine stranger turned Paul's world upside down. His hunt-and-destroy mission, executing Christians wherever he could find them, turned into a search-and-rescue mission, encouraging and making Christians wherever he could find them. His moment of abject fear gave him the opportunity to know and serve the God he had been persecuting.

Paul met Jesus personally and was inspired by God to teach theology to the world, in the end penning the majority of the New Testament. But at the climax of his most exhaustive theological treatise—the book of Romans—Paul provides not a series of convincing answers, but a series of irresistible questions. He effectively asks once again, "Who are you, Lord?" by declaring both what he does know about God and what he doesn't. Paul proclaims the God he loves to be a stranger—not in a dejected admission of defeat or a confession of confusion, but in an enthusiastic hymn of praise.

> Oh, the depth of the riches of the wisdom and knowledge
>   of God!
> How unsearchable his judgments,
>   and his paths beyond tracing out!
> "Who has known the mind of the Lord?
>   Or who has been his counselor?"
> "Who has ever given to God,
>   that God should repay them?"
> For from him and through him and for him are all things.
>   To him be the glory forever! Amen. (Romans 11:33-36)

This is our destination of mystery. As we travel together, we may find ourselves, like Paul, surprised by fresh encounters with God—filled, perhaps, with more questions than we started out with, but more importantly with overflowing wonder and praise for our mysterious, strangely present God.

ADAM AND THE STRANGER

The God who turns up only to drive us away

In which a naked man hides from a forbidding stranger
who throws him out of his home, and we ask why
friendship with God seems to be so impossible.

Sometimes the people we think we know the best turn out to be the ones we know the least. Recently I was shocked to hear the story of a young woman in my town. She was happily married to a commercial pilot. His shifts meant that most weeks he would be away from her and their young children a couple of nights at a time. But it was manageable. Then the opportunity came up for him to embark on further training that would boost his chances of getting more regular work, closer to home. Eventually they decided to go for it. It was a huge investment, but they reasoned it would benefit them all in the long run. They remortgaged the house, and he left for a couple of months, bound for Canada where he would take the course. One day she got a phone call. Her husband had been injured in an accident and was in the hospital. It was all going to be all right, the stranger on the phone told her, but his medical insurance had lapsed and so they needed her to wire money across to cover the bills. She took the details, but after the call ended she felt uncomfortable: something felt wrong. She checked the incoming number and discovered it was from Italy. What was going on? It felt like a scam.

Over the next few days she uncovered more details, but as she gradually pieced together the story, it was her husband who was the trickster. He had never intended to further his flying career. Instead he had taken their hard-earned money and used it to fund a whole secret other life. Another relationship. Another family. Suddenly the young woman found herself deserted. She and her children lost their home. What would become of them?

When she first told me the story, I struggled to believe her. It sounded like a plot for a novel written solely to be optioned by a Hollywood studio. But sometimes the truth is stranger than fiction; it is certainly more tragic. It is hard to imagine the betrayal this woman experienced. The person she thought she knew the best in the world, her closest friend and confidant, was actually a stranger to her. Their history together, their future together, everything she thought she could rely on, was blown out of the sky. His manipulating lies enabled him to live a double life, while she lost the only life she knew. Perhaps you know the pain of broken promises, betrayal, and abandonment. Perhaps you have been left high and dry to pick up the pieces in a world that suddenly looks very different. Or perhaps your biggest fear is finding out you have been betrayed by the ones you trusted the most. How would you cope if your nearest and dearest turned out to be strangers? At least God is there for us, even if everyone else fails us.

Right? God, the same yesterday, today, and forever, can be totally relied upon. He is that friend who sticks closer than a brother. He is our rock, our rampart, our refuge. He who loves us unconditionally will never leave us or forsake us. These are timeless, biblical truths that have helped countless Christians through the centuries. They are the promises we cling to when life takes unexpected turns.

But what if we have misjudged our relationship with God too? What if he doesn't seem to come through on those promises? What if he is not the friend we thought he was? What if the one being in the universe we have been told is utterly reliable actually turns out to be a stranger too?

I clearly remember the day I first decided to "make Jesus my friend." For several months my Sunday school teacher had made a persuasive case as to the immediate and eternal benefits of such a decision. So one Sunday morning, after the sermon, I made my way nervously up to the front of the building. It was a Salvation Army church a stone's throw from my home, and at the front of the hall was a polished dark wood bench into which were carved the words "Jesus Saves." I knelt down in front of it, and a dear elderly woman, dressed in the black Salvationist uniform, complete with bonnet and shiny black shoes, knelt alongside me and put her arm around me. She explained to me that Jesus would be the best friend I could ever hope for, because he had laid down his life for me. I sensed a ring of truth in what she was saying. Over the previous months I had received a warm welcome from this strange new community, even though, as the son of immigrants from different religious backgrounds, I stuck out like a sore brown thumb. The offer of a life-changing friendship with God sounded very attractive to a boy who felt socially isolated because of his skin color—and his annoying habit of asking too many questions.

Right from the outset of my newfound faith I had questions about what it meant for God to be a friend to me, and as I have grown up they have not entirely gone away, despite decades in full-time paid Christian ministry and the world of theological education. These questions keep coming up. Do I really know God? Does God really know me? To what extent is Jesus my friend? Is that expectation of mutual trust, support, and affection realistic? Why do I often feel so distant from God? Why does God often fail to turn up when I ask him to, and then turn up when I don't need him, often only to complicate things further? In my experience the nice and easy Sunday school idea of relationship with God does not work in the real world. It accounts neither for the complexity of the world nor, critically, for the complexity of God. And so our relationship with God can easily swing toward a desperate hope that it is all true or an obstinate determination to hold on come what may—a disgruntled resignation that this is not what we expected it to be. We can easily end up with a halfhearted faith in a God we only half believe in. We struggle to share this sort of faith with our friends and neighbors. We struggle to hold on to this sort of faith in difficult times. We struggle to rely on this sort of faith as we face the future. Despite the words of that godly elderly lady in that life-changing moment for me as a child, I have learned over the years that we can be profoundly mistaken about the God we claim to have a friendship with. And we can be profoundly confused about the nature of that friendship.

Last week my aunt was happy to sing the praises of the God who had been a trusted friend to her. This week she sits in a nursing home having lost her husband, her health, and her home within the course of a few days. Who could blame her for being angry that a lifetime of friendship with God has now turned out this way? I also spoke with a lady who stuck with God through the terrible years of young widowhood and then multiple sclerosis. But now she will not come to church any longer because of the atrocities of ISIS. She is ashamed of the way God seems to turn his back while terrible acts are committed in his name. As I listen to their accusations, I too wonder again why the God who is supposed to be our friend often feels quite the opposite—an enemy, or at least a stranger. Who is this God, who has the power of creation yet seems to be either powerless or uncaring when disaster strikes? Who is this God, who lets human beings wreak such destruction against each other? Who is this God, whose friendship seems so uncertain?

In some respects, it is no surprise that we struggle with the idea of friendship with God. His invisibility and intangibility are always going to be difficult for us, especially compared with the immediate presence of people around us. The instant gratification of an encouraging word, a warm welcome, or an affirming embrace can appear so much more real and meaningful. Or, in the absence of God's felt and seen presence, we can be in danger of refashioning God into a sophisticated form of imaginary friend. Just like a child's relationship with their self-generated illusory companion, we may end up substituting a friendlier, more manageable god, who asks very little of us, for the real and mighty God. When we are tempted to abandon friendship with God in favor of friendship with others, or when we are tempted to substitute friendship with an echo-chamber god who only speaks the words we give him, we are effectively acknowledging that the invisible God is a stranger to us.

The unpredictability of God is far more of a challenge to our friendship with him, though. An invisible God we can manipulate and misrepresent without obvious consequences. But when God actually turns up, when we see him in his true colors, he often appears to treat his friends pretty badly. In Scripture, Abraham and Sarah were summoned away from the safety and security of their homeland, then told to sacrifice their only son. When God turned up in Moses' life, he was driven away from the home he had made for himself in Midian and sent back to face the wrath of Pharaoh. Job was stripped of his wealth, health, and even his family because of a divine wager that God made with the devil. The list goes on. Jesus even admitted to sending his friends out "like sheep among wolves" (Matthew 10:16), more or less promising them persecution and pain. This pattern of behavior is a frightening one. The repeated occurrences in Scripture that seem to show God doing his best to drive his own people away could lead us to conclude that if God treats his friends like this, who needs enemies?

Perhaps more significantly even than God's invisibility and unpredictability, it is God's sheer incomprehensibility that makes friendship with him so difficult. God is just not like us. "'My thoughts are not your thoughts, neither are your ways my ways,' declares the LORD" (Isaiah 55:8). There is a bigger gap between us and God than there is between a human being and a bacterium. God is the Creator—we are the created. God is infinite—we are finite. God is spirit—we are embodied. God is eternal—we are temporal. It is no wonder that we face "crosscultural" communication issues, because God is simply a different order of being to us. When he graciously condescends to relate to us, it is not surprising that we find he is from a strange place, with a strange language and a strange way of doing things. He appears foreign, mysterious, and incomprehensible. And it is tempting to behave like the boorish tourist who shouts at the locals, complaining that they are backward and ignorant because they don't do things "our way," while he himself makes no attempt to understand and appreciate the host culture. So how should we, as guests in God's universe, make sense of a God who does not do things in the way we want or expect? How can a friendship be forged over such a great divide?

This hat trick of challenges makes the practical outworking of friendship with God, which seems so simple when we come to faith as a child, or when we introduce young children to faith, incredibly complex in actuality. Yes, we need to recapture the true meaning of friendship with God, but we also need to recognize and appreciate its limitations. God can be a friend to us, but he is also a stranger to us—and this is both bad news and good news. To start our exploration of these rich and vital themes, we need look no further than the strange first pages of the Bible. In its introductory chapters we are given an explanation of the sense of estrangement we feel from God and the world we live in. However familiar we may be with these chapters, the more we understand of them, the less we will see God as familiar and known, and the more we will see him as a stranger. The opening passages of Scripture offer us the origin story of the cosmos itself, so that we might be better able to discern our place in the universe.[1] Like the establishing shot of a movie that helps us to understand the context in which the ensuing drama will take place, in Genesis we are first presented with the backdrop of human history, with the creation of galaxies and stars, against which we quickly zoom in on the key theme—the interaction between God and humankind. The story starts so promisingly, yet within a couple of pages God is driving his people out of their home. Whichever way we interpret the opening chapters of Genesis, whether as historical narrative or as metaphorical parable, there is no doubt that they graphically portray something of the limitations of divine-human relationship.

The first humans begin by being utterly aware of God. Adam and Eve get to see God—visibly and with predictable regularity, it seems—as they walk with him in their perfect garden in the cool of the day. The designer world they lived in was in perfect sync with both human aspiration and divine purpose. A world with God present was all they knew, and friendship with God came naturally to them. Our ancient ancestors began their existence untroubled by the incomprehensibility of God we may struggle with, as he made himself accessible and available to human interaction.

It is hard not to be jealous of Adam and Eve. The privileges they enjoyed are what most of us long for in our relationship with God. They lived out the profound paradox of being both the dust of the earth and the image of God: humbly and yet wonderfully made, imbued with glory and knowing unspeakably great privilege, yet with no embarrassment, nor any need to prove themselves. Those first humans knew the honor of a face-to-face relationship with God himself. They knew the pitch and timbre of the very voice of their Creator. They were given clear direction from God as to how to invest their time and energy. They inhabited an environment that reflected God's glory in all its splendor. They had every good thing they could ever ask for. They enjoyed God's provision, sensed no shame or fear, and felt at home in God's company. God was no stranger to that first family.

Then, one day, the one fruit that was off-limits became the one fruit they had to have on the menu. A moment of weakness led to a bad decision. That was when God turned up to turn them out.

So the LORD God said to the serpent, "Because you have done this,

Cursed are you above all livestock
and all wild animals!
You will crawl on your belly
and you will eat dust
all the days of your life.
And I will put enmity
between you and the woman,
and between your offspring and hers;
he will crush your head,
and you will strike his heel."

To the woman he said,

"I will make your pains in childbearing very severe;
with painful labor you will give birth to children.
Your desire will be for your husband,
and he will rule over you."

To Adam he said, "Because you listened to your wife and ate fruit from the tree about which I commanded you, 'You must not eat from it,'

Cursed is the ground because of you;
through painful toil you will eat food from it
all the days of your life.
It will produce thorns and thistles for you,
and you will eat the plants of the field.
By the sweat of your brow

> you will eat your food
> until you return to the ground,
>   since from it you were taken;
> for dust you are
>   and to dust you will return." (Genesis 3:14-19)

This may well be a familiar passage, and yet it is surely one of the strangest in the Bible. What on earth is going on here? Why is there an evil snake in a perfect garden in the first place? And did animals really talk in Eden? Was there an anatomical change in the snake after human sin? How come the snake had legs to lose (or however it was getting around before it crawled on its belly), and how come it lost only them, while humans seemed to lose so much more—their home, their pain-free labor, their problem-free marriages, their weed-free gardens, their immortal bodies?

Of all the strange elements in this story, though, the thing that strikes me as strangest is the scale of God's reaction to the offense. The eating of the forbidden fruit seems such an inconsequential action compared with all that we see going on in the rest of Scripture and, for that matter, in the world right now. I can see that perhaps it warranted some kind of punishment, perhaps a skin rash, or an upset stomach. But here, plucking a fruit and consuming it was the act that did not just disrupt the perfect friendship and face-to-face intimacy Adam and Eve enjoyed with God, but also consigned humanity to mortality, pain, and conflict for the rest of history. It makes life from here onward a continual fight with the weeds to eke out a living where for many people on the planet, it would seem, the thorns always win. All this just for eating the wrong fruit?

Why is God's reaction so severe? Could he not have overlooked this one-off incident? Or instigated a "five-second rule" and quickly allowed them to eat of the Tree of Life? Perhaps a cooling-off period should have preceded judgment. Maybe God could have rebooted everything and returned creation to "factory settings," or remedied the glitch by means of an update? Instead, for their error of judgment, God enacts judgment of the severest kind, choosing to punish the whole of humanity by exile, making Adam and Eve homeless and effectively estranging everybody, everywhere from himself. This seems to be a gross, even malicious, overreaction to a minor infringement, one that makes us question God's very character.

Whether we read the opening chapters of Genesis as history or poetry, or even poetic history, we have to wrestle with the fact that Scripture depicts God here as one who creates the first refugees and curses them with hardship, conflict, weeds, labor pains, exile, and the promise of death itself. Why was humanity's rejection of God's command in taking the fruit, eating it, and then lying to cover their tracks so extreme that God intervened with the most severe punishment the world has ever seen? Why does the Creator God who has benevolently given human beings life, liberty, and everything they could ever need now reveal himself as a God of curses, who brings down judgment on all creation?

How can we find some context for this? There can be no doubt that eating the fruit was a kind of theft. God had given humanity freedom to eat from all the trees of the garden except this one. This one belonged to God alone, and human beings had no right to eat of it. This was explained to them clearly, at the same time that they were given the Garden of Eden containing everything they could ever want and more. They did not lack food that was both beautiful and tasty, but of course, as many of us can appreciate, they wanted the very thing they could not have. And so they took it.

God had created a wonderful planet to explore. He had hidden gold and onyx for our discovery, brought animals to the humans to name as part of the scientific enterprise, and offered his own face-to-face friendship, but none of that was good enough—the humans wanted more. Eating the fruit was a demonstration of dissatisfaction with and ingratitude for God's provision.

In fact, it could be seen as a betrayal. Take the young mother with her cheating husband. Her pilot partner had more than most people dream of: a good job, a lovely wife, a young family, a nice place to live, safety, and security; but that wasn't enough, so he took more. Through deception and betrayal, he took the precious family savings to spend on his own desires, breaking the trust on which those relationships were founded. It is natural and right for us to sympathize with the wife in this story. But just like the first human beings that Genesis describes here, we may be closer to the cheating husband in our natural reactions against God. Despite all God has given us, we all too often want more, too readily betraying our relationship with God for something we see as a better life.

This betrayal is on a different level to that of the pilot. We can all understand something of the temptation of a secret second life by the Mediterranean Sea. But to exchange devotion to the magnificent Creator God in order to follow the advice of some kind of puny snake creature is shocking. Put like that, it was clearly a substitution of something significantly inferior for the good things they knew.

Indeed, perhaps we might say it was more like a revolution. Instead of obeying God by ruling over creation as he'd asked them to, Adam and Eve obeyed the creation itself, overruling God's boundaries and putting his wishes at the bottom of their priorities. This turned the order of the universe upside down.

Then God turns up. Why could he not have turned up earlier and in a different mood? Why did he not intervene before the snake reared its ugly head? Or at least before Eve put the fruit to her lips? He must have known what was about to happen. Had he turned up earlier, he could have prevented all the heartache that was to follow. But no: God turns up after the crime, after the act of rebellion, after the onset of the terrible guilt that forced Adam and Eve into hiding. They really did not want God to turn up at all. They knew what they had done would wreck their friendship with him beyond measure. God was not overreacting to some trivial infraction; they did not know what to expect, but they knew enough to fear it.

In fact, God's reaction, though severe, was restrained. When God turns up to meet Adam and Eve, he does not kill them, but he does curse them. He does not execute them, but he does exile them. Human greed, human betrayal, and human rebellion are met with divine displeasure, divine judgment, and divine expulsion. But why choose this particular punishment of displacement, alienation, and estrangement? Especially since none of the day's events had caught God by surprise. He who sees the "end from the beginning" (Isaiah 46:10) knew before the creation of the world that this would happen, and as we learn in John's Gospel, had already chosen Jesus to be "the Lamb of God, who takes away the sin of the world" (John 1:29).

If this human betrayal was divinely foreseen, and somehow God made us as we are, all the while knowing we would rebel against him, knowing he would need to sacrifice his only Son to put it all right, why did he go ahead and do it anyway? What kind of strange logic is this? Why create a situation that is going to incur such a huge cost to fix? We will return to some of these questions later in the book, but for now we have to recognize that because of what happened that day in the Garden of Eden, we all begin life in this default position, suffering the consequences of this primal wound, cursed with estrangement from the God who made us and claims to seek our friendship.

※※※

The displacement of humanity in Genesis takes four distinct yet linked forms. First, Adam and Eve are displaced from the Garden of Eden, their home. Ironically, the God who wrote into the fabric of the universe the essential dignity of all human persons is the same God who creates the indignity of the first exiles. This is an archetype of much that follows throughout Scripture. Time and again, when God's people rebel against him, they are displaced and become strangers in a strange land. In the Old Testament the Canaanites' wanton rebellion toward God is the rationale given for removing them from the Promised Land in the time of Joshua.[2] Then, for their own unfaithfulness, the Jews are driven out of the Promised Land, first from the Northern Kingdom, by the Assyrians, and later from Judah, the Southern Kingdom, by the Babylonians (2 Kings 17:16-20). Throughout the Old Testament there is a strong connection between geography and theology, and it begins here, outside Eden.

This theme of displacement will confront us time and again as we thread our way through the stories where people encounter God as stranger in the course of this book. We will be forced to wrestle with the frightening question of how we love a God who not only allows the refugee crises today but who made refugees of the whole of humanity, so that we are all "strangers in a strange land," estranged from our Creator God. Fundamentally, we are all refugees from Eden, living in temporary accommodation on a planet that has been ravaged by the consequences of human sin. No amount of relocation, no degree of settling in to the place where we are, will remove our intrinsic home-sickness for that perfect place we have lost, where friendship with God comes naturally.

Adam and Eve had a premonition of this displacement even before they were expelled from Eden. As soon as they had eaten the fruit, they felt out of place in the garden, searching out somewhere to hide, no longer free to enjoy what had been their home. Their place of safety had become a place of danger. They knew this even before God cursed them and cast them out.

Imagine that my daughter, having been clearly told not to jump off the roof of our shed, does so anyway and breaks her leg. After the proper medical attention has been given, I sit her down for a talk. I explain to her that because she ignored my instructions, her leg is broken and she is not able to swim, compete in sports, play on the trampoline, or walk the dog for at least six weeks. My pronouncement is not a punishment, but rather a clarification of the consequences of her bad decision. It is not because I am vindictive that I explain this to her, but because I want to help her to accept the limitations caused by her disobedience. This is how I understand God in this chapter as he curses Adam and Eve and then expels them from Eden. God turned up not to cruelly punish them, but to help them come to terms with the extent of the inevitable consequence of their actions.

Second, as well as geographical displacement, there was also relational displacement. Like an extreme version of TV's *The Apprentice*, a boardroom fight breaks out, and the erstwhile partners in crime become staunchly independent in mutual con-frontation; Adam blames Eve, Eve blames the snake, and the snake has no one left to blame. This blame casting uncovers a fundamental disintegration of relationships. This point right here is ground zero for all human conflict. God spells out how their bad decision is going to impact all their relationships. The gender wars begin here as God's curse includes the tension between desiring and dominating. Interdependence is marred with interpersonal conflict, war, injustice, prejudice, turmoil, and betrayal. Xenophobia, literally "fear of the stranger," begins here when the very first human relationship breaks down and makes space for all sorts of relational tensions, from body-shaming to blame-shifting to boundary-building.

A third dislocation is within ourselves: internal alienation as personal shame and fear spoil the sense of fulfillment and contentment our first ancestors had previously known. Their sense of self is immediately perverted, and we see the damage to their self-image and the seeds of emotional and psychological breakdown. Adam and Eve, strangers to themselves as well as each other, have a sudden realization of nakedness and an instinct to hide when God comes calling. They hide from God, they hide their bodies from each other, and in denial they hide from themselves. Fear and shame begin before God's arrival to curse them, filtering down through humanity's history. When we look in the mirror and perceive ourselves as too fat or too thin, too dark or too pale, too old or too young, too loud or too quiet, it is because of what happened in Eden. When we fear the ghosts of our past or the unknowns of our future or the meaninglessness of it all, it is primarily because of Eden. What God formed from dust will return to dust. This phrase, often used in funerals, is a poetic but tragic description of a human life. Are we really just dust momentarily organized into a human life? Those we have loved and lost—are they really just ash now? Is human life really just a sweaty battle for survival, fueling ourselves with food until our molecules are recycled back into the soil? God's curse of mortality brings with it the challenge of finding meaning and hope in the face of death.

The fourth, final, and most significant dislocation is the one that helps us to understand best why God can seem more of a stranger than a friend. When Adam and Eve ignored God's command, their relationship with him changed immediately. Their attitude to God was altered—no longer could they even face, let alone enjoy, the privilege of a face-to-face encounter as he walked in the garden. They were rebels, hiding from the presence of God, yet knowing their lives would not make sense without him. They were made to image, or represent, God, and yet now, barely knowing why, they were terrified of his presence.

The paradox of humanity is that we are still, like Adam and Eve, both drawn to God and repelled by him. We are desperate to be closer to our loving Creator, but simultaneously we try to hide from him. Many of us try to hide in activity and busyness, effectively covering over our nakedness and feelings of meaninglessness by subsuming ourselves in family, friends, work, and recreation. Just as we both crave and dread peace, stillness, and silence, we can long for God's presence, but we also struggle with genuine prayer.

Attempting to hide from God is a surprisingly popular pursuit. We hide from God in our routines, religiosity, rituals, restlessness. We all hide from God just as Adam and Eve did in Eden. Moses did it when he killed a guard and fled to Midian. Jonah did it, jumping aboard a ship bound for Tarshish. Elijah did it when he cowered in a cave after defeating the prophets of Baal. One thing all these runaways have in common is their failure to escape from God. They could no more hide from God than lose their shadows. Like a toddler hiding her eyes behind her hands and believing she can't be seen, just because she can't herself see, like Adam and Eve's attempt to conceal themselves in God's own garden—so our efforts to avoid God's presence are futile.

By choosing to ignore God's rules, disobey him, and then hide from him, Adam and Eve no longer knew God as their friend—they had made him a stranger. And God, by casting them out of the garden, puts distance between him and them—he makes himself a stranger. Not like riled parents who declare they cannot stand to be near their belligerent teenager and dismiss him to his room where he can be out of sight and out of mind. No. More like a doctor who has been in contact with an infectious patient and needs to initiate emergency quarantine procedures. Not that our sin can contaminate God. But it is no longer safe for us to be in the presence of an utterly holy God. The Bible says, "God is light; in him there is no darkness at all" (1 John 1:5). The moral purity of God, his white-hot holiness, is not compatible with our sin-stained humanity. Unwittingly, Adam and Eve were jointly Patient Zero in a global pandemic that catches up with even the most apparently innocent. Their defiance triggered a cascade of evil and injustice, and God evacuated them from the garden and removed himself from them in order to protect us.

So where does that leave us? It all seems pretty final. Yet the Bible is filled with visible—albeit mysterious—manifestations of God, or "theophanies." Is God elsewhere, or not? Why does God seem to turn up when his people least expect it, and not to turn up when they desperately need him to?

Is God our "ever-present help in times of trouble," not far from each one of us? Or is he unsearchable, hidden, beyond measure and comprehension, dwelling in unapproachable light? Is he to be feared, or to be welcomed? Is he a friend, or is he a stranger?

We see both in the Garden of Eden. Adam and Eve recognize that they cannot draw near to God any longer, because his toxic glory is too much for their now sinful humanity, and yet God does come near them once more: he converses with Adam and Eve and fashions clothes for them. God later tells Moses outright that "no one may see me and live" (Exodus 33:20)—yet he puts him in a cleft of rock in order to allow him to see a glimpse of his glory (Exodus 33:22). When we get to the New Testament, the same kind of tension recurs. Those who followed Jesus heard him affirm that if they had seen him, they had seen the Father; yet they still expressed a longing to see God.[3] Even in Jesus' company, people felt God was a stranger.

All these conflicting things are equally true. This is the strange and exciting tension we must learn to face, not fear. God is both above and beyond us, and yet in and among us. He is away from us and alongside us. He is transcendent and immanent. In our estrangement—caused by both us and God—we long for him and he longs for us. God withholds the full manifestation of his glory, yet is always finding ways to be with us nonetheless. This side of heaven he will always be, simultaneously, a stranger and a friend.

This is what my Salvation-Army-bonneted friend should have told me at the altar that Sunday morning. It would have saved a lot of confusion and discouragement over the following months, years, and decades. Perhaps this is what our young people need to hear, what our churches need to grapple with, what our troubled communities need to know. The incredible promises of friendship with God we bandy about have serious limitations. Instead we continue to hear and to teach in misleading ways.

Jesus' death has reversed the curse, and therefore we will experience only blessing. Jesus' resurrection opens the way for all to know his perfect friendship right here, right now. When we become a Christian all our longings will be immediately fulfilled in a relationship with God. The Holy Spirit will make you feel close to God all the time.

These statements are simply not the whole story. There is more that we need to hear—more that we must say, if the big picture is to be understood.

I have met many people who commit their lives to Christ, fully expecting him to come good on the promise to be that friend who sticks closer than a brother. But a few years later they become disappointed and disillusioned with faith; the aches of alienation are as acute as ever, and despite some mountain highs, their relationship with God turned out not to be as all-transforming as they had been led to believe it would be. The first three chapters of our Bibles teach us that estrangement will necessarily be a permanent feature of life on earth. Christian or not, the consequences of human rebellion in Eden underlie the ongoing difficulties we experience in making friends, holding our families together, coping with work pressures, feeling we don't belong, struggling with addictions and phobias, and suffering in all its various and painful forms. And our relationship with God will always be a tension between knowing his presence and feeling his distance.

For many of us, when we "make Jesus our friend," life gets not easier but harder. As a seven-year-old who had already experienced some degree of racial abuse and alienation from my peers, God may have turned up in my life in a meaningful way, but I could never have imagined what would lie ahead of me. Would I be able to trust his friendship when he was apparently absent in times of bereavement? Would I be able to see his best interests for me when I found myself in danger in his name? Would I be able to know his protecting presence when I was cowering on the ground with bullets flying past my ears? Would I be able to feel the strength of his encouragement during dark days of depression? Will I still know him to be my friend even if I am stripped of health, ability to work, financial security, and family?

There are clues in these first pages of the Bible that although God may be as much a stranger as a friend, perhaps there is something bigger going on. If he loves us enough not to destroy us with his unfiltered glory, then perhaps he has a plan for us. Perhaps it is his bigness, his strangeness, that guarantee his ability to deliver. Perhaps God loves us enough to forgo our temporal well-being in order to ensure our eternal security. Perhaps the longing that we have for something better, some-where better, is legitimate, because there *is* something and some-where better. The fact that there are still a thousand or so pages of the Bible left following the calamitous event of Eden is a demonstration of hope in itself.

The rest of the Bible keeps on bringing us back to two strong themes: our current sense of dislocation, and our future secure destination; our estranged relationship with God now, and our eternal relationship with God to come. Throughout the Bible, God repeatedly seems to be driving his people away. Whether expelled from Eden, Ur, Sodom, Egypt, the wilderness, or the Promised Land (on multiple occasions), individually and collectively the people of God in the Old Testament constantly struggle to settle. On the other hand, God is always drawing them back to their promised security and place of rest. In the New Testament, alongside the clear hope of the coming kingdom, the people find themselves unsettled again—under the general Roman oppression, or under specific persecution from the Jewish and Roman authorities.

I mentioned in the introduction that it was the refugee crisis that prompted me to reexamine many of my assumptions about how we live out the Christian faith. What surprised me was the continual cycle of displacement in the Bible. It turns out that the Bible is full of refugees, people displaced from where they know: Adam, Eve, Cain, Noah, Abraham, Sarah, Lot, Hagar, Ishmael, Isaac, Rebekah, Jacob, Esau, Joseph, all the tribes of Israel, Moses, Naomi, Ruth, David, Elijah, Esther, Mordecai, Jeremiah, Ezekiel, Daniel, Shadrach, Meshach, Abednego, and of course Jesus, who fled as a refugee to Egypt as a young child, but with him Mary, Joseph, and then Philip, Peter, Aquila and Priscilla, and the majority of the early church spread around the Roman Empire.

Whether displaced by natural disaster, exploitation, people-trafficking, war, famine, or persecution, all these refugees make the Bible a most relevant book for our world today, with its 62 million physically displaced people—although, as we have seen, all 7 billion of us are in one way or another geographically, relationally, emotionally, and spiritually displaced from who we were first intended to be. We too are refugees, strangers in a strange land, wandering exiles.

The mass migrations and displacements of people groups in our world today are continued consequences of the fall of humanity. This is not the same as saying God is punishing or disciplining those who have been made homeless or exiles. Whether you are a refugee displaced from your homeland or have been driven out of your home by an abusive spouse or parent, Genesis teaches us that this can be traced back not to a particular sin in your life, but way, way back, to humanity's separation from God at the fall. The consequences and effects of sin are so far-reaching that we cannot separate cause from effect.

Between 2006 and 2011 Syria experienced its worst drought on record—nearly 85 percent of the livestock in the country died. Around a million villagers lost their farms and thus their livelihoods, and ended up in the already overcrowded cities. This put additional pressures on the water supplies, and so in 2011, fifteen teenage boys borrowed a slogan from the revolutions taking place in other parts of the Arab world and used spray paint to graffiti it on a wall in Daraa. After the boys were imprisoned, interrogated, and tortured, massive crowds took to the streets, and it wasn't long before the Assad regime clamped down in a way that led to the civil war that has so far claimed the lives of well over 200,000 civilians.

Was the president's overreaction to blame for the conflict? Was the underlying frustration at historical wrongs and political suppression to blame? Were those fifteen boys to blame for sparking the civil war? Or was it climate change and drought that really caused the Syrian conflict?[4] Or was it consumerism that fueled the climate change in the first place?[5] Or was it the greed that first manifested itself in the Garden of Eden that caused the consumerism, led to drought, and exacerbated the simmering conflicts such that more or less the whole country has been destroyed and so many of the people have fled? For Syria the causes are complex and intertwined. We cannot pass adequate judgment, because only God knows all the causal connections. What we can say is that every part of life everywhere has been affected by the consequences of that first rebellion in the garden. Just as dye dropped in a fish tank contaminates the whole ecosystem, so sin now touches every part of life in our universe. When God became a stranger, the whole world was in trouble.

In Genesis we see that alienation from God is both our choice and his action. Therefore worldwide conflict is both on us and on God. We may never know all the reasons behind the forced displacement of millions, but when Aleppo or Mosul are destroyed and Syrians and Iraqis find themselves the world's most unwanted refugees, it is as much God's presence in this as his absence that rightly troubles us. Yet when we ask what God is doing about it, we must ask, too, what we are doing about it.

Imagine two scenarios. In the first scenario your house burns down, and you lose everything you own and are made homeless. Dirty and stinking of smoke, you are shunned by your neighbors and forced to beg on the street corners where people are more likely to spit at you than offer you a sandwich. In the second scenario your house burns down, and you lose everything you own and are made homeless. Dirty and stinking of smoke, you are offered a shower by your neighbors, along with clean clothes and a bed for the night. Your community gathers around to help you get to work and find new accommodation.

In these two scenarios nobody can downplay the trauma of losing your home. A terrible tragedy has occurred that cannot be easily forgotten. However, in the second scenario it is not the end of the story. Discovering the kindness of strangers is more than a silver lining. It is more than a lifeline. It is a welcome that can restore faith in humanity, in community, and in God. It points to God's unconditional love and his invitation to a future home that can never burn down.

What if it is in sacrificial friendship toward one another that we can glimpse something of God's ultimate intention to restore us to perfect friendship with him? The terrible atrocities that go on around the world, and the sense of alienation that frustrates us all, are undoubtedly terrible things that stem from humanity's initial rebellion against God. But what if God is able to turn something terrible into something incredible? What if he could turn death to life?

After God cursed Adam and Eve, he clothed them. To do this he had to undertake the first recorded killing in his perfect creation. With the skins of dead animals, he provided a model of temporary mercy. When we clothe the naked, welcome the stranger, and feed the hungry, we provide for immediate needs with a hospitality that stems from and points to God's care for us. But God also, in this killing, provided a model of eternal mercy. One day his Son, the Lamb of God, would be killed to take away the stain of sin in humanity. The snake's head would be finally crushed, and we would be able once again to be in God's glorious presence, seeing him face-to-face without fear. In Eden we subtly begin to learn that God can turn death to life, bad news to good news, fear to opportunity, curses to blessings, despair to hope, temporary estrangement to eternal life.

As we live in anticipation of our eternal destiny, yet still blighted by the effects of sin, we can perhaps see God's presence and know God's friendship most clearly in the way we give and receive merciful hospitality. We started this chapter with an example of human alienation, seeing how those closest to us can turn out to be total strangers. But sometimes it is in our sense of displacement that we meet strangers who give us a glimpse of divine friendship. I saw something of this in a refugee camp in Lebanon. But I also experienced something of this on a dangerous night in Georgia.

It was a starry night in downtown Tbilisi, the perfect evening for an exchange student to explore the city and learn about the language, culture, and history of this part of the former Soviet empire. A few months earlier I had been the host and dutifully introduced a young Georgian student called Tamaz to my home culture, making sure he experienced fish and chips, English tea, the Church of England, and a Sunday roast. Now Tamaz was returning the favor, and he had taken me out to sample their national cherry tea, traditional haja puri breads, and an evening of singing folk songs, swapping favorite excerpts from great Russian literature and sharing hopes and dreams for the future of our nations.

As it got late, we began to saunter home. Suddenly a crowd rushed en masse from a café close by. There was a sound as though someone had fired a starting pistol, except these shots were no blanks, and any direction counted as everyone sprinted as fast as they could away from the café. I felt my legs running before I could work out why. Tamaz pulled me down behind a car for shelter, and squeezed between me and the ongoing chaos. Then he fell, clutching his leg and rolling on to the floor. His trouser fabric turned red, a patch of blood growing under his hands. I could see something of Tamaz's physical pain from his facial aerobics. As for me, I just felt helpless, alienated, and vulnerable. I prayed like never before as I knelt beside this relative stranger.

I discovered a lot more about Georgian culture that evening than I would have done on the original itinerary. I saw the inside of a hospital, experienced the suspicion of the police force, and learned several words that would not have gained me any extra marks in my Russian language exam. I learned that it was possible that a stranger I had known for only a few weeks was literally prepared to take a stray bullet for me. I realized how even in the midst of suffering, surprising true and sacrificial friendship can point us to a coming world where there will be no mass shootings, civil conflict, and pain.

In retrospect, what seemed to be a curse turned out to be a blessing in disguise. The man who had so recently been a stranger turned out to be a friend in disguise. When I felt most far away from home, I also felt most drawn to God. What I now describe as a near-near-death experience helped me to glimpse God's mercy and protection in a place and a person I did not expect to find them. Fear turned to opportunity. We may not yet know the privilege of the presence of God in all his glory as Adam and Eve did before the fall, but because of the curse we can perhaps in the meantime know the drive to share something of the mercy of a stranger God.

ABRAHAM AND
THE STRANGER

The God who turns up out of the blue

In which an old refugee invites three strangers for dinner
and gets more than he bargained for, and we see
that trusting God is never as simple as it seems.

Looking back, it seems a miracle that we survived. The only reason we got into a car driven by a total stranger that day was that he was a distant relative of our neighbor, and we knew it would have brought shame on the whole family if we had refused their hospitality. Fortunately that short trip to the airport remained a comedy of errors and avoided full-blown tragedy. Immediately, the man's erratic driving indicated this was not going to be a smooth taxi ride to the airport. Speeding down the narrow streets of Tirana, I could easily believe the rumors that bribery was the primary means of procuring a driving license in Albania at that time. We narrowly missed a horse-drawn cart laden with enormous watermelons traveling the wrong way down the country's only dual highway. Technically, of course, that wasn't our driver's fault, although it didn't help that he was consistently ignoring all road signs and speed limits. It was then that I noticed the indicator stalks were missing. In their place were bare wires that our driver pinched together when he wanted to signal. It was a difficult procedure as he was also holding a cigarette, so when he needed to steer and signal and smoke—all at speed—he came up at least one hand short, perhaps two.

Needless to say, I was not that surprised when the engine started to make strange noises and we were forced to pull over for some streetside repairs. Our driver pried open the hood and rearranged a large plastic Coke bottle, which was acting as a replacement for something important under the hood. As he did so, fuel leaked everywhere and all over our driver, but he was happy he had fixed the issue. He got back into the car and resumed smoking and indicating, weaving and speeding, and smoking and indicating some more, a thick smell of petrol exuding from his damp hands and clothes. I was convinced we were all about to be incinerated and whisked straight to heaven. I tried to reassure myself that I could trust my neighbor's judgment, but I have never been so relieved to arrive at an airport. A journey I will never forget thankfully ended without immolation or conflagration, although I fully blame it for my subsequent amaxophobia, a condition which up to that point I hadn't even known existed.

〰〰〰

Most adults I know suffer a mild form of amaxophobia, or fear of being a passenger, instinctively preferring to be in the driving seat than anywhere else in the car. The prospect of letting another person take control can be nerve-racking, if not terrifying, however competent the driver. And this can be just as true for life in general. It is far easier to trust in our own abilities than in those of another.

Of course things seem like they should be different when it comes to surrendering control to God and giving him the right to rule in our lives. God is omniscient—he isn't going to make a wrong move or inappropriate maneuver, right?

God is omnipresent, so nowhere is off-limits for him; no place will be unfamiliar or out of his reach. And God is omnipotent—he is never going to be caught out by circumstances out of his control, or overcome by conditions that go beyond his competencies.

And yet, looking at his track record in Scripture, God actually appears to be a really bad driver. For example, how on earth did it take forty years for God's people to travel the straight-line distance of 240 miles from Egypt to the Promised Land? They traveled an average of six miles a year. Some of us can run that distance before breakfast! I once heard of a driving test that took four hours because the examiner got lost, but even that seems like a minor navigational mishap compared to God's direction of Israel through the desert. Or what about Jesus and the disciples? They spent three years traveling with him and yet seemed to end up with very little idea of who he was or where he was going. How did they have so much intense tutelage and still miss that Jesus was going to die and rise again from the dead?

Or what about the strange story of Abraham, whom God uprooted from his home and family? God's first words to Abraham were not encouraging declarations of comfort and peace. Nor even a voice of promise and protection. Instead, God's voice brought disruption and displacement and caused Abraham and his wife to become wandering nomads: "Go from your country, your people and your father's household to the land I will show you" (Genesis 12:1). And this is just the beginning. Things get a whole lot more complicated as God leads Abraham (eventually) to his new home.

How would you feel if God asked you to suddenly relocate in your old age? How would you react if, despite being physically unable to have children, God nevertheless promised that you would parent a family that would outnumber the stars? How would you have coped if you felt the only means of survival, God being somehow unavailable to help, was to give your spouse to the local ruler under the pretense of being your sibling? And then how would you feel when God finally turns up to rescue both of you by inflicting serious diseases on those you had traded with?

What would you think of a God who turned up in the midst of your personal devotions in the form of a levitating, flaming torch? Would you trust a God who predicates ethnic cleansing in order for you to settle down in a new homeland? Or who asks you to demonstrate your allegiance through a form of genital mutilation? Or who lets you make a decision to go down the surrogacy route, despite the painful rejections it will entail? Or who asks you to trust his promise through child sacrifice? Trusting in the lordship of a God like this is risky business. Who would want a God like this in the driving seat of their lives?

Of course nobody pointed any of this out to me when I first became a Christian. I was taught that accepting God as Lord of my life would mean that I got to live life to the full, and that he would lead me beside quiet waters, along straight paths, away from temptation, and in the way everlasting. But these promises of the Bible do not come close to describing my life, or those of countless Christians around the world—and they certainly couldn't be used to describe Abraham's biography. Yet despite God's strange ways, Abraham continued to have trust in God's leadership, confidence in God's power, and faith in God's character.

He obeyed him despite all his difficulties and is held up in the New Testament as the ultimate example of a person of faith. How can we reconcile these tensions?

In the last few years, just in our small church, we have seen a young family coming to terms with a brain injury in a father of four, which left him not only physically incapacitated but incoherent in speech and needing full-time residential care. We have had to watch a young teenager dying a slow death from cancer, despite the fervent prayers of all who knew him. Our little church family has witnessed marriage failure, health crises, family breakdown, and children coming in and out of care in heartbreaking situations. I have seen firsthand the havoc wreaked on those who have faithfully entrusted themselves to God as their Lord. And I have been constantly amazed how my brothers and sisters in the most difficult of life circumstances have continued to follow God despite everything.

For many of us, though, this is not the life or the God we bargained on. This is not the Jesus we invited into our lives. This is not the way that the Holy Spirit was supposed to guide us through life. This is not the journey of faith that we signed up for. Is God still there during the tough times, or has a stranger hijacked the controls? If God himself is that stranger, how on earth is he to be trusted with the leadership of our lives? Why does he make himself so unrecognizable?

There is an incident in the Bible involving Abraham that gives us a fascinating perspective on how to trust God when to all intents and purposes he seems no more than a stranger. It comes about a year before Isaac is born, and several years before Abraham is asked to literally sacrifice him. This incident sees

God turning up unexpectedly, as a stranger, and it involves an invitation, an intercession, and, finally, an intervention.

The LORD appeared to Abraham near the great trees of Mamre while he was sitting at the entrance to his tent in the heat of the day. Abraham looked up and saw three men standing nearby. When he saw them, he hurried from the entrance of his tent to meet them and bowed low to the ground.

He said, "If I have found favor in your eyes, my lord, do not pass your servant by. Let a little water be brought, and then you may all wash your feet and rest under this tree. Let me get you something to eat, so you can be refreshed and then go on your way—now that you have come to your servant."

"Very well," they answered, "do as you say."

So Abraham hurried into the tent to Sarah. "Quick," he said, "get three seahs of the finest flour and knead it and bake some bread."

Then he ran to the herd and selected a choice, tender calf and gave it to a servant, who hurried to prepare it. He then brought some curds and milk and the calf that had been prepared, and set these before them. While they ate, he stood near them under a tree.

"Where is your wife Sarah?" they asked him. "There, in the tent," he said.

Then one of them said, "I will surely return to you about this time next year, and Sarah your wife will have a son."

Now Sarah was listening at the entrance to the tent, which was behind him. Abraham and Sarah were already very old, and Sarah was past the age of childbearing. So

Sarah laughed to herself as she thought, "After I am worn out and my lord is old, will I now have this pleasure?"

Then the LORD said to Abraham, "Why did Sarah laugh and say, 'Will I really have a child, now that I am old?' Is anything too hard for the LORD? I will return to you at the appointed time next year, and Sarah will have a son."

Sarah was afraid, so she lied and said, "I did not laugh." But he said, "Yes, you did laugh." (Genesis 18:1-15)

The setup reminds me of a good comic farce, where the audience is privy to information that the characters in the scene do not have. Conversations ensue that are laden with double meaning. This story begins by letting the readers into a secret that our protagonist is unaware of—it is the Lord himself who has turned up. God is coming to visit Abraham, but Abraham does not know that. In contrast to Adam and Eve hiding from God behind the trees of Eden, here God is hiding from Abraham near the trees of Mamre.

We are told at this point that the three visitors are "the Lord," and the issue of their identity seems deliberately obscure and mysterious. Sometimes we are told "they" speak, sometimes it is "the Lord" who speaks. When the three men leave, we are told Abraham "remained standing before the LORD" (Genesis 18:22). And later on there are just two men, who are described as angels. Some people have concluded that God has turned up in the form of three men to represent the Trinity. This is how Russian painter Andrei Rublev depicts it in his famous icon called, with his own appropriate ambiguity, *The Hospitality of Abraham*. In the background he paints the tree of Mamre, Mount Moriah, and Abraham's home, while the three visitors gather around the table in the forefront, symbolically presented as the three members of the Trinity. While the exact identity of the three visitors is partially obscured to us in the text of the Bible, it is fully obscured to Abraham, who just sees three male travelers. Abraham has never had any trouble recognizing God before, so why does God choose this occasion to come in disguise, as a stranger or three?

The incident reminds me of Shakespeare's rich historical drama *Henry V*, which contains clues that may help us understand what is going on with Abraham here. It is the night before the great battle of Agincourt, where the king's English army will be outnumbered by the mighty French battalions, and King Henry wishes to encourage his men. But as king he is unable to get as close as he would like. So he exchanges his royal robes for a borrowed cloak, disguising himself as a lowly soldier, to listen to the troops and spur them on for the battle the next day. By laying aside the privileges and honors of his regal standing, he can sit alongside the men who serve him and talk with them.

Another British royal did something similar at the end of another great battle. On May 8, 1945, Prime Minister Winston Churchill pronounced that the war in Europe was finally over. The streets of the nation's capital began to fill up as people sought out somewhere to congregate and celebrate the end of this most bloody conflict. Among the revelers were two young women aged nineteen and fourteen. They were the Princesses Elizabeth and Margaret. The elder would later become the longest-reigning monarch in English history. But that evening she walked out in the London air, wearing the humble uniform of the Auxiliary Territorial Service. Cap pulled down to avoid recognition, she was able to blend into the crowd and join the party.

The disguises used by both Henry V and Princess Elizabeth were intended not only to hide their identities but, at a critical moment in history, to make authentic connection more possible.

Something similar is going on in our Abraham story, as the Lord of the Universe disguises his glory and appears as three tired travelers seeking shelter, before embarking on a significant intervention in the way the world turns. Now that we, the readers of this text, are in on the secret and the stage is set, we are ready to see how Abraham will react.

It was customary at the time for strangers to make themselves known by standing in a visible public space and then waiting to be received.[1] This is why, years later, when Abraham is on a search for a potential bride for Isaac, his servant stands by the spring and prays to God that the designated woman would approach him and offer him (and his camels) a drink of water (Genesis 24). So it is that as soon as Abraham notices the men, he dutifully rushes over to them, bowing low and giving them the honorific greeting "lord." We know better than Abraham himself that this response is exactly what is required—he is in fact behaving and speaking better than he knows. Incidentally, the word used here for "bowing down"[2] is also the word translated "worship" when its object is God.[3] These are the most fitting ways for Abraham to greet God on the earth—with haste, with humility, and in honor.

Next comes the invitation. Abraham is not prepared to let these men pass without their permitting him to care for them. He presents his hospitality as a privilege rather than a burden. His offer is meager and modest in a bid not to overwhelm his guests but persuade them to at least receive from him the minimum of respite. As soon as they agree, Abraham puts all of his resources to work to make sure that they receive a banquet fit for a king. One biblical scholar notes that "to kill 'a bull' for just three visitors shows royal generosity: a lamb or a goat would have been more than adequate."[4] Abraham's enthusiastic reception for unannounced visitors at midday, when it would have been usual in the Middle East to take a siesta, becomes a role model. The writer to the Hebrews picks up on this event by reminding all of us: "Do not forget to show hospitality to strangers, for by so doing some people have shown hospitality to angels without knowing it" (Hebrews 13:2).

Abraham's hospitality is such that he treats his guests as well as if God himself were visiting—which is entirely appropriate as God himself has actually turned up! Abraham's story challenges us not to see the unexpected visitor as an interruption or an inconvenience but as an opportunity to show devotion to God. I wonder how we would fare in this "mystery shopper" test? Many houses today are set up to minimize the possibility of the uninvited turning up. Whether it's the forbidding metal gates, the long drive, the "Beware of the Dog" sign, or perhaps a "Polite Notice: No Canvassers, No Salesmen, No Cold Callers" sticker, many people feel it is imperative to protect their space from any unwanted invasion of the outside world. Even if we want to cultivate a countercultural open-door policy, where anyone is welcome at any time, it is difficult to find a balance between being at the mercy of door-to-door salespersons tempting us with forbidden fruit, and yet open to showing mercy to angels in disguise.

Maybe a bit of historical and cultural context will help here. Hospitality in the ancient Middle East, particularly toward travelers, played a vital role in the culture.[5] In the ancient world, before highways, satnav, police cars, and the mobile repair vans of the "fourth emergency service" existed, traveling between cities was a dangerous enterprise. It took something big for people to travel outside their hometown or its locality. One scholar put it like this: "Travel, in the ancient world, was only undertaken for grave reasons, often negative in nature, such as flight from persecution or search for food and survival. Hospitality, under those circumstances, has little to do with modern tourism, but embraces the biblical equivalent to our policies regarding refugees, immigrants and welfare."[6] There was no ancient equivalent of Airbnb, so welcoming travelers into your home, therefore, was not a question of helping them get a vacation on the cheap, but rather a form of refuge or shelter.

Here is a fascinating insight into the nature of God's leadership in our lives, which perhaps we can appreciate more fully as we today are faced with a refugee crisis like none other. God chooses to take on the persona of a hungry, tired, and thirsty traveler, a would-be refugee with no place to stay, and waits to be invited in. The God who, as we saw in the previous chapter, made us exiles, makes himself an exile too. Despite being the ruler of the universe, God hides his glory and status in order that he can receive hospitality from those he has created. What an incredible demonstration of the humility of God.

This incident involving Abraham is not an isolated occasion. Think of Jesus as a newborn baby dependent on the hospitality of an overstretched innkeeper. Remember him tired from his journey, sitting down by a well in Samaria and asking an ostracized local woman for a drink (John 4). Think of him pictured in Revelation saying, "Here I am! I stand at the door and knock. If anyone hears my voice and opens the door, I will come in and eat with that person, and they with me" (Revelation 3:20). God never *needs* to knock. As Lord of all, he could command and enter, but instead we find a God who waits to be invited and accepts hospitality not because he needs anything, but because there is something significant in this for us.

Abraham is given the amazing privilege of hosting God himself in the form of these three strangers. For those of us in on the secret of the identity of the visitors, the host-guest relationship is intriguingly reversed. It is surely Abraham who has been blessed by their company. But there is more blessing to come— the visitors' parting gift to their host is in the form of a promise: "I will surely return to you about this time next year, and Sarah your wife will have a son" (Genesis 18:10). God has already promised Abraham a son (Genesis 17:16), but this time he wants Sarah to hear it directly. Sarah does hear, but laughs to herself, because while Abraham has been entertaining strangers, she has been entertaining doubts and disappointments. However, the stranger is God himself, so he knows this already, and in a question that simultaneously chastises and reassures her, asks, "Is anything too hard for the LORD?" (Genesis 18:14). The omniscient God knows Sarah's secret thoughts, and the omnipotent God can even override Sarah's worn-out body. Surely now the hosts are beginning to realize who their guests that day really are?

Is anything too hard for the Lord? It's a powerful question. Of course, theoretically, we know the answer is no. What could be too hard for the one who spoke the universe into being with its uncountable galaxies and innumerable star systems? But, existentially—in the midst of real life—we are not so sure. Yes, theoretically God can do anything; but practically, it seems, we must get on with life and assume that he won't. I may pray that God would fix my dishwasher, heal my back, save my neighbors, find me a job, and pay off my credit card. But I don't really expect him to. I get on with life with all its troubles and pretty soon I stop praying altogether. God becomes an added extra, an afterthought, if a thought at all. We laugh inside, perhaps, when others suggest we pray about our problems. If we are not careful, we don't really allow God to lead in our lives at all.

As Abraham accompanies the angel visitors on their way, once again we are privy to information that Abraham does not have. God makes known to us, the readers, the unheard dialogue between the visitors:

> Shall I hide from Abraham what I am about to do? Abraham will surely become a great and powerful nation, and all nations on earth will be blessed through him. For I have chosen him, so that he will direct his children and his household after him to keep the way of the LORD by doing what is right and just, so that the LORD will bring about for Abraham what he has promised him. (Genesis 18:17-19)

God is conversing with himself, just as in the creation story, when he says, "Let us make mankind in our image" (Genesis 1:26), or again during the Tower of Babel debacle, when he says, "Come, let us go down and confuse their language" (Genesis 11:7). An imperative tense for an imperative occasion. This is God deliberately speaking out his plans in advance so we can understand what he is doing and why. But how should we understand this hesitation as to whether to share his plans with Abraham? Are we to conclude that there is an inner resistance or internal wrestling within the person of God himself? Or are we being invited to wrestle ourselves with the plan that God has—to destroy an entire city?

Now, this is where the chapter suddenly takes an unpredictable turn in the road. A God who turns up unannounced for dinner is one thing. A God who promises the impossible is something else. But neither of these traits of God make us question his lordship. The destruction of an entire city is quite a different matter. We have seen far too often in recent times the heart-wrenching images of rescuers desperately clawing through rubble with their bare hands, trying to find survivors after a city has been flattened by bombing or earthquake. We have seen them pull out bodies of men, women, and children. Most are already dead. And then, miraculously, we see one who is still alive, dazed and covered in blood and dust, having lost everything and everyone they know, but a life to celebrate nevertheless. Where do we see God in these tragedies? In the hands of the rescuers; in the final breaths of the deceased; in the miraculous stories of survival against all odds? Or, as this story suggests, in the forces that destroy?

By eavesdropping on the conversation as recorded in the story of Abraham, we hear God in dialogue, and it is on this hallowed ground that we need to wrestle with these most difficult questions. God is apparently trying to decide whether he should confide in Abraham about his plans of destruction. It could be the final straw for Abraham's already stretched faith. How could he trust a God who does what seems wrong and unfair? On the other hand, it could secure Abraham's already strong faith. It could help him continue to trust a God who does "what is right and just" (Genesis 18:19). Because of his great potential and future spiritual leadership, God concludes that Abraham needs to understand how God thinks and works, and that even in the midst of destruction, God's righteousness and justice are absolute. Things are not always what they seem—sometimes they are entirely the opposite.

This insight shapes the way we understand the next part of the conversation. At first sight it appears as though Abraham is bartering with God, as he would with a street seller to get the lowest price. This sounds a bit like a haggling match in which Abraham finally wins God over to his way of thinking when it comes to Sodom. No. That's not it. Rather, God intends to win

Abraham over to his higher way of thinking, and the first lesson on the curriculum is how to be "distinct from the ways of other gods or of other nations."[7]

The central aspect of this divinely inspired syllabus is to teach Abraham about the importance of living justly, so that he can pass this on to all those numerous descendants he has been promised. God explains that he cannot ignore the terrible state of Sodom and Gomorrah: he has heard the outcry from the cities. Old Testament scholar Chris Wright notes that "outcry" is a technical word "for the cry of pain or the cry for help from those who are being oppressed or violated."[8] There are terrible atrocities going on in that city, and God will not stand by and do nothing. This is surely relevant to our world today. When we see terrible things on our news feeds, we can feel desperate. Not only is there little we can do, but when we pray to the one who can intervene, he often seems to be silent and inactive. This story tells us that God hears not only our prayers, but also the outcry from those who are being violated. We can also take comfort that when we cry out in our own suffering to God he does hear us, despite appearances to the contrary, as his timescale is so often different from ours. But we must also take note from this that walking in God's ways must include being attentive to the cry of the poor and the marginalized, just as he is. There is a strange and very real tension in this story. God hears the outcry from the oppressed and answers, but God is going to cause an outcry as he visits judgment on the city.

By sharing his plans with Abraham, God invites him to get involved, to intervene and intercede. Commentator Gordon Wenham puts it well when he states, "It is God himself, who wants intercession made, and Abraham must be the intercessor."[9] While this divine ratification for the importance of prayer may encourage us on one hand, we must also face up to the criticism that it could appear that God is being manipulative. Why does God linger with Abraham, teasing this intercession for Sodom out of him? Why doesn't God just come straight out and tell Abraham to pray for the city? Or just do what he is going to do anyway? Why involve Abraham at all?

Let us pause here a moment. This passage has already shown us something about the power of invitation—how our hospitality toward the vulnerable brings with it the means of intimacy and blessing from God. Now we are being taught about the power of intercession—through our prayers we can draw close to God's heart for the vulnerable and learn directly from him about how to live justly. When it comes to surrendering to God's lordship, he seems to be delegating back to us this challenge and privilege of being the initiator, inviter, and intercessor.

God is more interested in forming character than in forcing control, more concerned about teaching us his ways of justice than enforcing his plans on us, more intent on molding us than manipulating or micromanaging us. But this begs the next question: if God wants us to learn to respond with him to the outcry of the marginalized, why does God plan to be so destructive? Why wipe out Sodom and Gomorrah—won't that cause even greater outcry? Now we will see Abraham wrestle with this problem, just as we must wrestle with it if we want to know and trust God.

Abraham rises to the challenge of intercession. He is fully aware that his nephew Lot has made his home in the city, but he does not simply pray for Lot's life. Rather, he first of all pleads on behalf of God's reputation, and secondly he pleads on behalf of the city, begging God not to sweep away the righteous and the wicked, but to be discriminating in his punishment. His question "Will not the Judge of all the earth do right?" (Genesis 18:25) is an important one as, like God's question of Sarah earlier, it could be read either as a reproach or as a reassurance. Either it was, as one commentator puts it, "a challenge hurled by Abraham toward God or . . . a testimony by Abraham about his belief in his God's integrity and predictability."[10] Perhaps, like a good double meaning, it can be both at the same time. Abraham can at the same time both doubt and declare God to be true to his character—consistent, good and fair, the righteous Judge of all the earth, no stranger to justice.[11] In fact, perhaps you too have used such a double-edged question in your own part-doubting, part-declaring prayers on behalf of those you know are suffering. Elsewhere in the Bible we see similar prayers recorded: a father praying for his son's healing confessed, "I do believe; help me overcome my unbelief!" (Mark 9:24). Shadrach, Meshach, and Abednego, facing the fiery furnace, defiantly cried, "The God we serve is able to deliver us. . . . But even if he does not . . . we will not serve your gods" (Daniel 3:17-18). We can pray honestly like this and take assurance that God hears.

Abraham makes six successive requests. Will God spare the wicked city for fifty righteous people? For forty-five? For forty? As his boldness grows, he reduces the requirement in greater increments. For thirty? For twenty? At ten righteous people, God ends the conversation—and goes on his way to fulfill his purposes in Sodom. Yet God's replies do not sound like the begrudging concessions of a hard-nosed salesman. The willingness with which he concedes to Abraham's requests negates the argument that this interchange is just about bartering with God in a bid to save Lot. Wrestling with God, as we will see even more clearly in the next chapter, is a vital part of forging a meaningful relationship with one who is so completely different from us.

Let us look at three interesting tensions in the way that Abraham wrestles with God in this episode, which may help us in our own struggles to understand God's leadership in our lives.

First, Abraham was called by God to leave his home and be a blessing to all the nations of the earth. By attempting to bless Sodom through his advocacy on their behalf, even in the face of God's apparent determined decision, he is fulfilling this vocation. He is seeking to save a pagan city from judgment, interceding on behalf of strangers for a stay of execution. But now his call did not match up with God's plan—that is, to bring final judgment. How is it that the God who called Abraham to bless the nations is the same God who is about to bring terrible judgment on a whole group of people? Is God a God of blessing or of destruction? A God of compassion or of judgment?

Somehow Abraham is caught up in the complexity of this as he wrestles with God in prayer. In some mysterious way, being caught in this paradox is the privilege and the vocation of all believers. Prayer and intercession are the meeting point between surrendering to the leadership of an all-knowing God and crying out to God on behalf of those who are suffering. It is the tension between trusting God's judgment and calling on God's mercy. In wrestling with God in prayer we may well, like Abraham, get more than we bargain for: a lesson from the One who always does what is both right and just.

Second, because God was willing to include Abraham in his decision-making process regarding the destiny of Sodom, we can see something of the potential influence the righteous might have on their community. If only ten righteous people were to be found in the whole city of Sodom, they would become the means through which the entire community was rescued. Commentator V. P. Hamilton puts it succinctly: "Just as the nations of the earth find blessing in Abraham . . . so the guilty in Sodom and Gomorrah find mercy in the lives of their fellow citizens who are innocent."[12] This is highly significant. Here is a precursor of Jesus' statement that God's people act as salt and light. It seems that a minority *can* bless the majority. Here we see the potential of the faithful presence of God's people, bringing hope and help to the wider population.[13] We begin to glimpse here how in God's economy, women and men seeking to live for him could have a pivotal importance in the communities in which they live, work, and play. Walter Brueggemann notes that "conventionally, a few guilty people can cause the destruction of the whole community and the power of innocence is limited to the persons themselves. . . . By the new mathematics . . . , one is enough to save (Rom. 5:15-17)."[14] Here, in the inhospitable psychological terrain that foreshadows the destruction of Sodom, we see something of God's view of hospitality: the few can save the many. Abraham is one man, who stands before God pleading for a whole city; the presence of ten righteous men and women could have saved that whole city. This points forward to the time when one man will save the many. We will explore this later in the book when we consider how Jesus the stranger becomes the one who saves all.

Third, we see a tension in the fact that, through this prayer of intercession, Abraham himself is learning about God. Abraham engages here with a God who is sympathetic to the outcry of the oppressed, who is a righteous judge, who is Lord of all the earth, and who is yet approachable and open to conversation and relationship. By letting Abraham into his plans and inviting him to pray, God is opening up a depth of relationship with Abraham that he could not have known otherwise. Prayer is not just the exchange of demands, a wishlist of things that we try to nag God into fulfilling. It is a transforming means of developing friendship with our Lord God. To Abraham, God first appeared as a stranger. Abraham has engaged with a God whom he can barely begin to understand. Even the expression of his conviction that God is the Judge of all the earth is framed in a question. There was a disparity between the God Abraham saw in front of him and the God Abraham may have thought he knew. This tension between the God we think we know and love and the God we don't yet know but want to trust is an ongoing one, this side of eternity. The dissonance we feel should drive the urgency and the intensity of our prayers.

These three tensions—of a God who calls us to things yet then seems to make it harder to achieve them, a God who pursues judgment yet wants us to plead for mercy, and a God whom we get to know even as we recognize our lack of understanding—must impact the way we respond to the lordship of God in our lives.

In the next part of the story we see how the same tensions come up again as the visitors—now as two angels—move on to Sodom.

The two angels arrived at Sodom in the evening, and Lot was sitting in the gateway of the city. When he saw them, he got up to meet them and bowed down with his face to the ground. "My lords," he said, "please turn aside to your servant's house. You can wash your feet and spend the night and then go on your way early in the morning."

"No," they answered, "we will spend the night in the square."

But he insisted so strongly that they did go with him and entered his house. He prepared a meal for them, baking bread without yeast, and they ate. Before they had gone

to bed, all the men from every part of the city of Sodom—
both young and old—surrounded the house. They called to
Lot, "Where are the men who came to you tonight? Bring
them out to us so that we can have sex with them."

Lot went outside to meet them and shut the door behind
him and said, "No, my friends. Don't do this wicked thing.
Look, I have two daughters who have never slept with a
man. Let me bring them out to you, and you can do what
you like with them. But don't do anything to these men,
for they have come under the protection of my roof."

"Get out of our way," they replied. "This fellow came here
as a foreigner, and now he wants to play the judge! We'll
treat you worse than them." They kept bringing pressure
on Lot and moved forward to break down the door.

But the men inside reached out and pulled Lot back into
the house and shut the door. Then they struck the men
who were at the door of the house, young and old, with
blindness so that they could not find the door.

The two men said to Lot, "Do you have anyone else here—
sons-in-law, sons or daughters, or anyone else in the city
who belongs to you? Get them out of here, because we are
going to destroy this place. The outcry to the LORD against
its people is so great that he has sent us to destroy it."
(Genesis 19:1-13)

Before we get into the stranger elements of this story, first
let us reflect on how the two angel strangers are received. There
are three facets to the welcome: how Lot responds, how the
wider city of Sodom responds, and how God responds.

Lot, like his uncle Abraham, offers the visitors welcome and
refuge. He comes with haste, getting up from his seat at the city

gate; approaches with humility, bowing low; and shows hospitality, imploring them to become his guests for the night. However, unlike Abraham, he offers only a simple meal. Perhaps this may imply that he had not grasped the significance of who these visitors were.

In striking contrast to both Abraham's and Lot's hospitality, the city of Sodom's response to these strangers is hostility. We are told that all the men of the city, both young and old, from the various districts, surround Lot's house and demand that the visitors be released to them so they can target them for gang rape.[15] It is possible that such abuse of passing travelers had become all too frequent and was the cause of the "outcry" from the violated that God spoke of with Abraham earlier. Interestingly, when the sin of Sodom is described by the prophet Ezekiel, he states, "Now this was the sin of your sister Sodom: She and her daughters were arrogant, overfed and unconcerned; they did not help the poor and needy. They were haughty and did detestable things before me" (Ezekiel 16:49-50). Passivity toward the poor and mistreatment of the needy—which would include these vulnerable travelers—lies at the heart of the sin of Sodom. The writer of Genesis could not make it any clearer that, with the single exception of Lot, all the men of the city were implicated in the abuse. Sodom is so endemically corrupt that strangers are systematically abused, and afforded not even the basic dignity one would offer to a fellow person, let alone the divine honor of which these particular visitors are worthy. If some have entertained angels without knowing it, then it seems others will have abused angels without realizing it either.

Lot, himself a foreigner, seems to show great courage as alone he steps outside to face the crowd, shutting the door behind him, giving a degree of protection to his guests, but leaving him with no place to go. One man versus the masses, now it is Lot's turn to intercede. He pleads God's case before the city, just as Abraham had pleaded the city's case before God.

What happens next in the story makes for extremely uncomfortable reading. Lot has taken the vulnerable visitors under his roof and feels morally obligated to protect them from harm. So much so, he callously offers his own daughters to slake the lust of the mob. Lot volunteers them without their consent, and without offering himself first. Perhaps he feels backed into a corner. Perhaps this speaks of an ancient misogyny. Perhaps he is unconsciously mirroring his uncle's behavior when he offered his wife to try to protect himself from the dangerous might of Pharaoh. In Abraham's case, God stepped in to protect Sarah, but here it is the crowd who rejects the exchange. They also reject Lot, threatening to treat him worse than they had been planning to treat the other visitors. As they cast out the one "righteous" person who could have averted the destruction of the city, we wait with bated breath: what will God do?

And so we come to God's response. At the last minute, when things could not get any worse, Lot is rescued by the angels, and the crowd is struck blind. Once they have escaped, fire rains down from heaven. The destruction of the city appears to be the only option left on the table. It is shown to be a severe retribution to meet a city so severely steeped in sin that despite warnings and intercessions and even an angelic visitation, it could not be saved.

There are other stories in the Bible where entire cities are doomed to destruction. Jonah reluctantly conveys God's warning and prevents the destruction of Nineveh as the whole city responds and turns to God in repentance. In the case of the destruction of Jericho, one woman, Rahab, was spared along with her family, as she had provided refuge to the foreign spies. In all three of these cities the righteous and repentant were rescued, at the same time that God leaves us in no doubt that there is a limit to his patience in dealing with the persistently wicked.

God rescues Lot, and his two daughters, perhaps striking home that God was more able to take care of those girls than their own father, who was prepared to toss them out to be violated. Now they, like Adam and Eve in our last chapter, like Abraham earlier in this chapter, and like Jacob, whom we will look at in our next chapter, are homeless outcasts, exiles, refugees. God by his mercy has deliberately displaced them, in the first place at least in order to rescue and protect them from the destruction of Sodom.

When we struggle with the lordship of God, not understanding where and why he is taking us through strange and difficult times, perhaps the idea that God is also stranger than we sometimes realize may in fact help us. There is so much to God that we cannot grasp. We cannot begin to imagine his comprehension of the grand scheme of things. One thing he wants us to be sure of, when we cannot fully understand what he is doing, is that we can trust that his ways are right and just, however inconceivable that may seem to us.

We have seen in this story the full contrast between the gentle grace of God to a childless geriatric couple and the destructive judgment of God on a depraved society.[16] We have seen the divine visitors enact their twin tasks, described well by Brueggemann: "One is to promise a beginning . . . the other is to effect an ending."[17] Through hospitality and a blessing we see the promise of a child and the birth of a dynasty to Abraham and Sarah, and through fire and destruction we see the end of a corrupt civilization in Sodom. At the heart of both stories lie the different responses that are shown to the incognito God, the God who is a stranger.

This topic of entertaining strangers and angels, and thereby unwittingly welcoming God, may not come up much on your church's curriculum. I have never seen it on any evangelism or discipleship course. Nor does it feature in many marriage, family, ministry, or theology courses. Yet here it is, at the heart of a critical episode in the Bible. Here it is intrinsically tied in to the conception of God's people, as well as connected with the judgment of Sodom that foreshadows the final judgment, and notably, it marks the first occasion in the Bible where God takes the form of man, prefiguring the incarnation of Jesus. How we should treat strangers is taught here—not just once, but twice—not just as a positive example, but as a negative example too. In chapter ten we will see how Jesus reiterates this really important doctrine. And in each of our chapters along the way we will see again and again that as we navigate the stranger, ostensibly inhospitable parts of our Bible, hospitality toward strangers may be more important than we have ever realized.

I have been reminded while writing this chapter of another aspect of life in Albania, one that is a far cry from our neighbor's relative's dangerous driving. Woven into the fabric of Albanian culture is a commitment to hospitality that was codified in the fifteenth century into thirty-eight articles, known as the Kanun of Leke.[18] Among these it states that "the house of the Albanian belongs to God and the guest."[19] This means that if a traveler turns up unexpectedly and asks to be your guest, it is unacceptable to turn him away, even if he is your worst enemy. You cannot refuse him hospitality, even if your families are engaged in a blood feud, a practice of vengeance that sounds medieval to us but still exists in some parts of the country. During the time I lived in Albania, it was far and away the poorest country in Europe, yet despite great poverty and trouble, I experienced an overwhelming hospitality and generosity from its people. I went there to help strangers know God better, but as I was welcomed into the homes of strangers, they taught me what it meant to trust God, not only to keep me safe on the roads, but in all sorts of hardships and crises. I learned much of value from these strangers.

JACOB AND
THE STRANGER

The God who turns up and picks a fight

In which a homeless outcast wrestles a stranger
and wins the fight but loses his name, and we learn
how being wounded may bring healing.

It was pitch black. The boy could see nothing, but he could sense someone was there. He thought he could hear breathing and began to imagine a giant stalking him. Having already fought off lions, his horse was too tired to outrun anyone, and so, when he could bear it no longer, the lad called out, "Who are you?" The answer from the stranger was to change his life forever.

In C. S. Lewis's *The Horse and His Boy* (incidentally my favorite of the Narnia stories[1]), young Shasta is on the run from his family. The boy and his horse have suffered a series of terrible misfortunes. Relieved that he is not about to be a giant's supper, but nevertheless scared, lost, and alone, he begins to cry. The stranger reassures Shasta and listens to him as he recounts his troubles: how he has been howled at in the desert, chased by lions, forced to swim for his life, and how, hungry, tired, and thirsty, on the verge of reaching safety, another lion attacked him and wounded his traveling companion, Aravis.

Finally, the listening stranger speaks and reveals his identity: "I was the Lion."

Shasta's jaw drops.

> I was the lion who forced you to join with Aravis. I was the cat who comforted you among the houses of the dead. I was the lion who drove the jackals from you as you slept. I was the lion who gave the Horses the new strength of fear for the last mile so that you should reach King Lune in time. And I was the lion you do not remember who pushed the boat in which you lay, a child near death, so that it came to shore where a man sat, wakeful at midnight, to receive you.[2]

I first came across this story during my primary school days, around the same time when I had just started to attend church. Coming from a multiethnic family, I understood neither the cultures nor the religions of either my parents or my peers, and certainly had no idea that this strange beast called Aslan was a picture of Christ. Nevertheless, I related to Shasta, and as I read about this ferocious lion in the night that scared and scarred and chased and injured in order to protect a young lad through the darkness, I can remember sensing something deeply ominous and profoundly comforting.

Perhaps we find ourselves at the beginning of Shasta's story. We lurch from one crisis to another and have little, if any, sense of the presence or protection of God. Instead of being our Savior, he is a stranger to us. In our fear, our doubt, or our anger, we cry out like Shasta, "Who are you?" Or perhaps we cry out to God like Jeremiah, "You who are the hope of Israel, its Savior in times of distress, why are you like a stranger in the land, like a traveler who stays only a night?" (Jeremiah 14:8). I have sat with many Christians as they have asked, "Who is this God?" Others have asked, "Where is God now?" Others again have shared that they can no longer believe in God, because he is not who they expected him to be. Some of these bear the scars inflicted by unwanted or unexpected singleness, childlessness, or other forms of brokenness. Others nurse wounds of grief after watching friends and family members suffer or die.

Some have filed a hefty personal injury claim with Jesus—and are demanding full compensation. They all thought that God would be there for them, whatever life had to throw at them, but when tragedy hit, they tell how God let them down because he failed to rescue them. Their faith seemed to make no positive difference at all; in fact, if anything, it made the situation worse. If we think someone is there to catch us when we fall, we are not prepared for a hard landing. Divinely inflicted disappointment can be the last straw for us in a crisis scenario. We find ourselves at the mercy of a God who wounds and feel let down, deceived even, by a Savior who does not save.

Whether wrestling with these issues is endemic to your current circumstances or merely an academic consideration at this point, there is a strange incident in the Bible that may offer us some surprisingly helpful perspectives. We will trace in the story something of what it is like to feel alone and scared, and to cry out for rescue. We will watch how things seem to get worse, not better, when God turns up. We will see the trouble caused by deception and disappointment. We will relate to one whose family was a frequent cause and catalyst of struggles. We will meet a savior who wounds. Like Shasta we will ask and be asked, "Who are you?" And the answer may change our lives too.

Because sometimes the stranger is not God, but us.

The prophet Hosea gives a two-line description of our unlikely hero, which acts as a helpful structure for our reflections. Like many of us, this hero struggled with human relationships and struggled with God: "In the womb he grasped his brother's heel; as a man he struggled with God" (Hosea 12:3).

Hosea is not very flattering about Jacob here, and the Genesis account is similarly honest when it comes to telling his backstory. Although sometimes known as "the deceiver" or "the grasper," his name literally means "may he be at the heels," not only referring to the unusual way he was born with his hand tightly grasping hold of his twin's foot, but also alluding to a double-edged theme in Jacob's life. In its negative rendering his name means that Jacob is a fighter, a troublemaker; in its more positive context it means that God will fight for the troublemaker. Throughout the story we will witness this twin struggle as Jacob tries to grasp hold of what he wants in life, and God tries to grasp hold of Jacob. Perhaps we can recognize this tug-of-war tension in our own stories and let it help us understand a little more of why we sense fluctuations in the closeness of God's presence.

In the grand scheme of things, it is God who wins, and Jacob goes down in history as one of the great Jewish patriarchs. Ironically, God's plan for Jacob's greatness is bigger than his own, for all his scheming. However, as we will see, this comes via a more surprising route than anyone could have predicted. The first half of Jacob's life is defined by the rivalry with his twin, Esau. He does not want his brother to get ahead of him in anything—from their entry into the world, right up to his father's blessing. It was the custom in those days that the oldest son received a double share of the estate and the greater honor in the family hierarchy. So despite arriving into the world only a few seconds later, Jacob's status in life was significantly lower than Esau's. He was going to have to do something radical in order to turn the tables on his brother and be in with a chance of grasping hold of what his twin was automatically going to inherit.

We might actually have a little sympathy with Jacob here, because his marginally older brother Esau was not easy to live with. His name meant "hairy" (Genesis 25:25), but I like to think of it more as "prickly." He fitted the stereotype of a man's man in the ancient world. Outdoorsy, physical, and big into killing things, he won huge favor with his father, who loved eating wild game. Jacob, on the other hand, was quiet, intellectual, and homely, which seemed to find him favor with his mother (Genesis 25:28). In a famous food-related episode, Esau, hungry from a hunting trip, was willing to exchange his status as firstborn son for a bowl of broth. Note the contrast here: Esau cares so little about his birthright that he sells it for soup, while Jacob cares so much about the birthright that he is willing to soil his soul to get it.

Perhaps we would have expected more from the family of the covenant of God and the promised offspring of Abraham—surely God's chosen would live pristine lives of beatific perfection? But the strikingly strange thing about this story of Abraham's grandson is how dysfunctional this family is, with damning indicators of disintegration. The destructive influence of favoritism on the part of the parents—"Isaac . . . loved Esau, but Rebekah loved Jacob" (Genesis 25:28)—makes some sense of this fierce sibling rivalry that lasts for decades (although everyone in the story is still ultimately held accountable for their actions). But what is most encouraging here is what all this can mean for us. Those of us from or in dysfunctional families are not disqualified from inclusion in God's plans. Whether we are by nature prickly or selfish, physical or intellectual, chip-on-shouldered by favoritism or predisposed to competitiveness, there is hope. Even if we are at times disappointed with God, God is not disappointed with us—he knows from the outset how messed up we are, both by nature and by nurture. Whether we are messing up in the way we treat the unlikely people around us, or if we consider ourselves unlikely choices for him, we can be assured that God consistently chooses unlikely candidates for his special attention and presence.

When Isaac calls for a tête-à-tête with Esau in his tent, Jacob and Rebekah are disappointed. This seems to have been irregular. Later, when Jacob is on his deathbed, he summons *all* of his sons to publicly bless them and allocate the succession (Genesis 49), and when Joseph knows he is about to die he gathers *all* of his sons (Genesis 50:24-25).[3] Isaac, reaching the end of his life and ready to formally confer blessings, probably should have invited both his boys into the room. With his mother's support, Jacob takes matters into his own hands. Mother and son launch a private mutiny, an intrafamilial coup, cooking up a plan to trick Esau out of what is rightfully his, albeit so little valued. Despite being his son, and helped by Isaac's partial blindness, Jacob is enough of a stranger to Isaac that he can impersonate his brother undetected. In this, the first recorded case of identity theft, Jacob receives Esau's blessing—illegitimately putting him at the head of the family.

Although the deception is soon uncovered, it cannot be undone. Isaac's word is his bond and cannot be broken, even though the blessing was secured under nefarious circumstances and would have dire consequences (Genesis 27:29). However, things begin to unravel for Jacob pretty quickly. Seeing Esau's rage at his brother's deception, and bearing in mind his proclivity for killing things and his solemn vow to murder his brother, Jacob goes into exile, fleeing to Mesopotamia for refuge.

Here is a mini reenactment of the expulsion from Eden as Jacob becomes an outcast and refugee, far from his home, from his immediate family, and apparently from his God. But even in the act of escaping from Esau, the renegade Jacob discovers the mercy of God as he makes this perilous solo journey. Unlike when Abraham's three visitors received his kind hospitality, there is nobody to offer Jacob refuge from the dangers of the darkness, and he has only a rock to call a pillow. We will get to the part where Jacob experiences disappointment with God, but at this point in his life, he is disappointed with himself. Knowing that the mess he is in is his own fault, he collapses in exhaustion and self-pity. In this state God visits him in a strange and symbolic dream.

Jacob left Beersheba and set out for Harran. When he reached a certain place, he stopped for the night because the sun had set. Taking one of the stones there, he put it under his head and lay down to sleep. He had a dream in which he saw a stairway resting on the earth, with its top reaching to heaven, and the angels of God were ascending and descending on it. There above it stood the LORD, and he said: "I am the LORD, the God of your father Abraham and the God of Isaac. I will give you and your descendants the land on which you are lying. Your descendants will be like the dust of the earth, and you will spread out to the west and to the east, to the north and to the south. All peoples on earth will be blessed through you and your offspring. I am with you and will watch over you wherever you go, and I will bring you back to this land. I will not leave you until I have done what I have promised you."

When Jacob awoke from his sleep, he thought, "Surely the LORD is in this place, and I was not aware of it." He was afraid and said, "How awesome is this place! This is none other than the house of God; this is the gate of heaven."

Early the next morning Jacob took the stone he had placed under his head and set it up as a pillar and poured oil on top of it. He called that place Bethel, though the city used to be called Luz.

Then Jacob made a vow, saying, "If God will be with me and will watch over me on this journey I am taking and will give me food to eat and clothes to wear so that I return safely to my father's household, then the LORD will be my God and this stone that I have set up as a pillar will be God's house, and of all that you give me I will give you a tenth." (Genesis 28:10-22)

Was this dream really a vision from God, or just a trick of the brain of the sort that may be quite likely when you sleep with a rock under your head? Why were there angels going up and down a stairway anyway? Had Jacob found a secret portal to heaven? Why on earth does he pour oil over a pile of stones? And then, is Jacob making a deal with God? Or is he bribing him? And why only offer a tenth? Would it not have made more of an impact to have said he would give half—or everything—if only he could return home?

I think we can safely conclude that there are some strange aspects to this story, which justify a closer look.

In this bizarre encounter, Jacob is utterly convinced that he has met with God. As a vulnerable traveler, he has been assured that the Lord himself will keep him safe. Through the vision of a ladder with angels ascending and descending, Jacob is given a visual aid to help him understand that a God with the power to save him is close by, even though sometimes he feels far away. As a runaway, far from the safety and familiarity of home, and painfully conscious of being far from the person he should be, he feels God drawing close and revealing his presence. Despite the deception he has practiced and his distance from the home he knows, Jacob hears God's voice, directly reassuring him that he is still included in the covenant family—more, that the covenant will center on him (Genesis 28:13). More importantly than the dishonestly acquired blessings inherited from his father Isaac, he will receive the distinctive blessing God conferred through his grandfather Abraham. Perhaps if Isaac had been able to tell him of this heavenly blessing earlier, it might have diminished Jacob's need to cheat his way to the earthly blessing. Perhaps, blinded by favoritism, Isaac had never helped Jacob fully grasp the great privilege and responsibility that was his as a descendant of Abraham.

Jacob reminds me of a boy who arrived on our doorstep straight from the emergency department of our local hospital. He had been seriously assaulted at home and run away in fear for his life, vowing never to return. Our home was a culture shock for him in many ways. Every mealtime for the next three weeks illustrated this. Whatever I plonked down in the middle of the table, he would immediately take the lion's share and stick it straight onto his plate or into his mouth, much to the indignation of our other teenagers. It was not because he was inordinately hungry or rude, just that his food supply had never been reliable in his home. This was a learned behavior, driven by self-preservation, and it was going to take a lot to persuade him that there would always be more than enough to go around, and a next meal just around the corner, for as long as he was living under our roof. If only we could have told him then what God already knew: the family who would give him an eventual permanent home loved to cook lavish meals, and every pot and pan they owned was industrial-sized. Perhaps we too have felt so starved of God's presence, we fail to see that whatever we have done or had done to us, God is still watching over us and waiting to welcome us into a feast of his presence when the right time comes.

Smash-and-grab Jacob was also going to need persistent persuasion that he was already blessed by God, as we will see when we fast-forward twenty years to Jacob's return journey. But God begins here by restating the promise he gave to Abraham: "All peoples on earth will be blessed through you and your offspring" (Genesis 28:14). To a desperate man sleeping under the stars, unsure whether he will survive the night, this would have been beyond his imaginings—a promise of descendants as numerous as the stars and a future far beyond the dawn. Then God gives the lonely Jacob far from home the most comforting of all promises, one of both immediacy and long-term benefit: "I will not leave you" (Genesis 28:15). As a refugee in his darkest hour, troubled Jacob is treated as God's honored guest. In the inhospitable desert, he senses something of God's hospitality—God's presence and protection and promises. This will be a lifeline for grasping Jacob to grasp on to during the difficult years ahead. (Or the skeptical may ask, will he toss it aside when God seems to fail to save and protect him?)

For now, reassured by his strange dream, Jacob decides it is safest to seek out relatives on his mother's side of the family and not only finds a warm welcome from her brother Laban, but an even warmer one from Laban's youngest daughter Rachel. A deal is struck, and Jacob works for seven years to win her hand in marriage. After a wonderful marriage celebration, he wakes up in the morning to find that he has received a taste of his own medicine. Jacob ends up on the wrong end of an identity theft.[4] Under cover of darkness, his sneaky uncle swapped the young and beautiful bride Rachel for her older, "weak-eyed" sister, Leah (Genesis 29:17). Coincidentally, "weak-eyed" is exactly how Isaac was described on the night that Jacob deceived him; now it is Jacob's eyes that have played him false. In his deceit Laban can be credited for at least trying to look out for the less-favored daughter, Leah, in a way that Isaac had failed to do for his less-favored son, Jacob.

Jacob works another seven years to pay for the hand of Rachel, and meanwhile reinforces the family flaw of favoritism in his new family unit. God intervenes by allowing Leah to bear the first, and the most, children, and this initiates a form of competitive childbearing. The names of the children bear striking testimony to the dysfunction within the family. Each one is deliberately chosen as a form of one-upmanship, to remind the rival of who is winning the struggle to secure Jacob's affections (Genesis 29–30). In fact, all the names in the story of Jacob are heavily laden with significance, underlining the key theme of how we find and shape identity, which we will explore shortly. In a foreshadowing of what will be a defining moment in Jacob's life, the middle child born to Rachel's servant Bilhah is called Naphtali. Naphtali means "wrestling" or "struggle," and on his birth Rachel declared, "I have had a great struggle with my sister, and I have won" (Genesis 30:8). Such scheming and grudge-bearing in this ongoing feud between the wives and within this polygamous family is clearly shown to sow the seeds of trouble into the next generation.[5]

Before we move on with the story, we need to tackle this question of favoritism. We see in the stories of Jacob and Esau and of Jacob and his wives and children just how much damage favoritism can do. Many of us know from bitter experience in our own childhoods the pain it can cause, and perhaps we too have asked why God would allow children to suffer like this. According to the Bible, "God does not show favoritism" (Romans 2:11).[6] Whether male or female, Jew or Gentile, rich or poor, we are all considered equal in God's eyes. But the story of Jacob indicates favoritism to be rife in God's own chosen family. Not only that, but it even seems to bring out favoritism in God, articulated clearly in the prophecy of Malachi: "I have loved Jacob, but Esau I have hated" (Malachi 1:2-3).

These words of Malachi are certainly not highlighted in that old Bible of mine, nor would I ever consider including them in a baptism blessing or a wedding sermon. They seem mean-spirited and nasty. Maybe if we dig down a little into the historical context, we can see why they could possibly be included in Scripture. By the point of Malachi's prophecy the enmity between "Jacob" and "Esau" was really between their numerous descendants—the Israelites and the Edomites. So much so that, when the Israelites asked for help from the Edomites against the international superpower that was Babylon, they not only refused but joined the opposition, taking full advantage of Israel's vacated land when the Jews were taken into exile. Sixty years later, the Israelites return to reclaim their land and rebuild the temple and the city walls, only to find that the Edomites themselves have been defeated and dispersed, and there is little left to show for their existence. Israel may have complained about their fate—but they had in fact fared significantly better than the Edomites. In other words, despite everything that had happened, Jacob's tribe had thrived, while Esau's tribe had barely survived.

If you have seen the video for Radiohead's exquisite song "All I Need,"[7] you will know that they employ a split-screen format to show the parallel lives of two children, one living in middle-class America, the other in a sweatshop in Asia. One has time to draw and color and play, the other slaves from dawn to dusk. One gets to eat a lavish meal with his family, the other shares a crust with his fellow child-slaves. We are blind to our own privileges and the poverty of others, until we compare like for like. Commentators explain that this is what is going on in this verse from Malachi: it is supposed to provoke a side-by-side comparison of the outcomes of the two tribes that remind God's people to count—and indeed share—their blessings. Old Testament commentator Joyce Baldwin puts it well: "If Israel were more outward-looking she would come closer to a knowledge of God's love, and see, by contrast with the experiences of other nations, how wonderfully God had dealt with her."[8] Perhaps when we feel like complaining at God's apparent lack of attention to us, we should compare ourselves with our brothers and sisters around the globe whose faith remains whole in far tougher conditions.

The apostle Paul, however, seems to read this verse through an entirely different lens when he writes in his letter to the Romans:

Yet, before the twins were born or had done anything good
or bad—in order that God's purpose in election might stand:
not by works but by him who calls—she was told, "The
older will serve the younger." Just as it is written: "Jacob
I loved, but Esau I hated."

What then shall we say? Is God unjust? (Romans 9:11-14)

This raises more questions. If God knew all that would happen,
why plan in advance for the normal birth precedence to be
reversed in the way things played out, despite the pain and
conflict this would cause? Was it really just to help Paul illustrate
the difficult-to-grasp theology of predestination and human
freedom and the doctrines of divine foreknowledge and election?
However we understand Paul's words here, the conclusion he
comes to is not dissimilar to Malachi's teaching, and it has to do
with our ability to identify with God's justice.

In a world that seems unfair, where not only families but
entire nations struggle with inequality, the question he poses
seems highly relevant: is God unjust?

I have no doubt that Jacob asked that question many times
in his life. As a child, life seemed so unfair that he became expert
in helping himself to whatever he wanted. And these attitudes
travel with him into adulthood. As if the internal dynamics of
his family life are not complicated enough, with an ongoing feud
not only with his brother, but also between his wives, Jacob
cheats his father-in-law out of his flock through an ingenious
selective breeding program. When Laban discovers the betrayal,
Jacob is once more forced to go on the run. Can he really be
trusting in the lordship of his God now? Twenty years after
arriving as a lone exile in Mesopotamia, Jacob starts his journey
home (Genesis 31:3). He had snuck away as a scoundrel fleeing

death, but is returning as a married man of means, albeit still under a cloak of duplicity. Moving his family and herds over a long distance is not without danger and peril. Jacob is again a wanderer as his nomad grandfather Abraham had been, and as he moves into an uncertain future, he is in some sense a refugee for the second time (Genesis 31:1-3). The first time he was running away from the murderous threats of his brother; now he is returning home, fully expecting those murderous threats to be repeated, and perhaps realized.

As Jacob travels, he comes to a border crossing and again his geographical and theological journeys coincide. He had seen the vision of angels on the ladder to heaven on his way out of Canaan and now, as he heads back, angels interrupt his journey again. Some might say these visitations display only wishful thinking, that Jacob must have been imagining things. But often it is in the destabilizing transitions of our lives that we are not only most aware of our need of God, but also more alive to his presence. This time the angels tell him that the place where he stands is the "camp of God" (Genesis 32:2). Jacob names it Mahanaim, "twin camps," acknowledging this place as the overlap between where God and humans reside. It was just the message he needed to hear. Sometimes the presence of trouble in our lives seems to preclude the presence of God in our lives, as if we can only focus on one thing at a time. Of course the two can—indeed must—coexist, but we may need a Mahanaim moment to recognize it.

Before Jacob can return home, there is one last broken human relationship that needs to be confronted. The encounter with the angels and the vision of the "twin camps" seems to be the trigger for Jacob to begin to make a plan to sort things out with his own twin. Jacob has a threefold campaign to win over Esau. He delivers a message, he divides up his family, and he depends on God. Some people see a lack of faith in the first two responses, but it is well to be wise as well as holy. Old Testament scholar Derek Kidner helpfully points out, "It is over-facile to condemn [Jacob's] elaborate moves as faithless, for Scripture approves of strategy when it is a tool rather than a substitute for God."[9] Jacob seeks to win favor by sending a calming and humble message to his brother, but he also prepares for the worst by dividing his possessions and people into two groups, so if one is attacked, the other might survive. This practical precaution may even have been divinely inspired: when he looks at his family he sees that he has been blessed with "two camps" (Genesis 32:10)—twice as much as he could ever have hoped for.

"There are no atheists in foxholes,'" the old saying goes. Shamefully, it can take the threat of tragedy to drive us to prayer and to seek out God. Jacob has not displayed the characteristic of prayerfulness so far in his biography—there is a lot more focus on his cunning and deceit than on any form of spiritual discipline. But as a vulnerable refugee at risk of harm from his estranged brother, and beginning to appreciate the blessing that is his family and the Presence that is his God, Jacob is forced to cry out, fearfully, "Save me, I pray, from the hand of my brother Esau, for I am afraid he will come and attack me, and also the mothers with their children" (Genesis 32:11).

If my children never said a word to me except when the car broke down or the money ran out, it would certainly sour our relationship. Their behavior would indicate that they see me not as a person but more as a taxi service or a cash machine; not as their father, but as a relative stranger (pun intended). Yet so many of us explain our journey to faith in terms of a crisis point:

a tragedy that opens our eyes to our need of God and opens our mouths to cry out to him. And God does not seem to hold this against us. We are often more interested in the rescue than the Rescuer, and choose to treat God as a stranger when all is well. He sometimes graciously and humbly chooses not to be a stranger to us in our time of need, and does not play hard to get when the going gets hard. But at other times, he does seem far away. When Jacob asks God to save him, God decides to remain a stranger for a bit longer.

This long journey seems to be changing Jacob, the deceiver and grasper. He has finally come to a point where he is concerned for protection not just over his own life but over the lives of his dependents. I have been on journeys like that. I remember a particular long-haul flight where the plane began to experience turbulence. The plane was juddering so violently that holding a coffee cup was proving impossible and the drinks service was put on hold. I am not normally an anxious traveler, but I could see that the smiles of the cabin crew were wearing a little thin. My thoughts went to my hand luggage, and I feared for the safety of my new laptop; all of this shaking would be doing strange things to its internal architecture. But as the turbulence worsened, my laptop dropped to the bottom of my list of worries. I began to think about my children and my wife and how they were going to manage if I died that day. I began praying fervently for their safety, for their futures, for their ongoing relationship with God. Sometimes it takes the threat of tragedy for us to be aware of what really matters in life.

Just as personal suffering can heighten our awareness of whom we really love, so too when those we love are suffering, our awareness of God can be heightened. But what C. S. Lewis calls the megaphone of suffering that awakens us to our need of God can also alert us to his absence.[10] So many of my friends have arrived at the place where Jacob is at this point in the story. They may have led a life that has been off and on with God. They may have appreciated the presence and promises of God in the distant past, but then gone on to build families and lives without God at the center. Then tragedy strikes and the things that seemed important to them before suddenly seem irrelevant. In their powerlessness they cry out to the God they remember from years previously. Sometimes God graciously intervenes. But sometimes they cry out to God and their dire circumstances remain dire. Or they pray and things get even worse. This is what happens now to Jacob.

Jacob sends his wife and family on ahead of him, and eventually he is the last man standing on the far side of the river. He has to cross the Jabbok River in the middle of the night, alone. This may not have been the wisest course of action. It is at this point, when he is at his most vulnerable, that he is attacked by a stranger.

> That night Jacob got up and took his two wives, his two female servants and his eleven sons and crossed the ford of the Jabbok. After he had sent them across the stream, he sent over all his possessions. So Jacob was left alone, and a man wrestled with him till daybreak. When the man saw that he could not overpower him, he touched the socket of Jacob's hip so that his hip was wrenched as he wrestled with the man. Then the man said, "Let me go, for it is daybreak."
>
> But Jacob replied, "I will not let you go unless you bless me."
> The man asked him, "What is your name?"
> "Jacob," he answered.

Then the man said, "Your name will no longer be Jacob, but Israel, because you have struggled with God and with humans and have overcome."

Jacob said, "Please tell me your name."

But he replied, "Why do you ask my name?" Then he blessed him there.

So Jacob called the place Peniel, saying, "It is because I saw God face to face, and yet my life was spared."

The sun rose above him as he passed Peniel, and he was limping because of his hip. (Genesis 32:22-31)

We know that Jacob was doggedly persistent. It takes gritty determination and resolve to work fourteen years for the hand of the woman you love, and six more to change the balance of ownership of the flocks. Jacob is not going to let this man win the fight, so he grabs hold and refuses to let go for hours. At daybreak, the man simply touches Jacob's hip and dislocates it. But Jacob, even with his injury, even knowing that he is wrestling no mere human, still does not let go. In fact, he grasps even more firmly. The one who has been chasing blessing all his life now realizes he has the opportunity to secure an even greater blessing, and pins his attacker to the ground to get it.

In response to Jacob's demand, the stranger asks his name. This seems to be an odd turn in the conversation. God knows that the question of Jacob's identity has been a lifelong struggle for him. In this defining moment of his life, Jacob is forced to wrestle with what lies at the heart of his issues.

Being asked his name, Jacob is forced to confront his past. His name is synonymous with his lifetime of cheating and grabbing.[11]

"Isn't he rightly named Jacob? This is the second time he has taken advantage of me," Esau declared when he discovered that his brother had stolen his blessing (Genesis 27:36), a remark that no doubt echoed in Jacob's mind when asked his name. Jacob is also being asked to do something uncharacteristic—give something up. When he gives up his name to the stranger, he gives it away for the last time. Because the name Jacob, which sounds uncannily like the name of the river behind him, Jabbok,[12] also needed to be put behind him. He loses his old name, and gains a new one—Israel.

If Jacob's old name reflected his old character of struggling, grasping, and deceiving, perhaps his new name—which means "wrestles with God"—will reflect a new character. Note that he is still struggling, but no longer in a wrongful relationship with his brother, rather in a legitimate if challenging mode of relationship with God. The stranger by the river says, "Your name will no longer be Jacob, but Israel, because you have struggled with God and with humans and have overcome" (Genesis 32:28).

This is a strange statement. On the one hand, Jacob does seem to have come out more or less on top in his struggles with human beings. He cajoled his brother into swapping his birthright for a bowl of soup. He cheated his father to receive his brother's blessing. He earned—eventually—the girl of his dreams. And he even beat Laban, taking his daughters and his riches. But at this point in the story Jacob feels helpless, at the mercy of his rightfully angry brother, and not yet free of this menacing stranger. So why does the stranger declare that Jacob has overcome God?

It is because Jacob has been wrestling with God, not just that one night in the ford, but all his life. At any point God could have found him and straightened him out, while barely raising a finger.[13] It is clear that the stranger has power over Jacob: he wounds him with a touch, giving him a lifelong injury, and he assigns him a new identity. Yet the stranger declares Jacob the winner. We see here another example of the grace and humility of God. Just as God got close to Abraham by turning up as a guest, rather than the host, now God gets close to Jacob by turning up as the loser, not the winner. Walter Brueggemann describes it well: "The new name cannot be separated from the new crippling for the crippling is the substance of the name . . . his prevailing is a defeat as well as a victory."[14] Or, as another scholar put it, "Jacob has won not because God has surrendered but because Jacob has conceded . . . with God one has to lose in order to win."[15]

This wrestling competition reminds me of the ones I regularly used to have with my children when they were toddlers. Usually around bedtime, on the softest carpet in the house, I would firmly wrangle them to the ground and encourage them to try and take me down too. I would eke it out as long as possible, always letting them feel they had won in the end. It was not really a competition of strength, though; I deliberately restrained my strength to appear to be on equal terms. On my part the wrestling match was really an excuse to be close enough to hug them and to see the delight in their faces through this mock battling. There is something similar going on with God, and Jacob—now Israel—knows it. To mark this encounter he names the place "Peniel," which means "face of God." He understands the great privilege he has been given: "I saw God face to face, and yet my life was spared" (Genesis 32:30).

Israel does not celebrate a victory over God as a boxer celebrates defeating a lesser opponent, arms held high in pride at his own prowess and glory. Rather, he has been humbled by the experience and realizes that it is only by the grace of God that he is still breathing. Strangely this does not stop him requesting blessing from God. Perhaps he figured that if God wasn't going to kill him then and there, he might as well risk asking for more. Perhaps he remembered the blessing that he had been promised and was yet to see the fruit of some twenty years on. Perhaps it was his old opportunistic grasping nature, which would take longer to change than his name.

The stranger does bless, but first Jacob echoes his own question back to him, asking him for his name. Jacob has no need to inquire; he knows and declares that he has seen God face-to-face. God has no need to answer. Just like the wrestling match, the question serves another function beyond the obvious. Jacob is articulating the fact that God is not who he expected him to be. He has discovered, like Adam and Eve and Abraham and Lot, that God comes closer, yet is stranger, than he had imagined. Not just a higher being somewhere out in the far reaches of time and space. Not just a divine entity we can take or leave, who may or may not turn up when we need him. This is a God who fights, who wounds, who lets us win sometimes, who helps us understand who we really are and who we should be, who cares about our lives as a whole, not just as a series of crises, and who sees how our lives fit together with those around us.

Jacob asked God to bless him, but the blessing he had earlier been promised was not to be merely the object of blessing, but also the means of blessing the nations of the world (Genesis 28:14). Jacob asked God to save him from Esau's wrath, but he needed saving from his own failings. Jacob asked God to protect him from injury at the hands of his brother, but he received injury at the hand of God. Jacob asked for salvation, and got suffering. From that moment on he walked with a limp. His dislocated hip would be a constant reminder of his past dislocation as an exile, the times when he was alienated from God, his family, and his country, and it would be a reminder of his dislocation with his difficult past. It was a physical reminder to him and a visual reminder to others of his true identity, his true character, and his true calling. Now it is time for him to be that blessing to all nations that God called him to be.

Jacob, the prodigal son, who had rudely snatched at his brother's inheritance and then run away to a distant country, now comes back home repentant. The one he had wronged sees him coming and surprises him by running to meet him, embracing him, kissing him, and celebrating. Jacob was reconciled with his brother, and received the blessing of his father. Looking back with the hindsight of history, we can see how the most difficult and painful moments of Jacob's life are woven together into a beautiful story of poetic justice. It can be difficult in the dark times of our lives to see how the threads of our lives will be resolved. But we should take heart from God's track record in Jacob's life to trust that even though it takes decades, even though it takes pain, even though we may need to wrestle with our own identity and God's, God has everything securely in hand.

This is the fairy-tale happy ending for Jacob. Except it isn't. Jacob's problems will only get worse. He will experience what it is like to be on the verge of destitution, as his country runs out of food. He will, ironically, be deceived by his own children into believing that his favorite son—yes, that favoritism problem still has not gone away—has been killed by wild animals. After years of grief, he will discover their lies and learn that Joseph had in fact been trafficked by his brothers and spent years wrongfully imprisoned. Yet in this wrong their future is secured. Then, once again, Jacob will have to leave his country behind and seek refuge in a neighboring one. Throughout these difficult times, Jacob will need that limp to remind him to trust in a God who wounds and blesses and who promises ultimately to save, but occasionally seems to make things worse along the way.

My mother's favorite picture of the Christian faith was the "Footsteps" poem.[16] It tells of a person who looks back at his life as a series of footprints in the sand. There were two sets of footprints; one belonged to him and the other to God. Then he notices that in the hardest times of his life, there was only one set of footprints. He is puzzled and asks God where he was in those dark and difficult days. The Lord's answer is: "It was then that I carried you." Perhaps this poem gives us another angle on C. S. Lewis's story of Shasta, who also thought he was alone against the wicked giants and lions, when all along the Lion was protecting him. But this is not the experience of Jacob. At this most difficult of times in his life, Jacob is attacked by God and left permanently wounded. Jacob's footstep trail after the river crossing would show a man limping through the sand.

That limping trail of footprints, however, would lead others to know the God of Jacob. As I reflect on Jacob's story, I wonder if making an impression on the world will require that we need to walk differently from those around us. Miguel D'Escota, a Nicaraguan Christian leader, argues that not only do our wounds catch the attention of the world; they actually authenticate our message. He says, "We preach the message of our Lord. But the people want credentials. Where are our wounds; what are we suffering?"[17] Just as Jesus showed his disciples the scars in his hands to help them believe, so our tough stories, even our wounds, can both be and bring good news. This was certainly true of the early church. Luke records in Acts that, "When they saw the courage of Peter and John and realized that they were unschooled, ordinary men, they were astonished and they took note that these men had been with Jesus" (Acts 4:13). And when facing persecution from the might of the ruling authorities, it was the disciples' willingness to face suffering that impressed their persecutors.

Hosea prophesies—centuries after Jacob but centuries before the events of the New Testament—as follows:

> Come, let us return to the LORD.
> He has torn us to pieces
>   but he will heal us;
> he has injured us
>   but he will bind up our wounds.
> After two days he will revive us;
>   on the third day he will restore us,
>   that we may live in his presence. (Hosea 6:1-2)

Hosea is pointing forward to the one who will heal our wounds, the one who would himself be wounded to bring that restoration. Jesus' death and resurrection three days later shows us a Savior who ultimately does not disappoint, because through his perfect sacrifice he embraces all our wounds and ensures our welcome into God's eternal presence.

There are some surprising acts of hospitality in this passage. God personally welcomes the unlikely Jacob into his covenant family, even though he has stolen his brother's birthright and has run away from home. Jacob learns to welcome a stranger intent on harming him, and accepts a new name, a wound, and a new outlook on life from him. Jacob learns to accept himself, his reprobate past, and his risky future. Then, to Jacob's absolute surprise, his wronged brother Esau accepts him back as a long-lost brother instead of seeing only a target for revenge. Can we too, through wrestling with God's identity and ours, learn to accept ourselves and to reach out to others for his name's sake?

The strange providence of a God who can see beyond what we know and see, and who may therefore wound us not carelessly but precisely to save us, is a rich and profound mystery. When we face difficult situations and God does not seem to intervene, perhaps it is not because we expect too much, but because we expect too little. The monster chasing us in the dark may turn out to be a lion protecting us, and the God who seems so elusive may be right beside us. Our Savior may be doing something that exceeds anything we could ever expect or dream. With the fullness of God's plans as yet unknown to us, we, like Jacob, may need to wrestle with and hold tight to the truths in this story, before claiming, and indeed sharing, the blessing that God is working out in our lives.

GIDEON AND THE STRANGER

The God who turns up way too late

In which an internally displaced coward complains
to a passing stranger, and we learn that the least
likely person can change a nation—or not.

I'm almost too embarrassed to admit it, but one of the values that defines my daily life is an overwhelming determination not to be late. I get so worried about the possibility of appearing tardy that I plan to ensure I arrive everywhere early. I factor in the probabilities of the train breaking down, the bike getting a puncture, Google Maps getting hacked, accidentally turning up at the wrong airport, and any number of unknown unknowns that could impede me on my journeys from meeting to meeting. The early bird catches the worm: that is what my mother always told me. She was not wrong. Arriving early to a meeting means I get to choose my seat (near a power socket, close enough to the front but not too close to look as if I am overly enthusiastic), my pick of the snacks, and that crucial conversation with the civil servant before anyone else arrives. I am with Shakespeare, who had one of his characters proclaim, "Better three hours too early than one minute too late."[1]

My family, on the other hand, do not like being early. They are purist punctualists, aiming to arrive at precisely the agreed time. They do this to avoid small talk, the awkwardness of hanging around, and the possibility that they will put somebody out. To arrive places at a time that everyone feels comfortable with is quite difficult, but what we do all agree on is that we cannot under any circumstance be late. To those of us who have been brought up in a culture where timing is deemed important, being late is rude. It devalues the occasion, it signals to everyone else in attendance that they are second best, and it demonstrates an unwillingness to think ahead and make plans. Latecomers frustrate early birds like me because that all-important issue of timing is sabotaged before the meeting even gets started. Whatever their excuse—"traffic," "family," "unavoidable delay," "weather"—it is just not good enough for me, not when the room is full of people who have managed to beat those same odds and arrive on time. Unless, of course, that latecomer with the excuse is me. Because sometimes even I, for all my inordinate forward planning, get stuck in the wake of a traffic accident, struggle to locate a venue, or spend what seems like hours trying to find a parking place.

For those of us who find the tardiness of others inexcusable, how do we even start when it comes to the tardiness of God? Considering he is the Creator of time itself, it often seems as if he has little respect for this aspect of his creation. Recently our family increased suddenly from six to eight, as we received two extra foster children into our household, and we realized we could not go on vacation in our then family car. After much searching I found a secondhand nine-seater van within my budget, delivered them my seven-seater in part exchange, and paid the balance in full. A week later the new van was still not on my driveway. The vacation loomed closer and closer, and we had no transport. Despite hours of difficult phone calls and stressed praying, and even legal advice from friends, the dealer refused to release our vehicle to us. This went on day after day until suddenly, within twenty-four hours of our vacation, the dealer miraculously relented and our van finally appeared on our driveway. Why couldn't God have done that sooner? Why did he leave us feeling stressed for so long for no apparent reason? He can't fall back on train delays or traffic jams as an excuse. An omniscient eternal being cannot claim lack of foresight regarding what might go wrong. For one whose timing is supposed to be perfect, God often seems to come across as rather disorganized. If something trivial can raise questions in my mind about God's timing, I wonder, what will it be like when I have something serious to face?

I have spent decades praying for members of my family to become Christians, and while I partly agree with the "better late than never" sentiment, I still much prefer the "better three hours early than one minute late" approach. If only God would hear my prayers and my worries and save my family right now. When God is late, I am left with the nagging suspicion that he may not come through for me at all. Maybe you are one of many who have found the tardiness of God unforgiveable, because he turned up too late for you. Where was God when your marriage was still salvageable? Where was God when your mental health was passing the point of no return? Where was God when you were putting all your eggs in the wrong financial basket?

As a foster parent, I often hear stories that make me want to shout at God for turning up far, far too late. Why couldn't he have intervened sooner—before the drug addiction stole the parent away from a child who needed them? Before the beatings and the violence? Before the burn marks and other injuries? Before the infliction of such terrible emotional scars that they will last a lifetime? We do our best to pour love into the children when they come into our care, but nothing can undo what has already happened to them. Why has God turned up for them only now and not earlier? Isn't it too little, too late?

And still there is more, so much more. Where was God when the bombs were falling on Aleppo? Where was God when the family were running for their lives hiding from ISIS and Assad? Where was God when they paid all they had for passage on a secondhand boat, but with no helmsman the refugees had to learn on the job and steer the dinghy through the night? Where was God when the waves came over the side? Where was God when the men and women screamed and the children cried? Where was God when the boat capsized and the cold of the water and the dark of the night immersed everything and everyone in terror? Where was God when the mother lost grip of her child and she was gulping water instead of air? Where was God when the toddler couldn't breathe and the water was cold and the night was dark and there was nobody to hold on to?

Where was God when a boy washed up on a beach in his red T-shirt and blue jeans? His picture broke a billion hearts and yet, for all the tears and sorrow, most refugees still have nowhere to go and nothing to eat. People marched on the streets, we said our prayers, we lobbied our government, we took an offering, we welcomed in foster children—but it was all too late for Aylan Kurdi, and thousands like him. Where was God in all that?

Suddenly my vacation transport deadline crisis pales into insignificance. But it doesn't matter if it is heartbreaking global issues, or the personal challenges in our immediate circumstances, or the perfect storm of both: stuff happens that can make us seriously question God's timing. Let's assume he is going to help, in the end; but why does he have to wait so long and let things get so bad?

Gideon's story might help us explore this problem of the God who turns up long after his help was needed. Gideon's story combines both a personal insecurity crisis and a national security crisis. He believes that God has abandoned both him and his country. The story of Gideon is undoubtedly a strange one. Set in a dark time of Israel's history, it contains scenes of soldiers drinking like dogs, child soldiers involved in executions, bounty hunters, sheepskins, dreams, and a last-minute unhappily ever-after ending. As in our previous two chapters, God turns up incognito for a face-to-face conversation, but for Gideon things may be about to go from bad to worse.

A lot has happened in Israel's history since our last chapter. The favoritism that so blighted Jacob's upbringing duly worked its wicked way with the next generation, leading to Joseph being trafficked by his own brothers and sold into Egyptian slavery. God turns the tables on these terrible circumstances by paving the way for the rest of Jacob's family to escape famine by coming to Egypt as asylum seekers. God blesses Egypt through this family, and he also blesses his people by giving them safety and shelter and sons, just as he promised. Although Joseph's Pharaoh sees the immigrants positively, Moses' Pharaoh, some generations later, sees these foreigners in their midst as a threat and so enslaves them and tries to exterminate their children. God rescues Moses so that he in turn could rescue his people from slavery, but then through stubbornness and faithlessness a whole generation dies as wandering refugees in the desert. Joshua leads the Israelites back to the Promised Land, but when he dies the nation goes into a tailspin, leading to a period of disaster, disorganization, discord, and defeat.[2] Without a clear successor to Joshua, chaos breaks out and the nation falls into a cycle of rebellion, retribution, repentance, and rescue. Around and around it goes like a broken record. Israel forgets God and worships other gods in the most degraded and despicable ways. God punishes his people by allowing another nation to occupy the Promised Land. This inevitably reminds the Israelites to cry out to God for help. So God raises up a leader, a judge, who rescues the people and brings order, peace, and stability back to the country. But only briefly, until they forget God's provision and the cycle begins again.

By the time we get to Gideon, God's people are on the downturn of this cycle, again estranged from him, and under oppression from the Midianites. They had forgotten all the previous rebellions. They had ignored all the warnings and chances. So now they find themselves refugees in their own country, internally displaced fugitives, hiding out in caves and mountains. The invaders try systematically to smoke them out. They wipe out the Israelite livestock to undermine their economic base.[3] Like a locust plague, the ubiquitous Midianites ruthlessly loot, raid, and strip the land bare, in their quest to starve the people to extinction (Judges 6:5). According to the United Nations High Commission for Refugees, 38 million people around the world today can relate to Gideon's situation.[4] They too have been forced to flee their homes because of conflict, poverty, or persecution in search of shelter in other regions of their own country. So this story may be more relevant than we have generally given it credit for.

We cannot, however, equate today's terrible global atrocities with God's direct punishment of Israel in Gideon's time. The "broken record" syndrome evident in the book of Judges is proof of the unique connection between Israel's national security and their national fidelity to God. We cannot extrapolate from this onto countries in crisis today. In 2013 the country of Haiti was hit with a massive earthquake. Around 300,000 people died and 1.5 million people were internally displaced in a single day. The suffering continued as a devastating outbreak of disease broke out in the aftermath. Many church leaders were quick to blame Haiti's religious practice as the cause for the disaster. Their condemnatory remarks were ill-timed—a nation in grief and disaster recovery mode does not need judgment and criticism from wealthy Westerners. They were also ill-informed, using the same misplaced logic as Job's so-called comforters who automatically and wrongly blamed his suffering on his sin. We know from the suffering of Job and indeed the agony of Jesus that it is not unusual for the innocent to suffer. We therefore must not jump to judgmental conclusions when individuals or entire populations face tragedy.[5]

The Israelites, on the other hand, were under no illusion that they were being punished. God had even sent a prophet to tell them as much. Like a parent talking to a child sitting on a "naughty step," he explained that God loved them, but there were consequences for worshiping other gods. This included time out hiding in the uncomfortable dark corners of their homeland. The anonymous prophet's last recorded words are, "But you have not listened to me" (Judges 6:10). It seems like a strange and abrupt place to end his message from God—until we see what is coming next.

The stage is set for Gideon to enter; but will he pay attention to God's voice? The stage is set for God to turn up; but will it be too late?

The angel of the LORD came and sat down under the oak in Ophrah that belonged to Joash the Abiezrite, where his son Gideon was threshing wheat in a winepress to keep it from the Midianites. When the angel of the LORD appeared to Gideon, he said, "The LORD is with you, mighty warrior."

"Pardon me, my lord," Gideon replied, "but if the LORD is with us, why has all this happened to us? Where are all his wonders that our ancestors told us about when they said, 'Did not the LORD bring us up out of Egypt?' But now the LORD has abandoned us and given us into the hand of Midian."

The LORD turned to him and said, "Go in the strength you have and save Israel out of Midian's hand. Am I not sending you?"

"Pardon me, my lord," Gideon replied, "but how can I save Israel? My clan is the weakest in Manasseh, and I am the least in my family."

The LORD answered, "I will be with you, and you will strike down all the Midianites, leaving none alive." (Judges 6:11-16)

God chooses a strange time to meet Gideon: he is busy secretly trying to thresh wheat in a winepress. Wheat threshing needs an airy open space to help separate the lighter chaff from the heavier grain. A Middle Eastern winepress was not by any stretch an airy open space. It was a deep hole in the ground. This is a picture of desperation. Poor Gideon may as well have tried peeling each individual grain with a garden spade in his nearly futile bid to eke out an existence in this occupied territory where anything edible might be snatched away.

I once visited a man in a shanty town in Cape Town who raided trash cans for soda cans he could turn into art and sell.

I have seen children in Albania rolling an abandoned car wheel in the dust because they had no toys to play with, their parents working from dawn until dusk and still unable to make ends meet. I met a man in Burkina Faso who fed his entire family with leaves from a hedge because there was nothing else to eat when drought hit his nation. We may laugh at Gideon's desperate measures, but we cannot berate him for the gritty determination and resourcefulness that so many persecuted and impoverished people of the world display as they try to survive.

In one way Gideon is just like others in the Bible: when God interrupts him, he is simply going about his everyday work. Moses was feeding his father-in-law's sheep. The first disciples were mending their nets or collecting taxes. A Samaritan woman was fetching water. Gideon was prepping his supper in his makeshift kitchen. The significant encounters of God in our lives are not restricted to the times when we are in church or even in prayer. God has a habit of connecting with us at the most mundane and unlikely times and places. I wonder how often we have missed God turning up to speak to us because somehow we have come to think that we only find God in church. How many times has God sought to challenge, encourage, and inspire us and found that we weren't listening because we had our work mindset in place? Perhaps because we only really expect to see God's interaction with our lives in our personal prayer times or church services (and often that in itself is hard to discern), we therefore do not recognize God when he approaches us at work, in our studies, or in our leisure pursuits. Yet the problem may be precisely that it is more in our "real lives"—workplaces, kitchens, gardens, or car journeys—than in the detached context of church that he chooses to speak to us. Theologian Christine Pohl writes of a sacred mystery to

hospitality—showing and sharing our faith in the midst of life—and discovers "how often one senses God's presence in the midst of very ordinary activities."[6]

Gideon may be engaged in a very ordinary activity when God shows up, but God's salutation to Gideon is far from ordinary, declaring, "The LORD is with you, mighty warrior" (Judges 6:12). Sometimes God needs to be provocative to get our attention, especially when we are busy. By using the third person "the Lord" and not the first person "I," God hides his identity from Gideon. Gideon is outraged. He sees straightaway the irony of calling an anxious man clumsily threshing wheat in a small pit a "mighty warrior." He thinks the stranger is being sarcastic. Especially since Gideon does not at all believe that the Lord is with him, either right there at that specific moment in time, or anywhere nearby at that moment in history.

Yet God is indeed with Gideon—and closer than Gideon could imagine. He has just demonstrated that he is within greeting distance; and he is about to transform Gideon into more than he thinks he ever could be. The stranger's polite greeting should have been returned according to the normal rules of etiquette. We will see in the next chapter that when Boaz greets his workers in the field with the words "The LORD be with you!" they answer, "The LORD bless you!" (Ruth 2:4). Instead Gideon responds to what he perceives as a sarcastic greeting with his own biting retort: "Pardon me, my lord, but if the LORD is with us, why has all this happened to us? Where are all his wonders that our ancestors told us about?" (Judges 6:13).

I have some sympathy with Gideon here. Maybe you do too. Perhaps, like me, you find yourself internally talking back to the song lyrics at church. You are not sure you can sing "How Great Thou Art" to God when you look around at the circumstances of the world. You struggle to think of ten, let alone ten thousand "reasons for my heart to sing." Or perhaps you recite the Lord's Prayer, but you stumble over the first two words; you cannot quite bring yourself to call God your Father. Then you listen to the sermon, punctuated with amazing Old and New Testament miracles, and wonder what on earth happened to that sort of faith. It is hard enough to admit these worries to ourselves; would we really be able to raise these questions and concerns directly with God?

By appearing to Gideon incognito, God is allowing him to openly voice and wrestle with his doubts and fears. And his particular gripe in this particular fix is not uncommon today. Gideon asks the question that was on everybody's mind: where is the mighty God of the exodus? Surely a God who rescued a nation of slaves from Egypt would not look on our suffering today and do nothing? Why has he abandoned us now, when we need him most? Although God replies to Gideon, he does so while seemingly ignoring the actual question: "Go in the strength you have and save Israel out of Midian's hand. Am I not sending you?" (Judges 6:14). Why does God allow Gideon to vent his frustration yet not give him any explanation whatsoever? Does he have no answer? Why does God not explain why he has abandoned his people? Why does he not defend his good name? Why would he answer such a big question with a question of his own? Is he deliberately shifting focus because he has been caught out? Or is he in a huff, taking a line more like "Well, see if you can do better yourself, then"?

God does not give any reasons for Gideon's sufferings; instead he commissions Gideon to bring the relief and rescue. But Gideon is still unconvinced: perhaps this stranger is taking him for a fool. Of course *he* can't save his people. He is the lowest of the low—he is the least in his family, and his tribe is the least in Israel. God may see him as a mighty warrior; he sees himself as a genetically inferior runt.

Self-doubt is a surprisingly common reaction when people are called by God. Sarah laughs when God tells her she is going to be the mother of a nation (Genesis 18:12). Moses argues with God (somewhat ironically) in a bid to prove he is no good at arguing, and therefore not the right person to confront Pharaoh and secure the liberation of the Israelites (Exodus 3). Isaiah cries out to God because he feels utterly unworthy to have even seen God, let alone to be sent by him (Isaiah 6). Jeremiah laments to God that he is too young to be his messenger (Jeremiah 1:6). All of these leaders who were mightily used by God considered themselves utterly inadequate or too insignificant to be of any use to anyone.

Perhaps this is exactly the reason why they were chosen, and why they were so effective in their work for God. God's *modus operandi* is, according to James, Jeremiah, and Paul, to give grace to the humble (James 4:6), raise up the outcast (Jeremiah 30:17), and use the foolish things of the world to shame the wise (1 Corinthians 1:27). Nowhere is this clearer than in the book of Judges. In a culture that saw left-handed people as freaks, God chooses leftie Ehud as the rescuer of his people. At a time when military hardware—albeit spears and chariots rather than tanks and missiles—was the mark of a nation's prowess, God raises up Shamgar, whose only weapon was an ox-goad. In a patriarchal society, God chooses a female prophet called Deborah to lead his nation. In a time when lofty family pedigree was all-important, he chooses lowly Gideon. God's strange recruitment criteria should come as no surprise, mind you. He chose barren retirement-age refugees Abraham and Sarah to birth a nation. He chose blessing-thief Jacob to be the means of blessing the nations.

He consistently chooses and uses the least likely people, just as he chooses to turn up in the least likely times and places.

If, reading this, you think this does not apply to you—watch out! Have you dismissed the possibility of being used by God because you think you are from the wrong background, have the wrong education, are of the wrong gender, or have the wrong physical appearance or abilities? Or perhaps you have ruled out the idea of being used by God because belief in God no longer seems viable anyway. Perhaps you think he abandoned you long ago, so why would he suddenly turn up now to recruit you to his service? Watch out! Lack of credentials and lack of faith are no obstacle for God. His track record shows that he is far more likely to use people like you for his purposes than the rich or powerful or "spiritual" people you may see around you.

In the whole of the book of Judges, Gideon is the only leader to get a personal face-to-face commission from God himself, as far as we know. The other eleven political, military, and spiritual leaders in the book just get on with the obvious task ahead of them, to overthrow the invading nations and their armies. But despite, or maybe because of, his unique personal visit from God, Gideon laughs it all off. He cannot consider himself a warrior, let alone a mighty one. But God has not chosen Gideon because Gideon is mighty, but because God is mighty. The words "I will be with you" (Judges 6:16) seem to put Gideon on the alert: he may finally be catching on to the possibility that this stranger is more than he appears. Hedging his bets, he both prepares a sacrifice and requests a sign. God graciously causes fire to burst from a rock to consume the sacrifice. Whether the flame reminded him of Moses' encounter with the burning bush, or if it was just the absurdity of a rock bonfire, Gideon realizes the mortal danger he is in and cries out, "Alas, Sovereign LORD! I have seen the angel of the LORD face to face!" (Judges 6:22).

Now he knows. Gideon has conversed not with a stranger, but with God himself. Like Jacob, he builds an altar to mark the occasion and location of what he now realizes is a momentous event. God has patiently listened to Gideon's complaints and self-doubts, graciously acquiesced to Gideon's demands for a sign, and graced Gideon with his presence. He has recruited him for a mission and promised to be with him. This encounter is not a private spiritual pick-me-up. This is God himself, enlisting Gideon to act on behalf of his people. He has seen their pain; he has not abandoned them—he is going to bring liberation. Perhaps we need to be careful what we wish for: when we ask God to make himself present to us, we could find ourselves with a job to do.

Gideon's first task was not to liberate the people from physical oppression by the Midianite army, but to liberate them from the spiritual oppression of the Midianite gods. More specifically, he was asked to go and destroy an altar to Baal. With our modern sensibilities this seems like a singularly insensitive thing to do. It sounds like a deliberate aggravation, along the lines of burning a Qur'an or banning the burkini. How dare Gideon curtail someone else's freedom to worship in the way that they see fit?

This is an important issue for me, because I spend a lot of time advocating strongly for the freedom of religion, particularly for minority and oppressed groups. As a foster parent, I want to ensure that children who come under my family's care and pro-tection have the opportunity to pursue whatever faith they adhere to. So what is the deal with Gideon and the worship of Baal? Why can't he just build an alternative altar to the true God, and let the people choose for themselves who they want to worship?

This is the Promised Land, a place that God had entrusted to Israel. God's chosen people made a covenant promise to be faithful to God no matter what happened. It is because of their rebellion against God that the land was occupied by the Midianites. To then go and worship their Baals, their idol-gods, only shows further ingratitude and betrayal. What Gideon is being asked to do is not the equivalent of graffitiing anti-Hindu messages on the side of a temple; rather, it is the equivalent of removing anti-Christian graffiti on the side of a church. Seen from this perspective, God is the victim of a public smear campaign who now gets to set about putting the record straight, not an intolerant religious bigot. And Gideon, as a recruit into his heavenly Father's family business, gets to join in the liberation by exposing the lies and misinformation of idolatry.

However, there may be more to it than that. Baal worship involved horrific practices, such as the ritual sacrifice of children. Ahaz, a later king of Israel, is said to have "made idols for worshiping the Baals. He burned sacrifices in the Valley of Ben Hinnom and sacrificed his children in the fire, engaging in the detestable practices of the nations that the LORD had driven out before the Israelites" (2 Chronicles 28:2-3). William Wilberforce's campaign to end slavery is not seen now as a restriction on the free market, but as a defense of fundamental human rights. In the same vein, if the destruction of the shrines for Baal worship was a means of child protection, then this is political activism in defense of fundamental human rights. Some things need to be challenged and opposed even against a majority view in a democratic society—which this, of course, was far from being. It is not intolerant to oppose injustice and wickedness, however widespread the practice. So Gideon's actions against Baal worship can be seen as action against an oppressive and cruel system.

Yet if this practice of child sacrifice was prolific in the Baal worship of the time, why is God intervening only now, and to destroy only one altar? What about all the children who have already unnecessarily lost their lives? These are the mysteries we have to grapple with. It appears that the altar Gideon has to destroy belongs to his own father. His own family has been drawn to take part in this fertility cult. Time and again God has asked the nation of Israel not to get involved in Baal worship, but they have continued to ignore him. This time he is trying a different tactic. He wants Gideon to care about this issue and so, before he can bring renewal to the nation, he first has to challenge idolatry closer to home. Frankly, sometimes it is harder to confront a few relatives than a host of strangers, and nervous Gideon, fearful of repercussions, gets the job done—but under the cover of nightfall. When his actions are discovered and the whole town sets out to lynch him, his father intervenes, arguing that if Baal is powerless to protect even his own shrine, then he is not really worth getting upset about. Now, perhaps, Gideon is ready to rid the country of Baal worship once and for all?

We might expect that, having successfully completed his first mission, the unlikely hero Gideon would grow in confidence in his relationship with God. We might think his brush with death, combined with his own father's unlikely change of heart, would have reassured Gideon of God's power as he readies to rally the nation. But no. Gideon wants another sign from God and lays out a fleece with his terms and conditions.

Gideon said to God, "If you will save Israel by my hand as you have promised—look, I will place a wool fleece on the threshing floor. If there is dew only on the fleece and all the ground is dry, then I will know that you will save Israel by my hand, as you said." And that is what happened. Gideon rose early the next day; he squeezed the fleece and wrung out the dew—a bowlful of water.

Then Gideon said to God, "Do not be angry with me. Let me make just one more request. Allow me one more test with the fleece, but this time make the fleece dry and let the ground be covered with dew." That night God did so. Only the fleece was dry; all the ground was covered with dew. (Judges 6:36-40)

The idea of "laying a fleece" has become proverbial, but I did once hear of a man who literally decided to follow Gideon's example. This new and enthusiastic convert lived in a part of Albania that was not only impoverished but had a reputation for widespread corruption. He was facing a difficult decision and as a majority of his community were shepherds, a fleece was not hard to find. He prayed fervently, placed his fleece on his field, and left it overnight. Waking early, he ventured outside to see what God had done and which way his decision would lie. Would his fleece be wet and the ground dry? Or would the fleece be dry and the ground wet? Of course, what he discovered was what every other Albanian throughout the country already knew: if you leave a fleece on a field overnight, it won't be either damp or dry the next morning—it will be gone.

Even a tangible overnight mini-miracle like this is not good enough for Gideon, who we might note has already had more direct guidance from God than most Christians could possibly hope for. He struggles so much with self-doubt, it seems no amount of evidence will convince him that God's presence and power really is with him. After the first damp fleece, he decides to be a good empirical scientist by testing for the possibility of a false positive and demanding as a second test the reverse of the first. Surely Gideon is stalling under the guise of seeking spiritual guidance? God is once again incredibly patient and humble with Gideon, giving way to his demands. When the second fleece is dry but the ground is damp, Gideon finally has no choice but to lead the men of Israel to face the massed armies of Midian and their allies.

Now the strangeness of God is displayed once again, as he offers what must be the worst military advice ever. Just as faithless Gideon went to ridiculous lengths to test God's presence, now it seems that the all-powerful God is going to ridiculous lengths to test Gideon's faith. Gideon, struggling with a keen sense of personal inferiority at the beginning of the story, is about to see what inferiority really means. Up against a Midianite army of over 135,000, God reduces Gideon's already-small-in-comparison army of 32,000 bit by bit by bit until he has only 300 men left (Judges 7:2-7). God's strange tactics, albeit illogical and ridiculous to Gideon, were reasoned. God explains, "You have too many men. I cannot deliver Midian into their hands, or Israel would boast against me, 'My own strength has saved me'" (Judges 7:2). God had no doubt that the battle would be won; what concerned him was who was going to get the credit. Once again, God deliberately chooses the weak to shame the strong, to help his people realize exactly that, contrary to all the rumors, God is very much still present with them.

This determined whittling down of the army does nothing to reassure Gideon at this point. Still he is afraid—and not of the omnipotent God. The Israelites were not known for their military expertise, and they were certainly no match for the Midianites under ordinary circumstances. Having made innovative use of camel-based warfare, the Midianites had both numerical and technological advantages over the Israelites. So Gideon jumps at the chance to do some God-ordained midnight reconnaissance. Trespassing into enemy territory together with his servant, Gideon gets so close to the soldiers that they can overhear a man recounting his dream of a "round loaf of barley bread . . . tumbling into the Midianite camp" and a second man interpreting the dream to mean that "this can be nothing other than the sword of Gideon. . . . God has given the Midianites and the whole camp into his hands" (Judges 7:13-14).

Strange. Does God give dreams to a pagan people? Why let the enemy know what he is about to do? Is this dream of impending doom for the Midianites an early warning system that might cause a change of heart in the enemies of God's people? Is this conversation engineered by God just for Gideon's benefit—an eleventh-hour lifting of the spirits before battle? Or is it a stunt to secure Gideon's execution of the mission he has been given? How strange it is that in a story where Gideon has doubted God's presence and power despite a great deal of evidence, this Midianite soldier with his short dream has no doubt at all of either.

Sometimes those of us who think we know God and how he works may find ourselves, like Gideon, missing what God is really like or really doing because of our preconceived ideas and expectations. Sometimes God needs to turn up as a stranger to provoke us into seeing him afresh. And sometimes it is the most unlikely strangers who encounter God more clearly than us and can thus help us finally grasp the truth about God. We will see this again in our later chapters, when Jesus comes on the scene. Those who understand best who Jesus is are not by any means the most learned, most religious, or most important.

Hundreds of years prior to Gideon's time, God spoke through a donkey to get the attention of a pagan prophet. Commissioned by an unholy alliance of the Moabites and Midianites, Balaam nonetheless refused to curse Israel, because he believed them to be God's people (Numbers 22). We might expect that a story about a talking donkey would have been remembered, but this peculiar episode in Midian's history doesn't seem to have stood in the way of their attacking Israel with impunity. By now they too have surely concluded after seven years of imposing siege, suppression, and starvation that God has abandoned his people. Perhaps the soldier's dream is a reminder to them of Balaam's warning and God's power to protect and liberate his people.

The prophetic dream turns into fact as God's promises are fulfilled. Gideon's tiny army, divided into three with their paltry trumpets, clay jars, and lights—weapons of mass disorientation, as it turns out—cause so much confusion and panic that the Midianites, already jumpy, turn on each other and defeat themselves.

What a great end to the story! God, despite appearances, does not abandon his people. His period of apparent absence teaches his people not to take him for granted and prepares them to engage with him afresh. God's incognito appearance initiates reconciliation and liberation. Through his surprising recruitment strategy and unusual military tactics, God gets the rightful credit for finally routing the Midianites, while we get an insight into what it means to wrestle with God—who seemed to have turned up too late, but whose timing is shown to be impeccable.

It is tempting to end the story with Gideon set up as a hero. He is the little guy from the wrong background with trust issues who is used by God to turn his nation from idols and bring about a colossal victory for the kingdom. But the end of the story is more strange, complicated, and frightening than our Sunday school versions, and we need to wrestle with it to the bitter end to understand why God often feels so far away when we need him most.

I'm afraid this is not a happily ever-after story. There is a clue in the report of the battle itself that perhaps not everything is quite right. As his men charge the Midianite camp, twice we are told that their rallying cry is "A sword for the LORD and for Gideon!" (Judges 7:20). No doubt it was commonplace for soldiers to shout the name of their military leader, but there is something uncomfortable about hearing Gideon's name alongside the name of the Lord: on Israel's lips it sounds like blasphemy, a transgression of the first commandment that Israel were to have no other gods but God. Israel may have abandoned their idol worship, but are they just going to replace it with idolatry of a different kind?

Gideon, despite having won the battle God gave him to fight, begins a personal quest to track down the Midianite kings. First he comes to Sukkoth, where Jacob once found refuge after he had made peace with his brother. Gideon and his men are refused shelter here, perhaps because of his unfeasible claim that he and his tiny, ill-equipped army of 300 had defeated the Midianite hordes.[7] This disgusts Gideon, and he swears to avenge their lack of hospitality when he has finished with his mission. Then they proceed to Peniel, the place where Jacob wrestled with God, receive the same cold shoulder—and issue the same threats. We know from his wheat threshing in the winepress that Gideon is resourceful and determined. He drives on his tired and hungry band until they eventually track down and overthrow the last 15,000-strong remnant of the Midianite force (Judges 8:12). Now it is down to a manhunt for the two kings themselves. Gideon relentlessly pursues them until they are captured, before returning to Sukkoth and Peniel to exact his revenge—torture and death for their male populations. This remorselessness, this mean streak in Gideon, makes for uncomfortable reading.

These are dark times, more closely resembling a savage plotline from *Game of Thrones* than a story helping us to understand that our Father God, the Prince of Peace, does not abandon us. But the Bible is an honest book, and the book of Judges is recording history, not telling nice stories for children. Gideon is descending into a dark spiral. He started off with his insecurities coming out in self-doubt; now they reveal themselves in the form of self-importance. Nobody is going to accuse *him* of doing too little too late. His anger at God for abandoning him turns into anger at the Midianites for oppressing him. The unrelenting hunger that encouraged his clumsy attempts at threshing at the beginning of the story turns into an unrelenting thirst for vengeance. The man famous for laying out a sheepskin to test God now turns out to be a wolf in sheep's clothing.

Why did Gideon go off script, not merely saving Israel out of Midian's hand as instructed, but then pursuing them beyond Israel's boundaries? We do find out during the course of the manhunt that the Midianites had killed Gideon's own brothers (Judges 8:19). So this fight was personal. In fact, Gideon gives his own young son the honor of finally decapitating the two kings. But the child is too frightened to lift his sword. The kings, perhaps fearful of a bungled beheading or the shame of being finished off by a boy, challenge Gideon to do his own dirty work, which he duly does. Gideon's allegiance is still very much with thoughts of his earthly family rather than with his Father God's.

> The Israelites said to Gideon, "Rule over us—you, your son and your grandson—because you have saved us from the hand of Midian."

But Gideon told them, "I will not rule over you, nor will my son rule over you. The LORD will rule over you." And he said, "I do have one request, that each of you give me an earring from your share of the plunder." (It was the custom of the Ishmaelites to wear gold earrings.)

They answered, "We'll be glad to give them." So they spread out a garment, and each of them threw a ring from his plunder onto it. The weight of the gold rings he asked for came to seventeen hundred shekels, not counting the ornaments, the pendants and the purple garments worn by the kings of Midian or the chains that were on their camels' necks. Gideon made the gold into an ephod, which he placed in Ophrah, his town. All Israel prostituted themselves by worshiping it there, and it became a snare to Gideon and his family. (Judges 8:22-27)

When the dust settles, the people of Israel ask Gideon to be their king. Indeed, they offer Gideon not just kingship for himself but the dynasty for his children and grandchildren (Judges 8:22). What a tempting offer to Gideon, who had seen himself and his tribe as the runts and the rejects, but who later enjoyed hearing his name called out alongside God's in battle. Yet Gideon turns the offer down. Perhaps he still has just enough theology to recognize that such is not his rightful place; this is not something the Lord has offered him. Or perhaps there are politics in play, since there is unfinished business with the even mightier tribe of Ephraim. Perhaps Gideon does still suffer a little from self-doubt. Or most likely, perhaps he sees an opportunity for a reward he'll enjoy more than the responsibilities of royalty.

Instead of a throne, Gideon asks for a share of the plunder (Judges 8:24). Just something small, like an earring from each of the citizens. One earring does not sound like a big deal. Then again, neither did the mention of Gideon's name alongside God's as the soldiers marched into battle. The citizens thought this was fair enough and happily handed over their share. In total it amounted to the equivalent of thirty bars of gold, a bounty that today would be worth well over a million dollars. It was a huge amount, and it was a huge deal. God had gone to extreme lengths to make sure that everyone knew the victory was won in his power, not Gideon's. Gideon had no right to ask for payment. Worse, next the new millionaire is using his ill-gotten fortune to acquire an ephod, a tunic normally only worn by a priest, made out of solid gold. He installs it as a public trophy in his hometown of Ophrah, the very place where God had asked Gideon to destroy his father's Baal altar. Now he is back where he came from, flashing this pseudo-religious centerpiece paid for by his illegitimately acquired blood money, and the Bible says, "All Israel prostituted themselves by worshiping it there" (Judges 8:27). The iconoclast has become the idol-builder.

The tale has come full circle. Gideon leads the people out of idolatry, then leads them right back into it. At the beginning of the story, Gideon, like most of Israel, was living with geographical displacement, hiding in mountains and caves (Judges 6:2). Now the mighty Midian military has gone, Gideon and Israel are safely settled back in their homes—yet they are spiritually displaced. Disappointed with God for seemingly abandoning them, now they have been rescued they are once again abandoning God. The disastrous ending to Gideon's story stands as a warning to all of us. God was willing to use Gideon, despite his low opinion of himself and his family. God was willing to be patient with Gideon, despite all his doubt and questioning. God was willing to use Gideon to lead Israel to a famous victory, despite his bid for personal recognition. Yet Gideon, recipient of all this favor and a face-to-face encounter with God, ends up leading the nation into idolatry.

When the victory was won, Gideon fell. Not in the heat of the battle, but on the safety of his home turf. Mind you, he was not the first person to find it easier to obey God in times of adversity than in the tests of prosperity.[8] Gideon's life has become a microcosm of Israel's. He doubts and questions God, demands signs, wavers and stalls, enjoys God's protection briefly, but then forgets God and falls from grace. It is too late for Gideon now. He has become ensnared in his own personal ambitions.

Perhaps we can relate to Gideon, struggling with the hardships of life and feeling as if God has abandoned us, even though he is there all along. Perhaps like Gideon we can look back and remember when we first met God and knew his presence and protection. Perhaps we remember times when God's presence and power were incredibly tangible. For those of us who have enjoyed this intimacy with God in the past, we must take heed from the pitfalls that trapped Gideon. Have we begun to presume on God's presence with us, even as we go our own way in life? Have we, because of God's blessing, begun to accept the admiration of those around us as our right? Have we allowed our own reputation to creep up in importance alongside God's reputation? Have we crossed a line between true worship and false worship, perhaps without even realizing it? Do we have our own "golden ephods" that may lead others astray—gilded, shiny, precious tokens of faith that are little more than idols in disguise? Have we become so overly familiar with God that we are in fact becoming estranged from him unawares, and are estranging others too? Have we accused God of abandoning us, when we are the ones who have abandoned him?

These are critical lessons to learn from Gideon. His story is all the more tragic because of how well it started. Gideon was right to sense his own inadequacy. This interplay of doubt and faith should have been the defining feature of his life's achievements, but he quickly forgot such vulnerability once he was on the winning side, when the oppressed became the oppressors. Prosperity and humility are not easy friends.

Paul seems to have grasped something profound in the warning of the Gideon story when he writes, "We have this treasure in jars of clay to show that this all-surpassing power is from God and not from us" (2 Corinthians 4:7). God whittled Gideon's fighting force down to a couple of hundred soldiers with little more than their clay jars and a candle to go in each for weaponry. So we too need the humility to recognize and remember God's power at work in our own lives, now and in the future.

God showed incredible generosity to Gideon, affirming his presence to him time and again and giving this self-doubting man from the wrong tribe every opportunity to be the hero, unlikely though it seemed. Yet in the end God demonstrated the ultimate generosity by giving Gideon the freedom to reject all he had given, even though this would lead to catastrophic consequences for his family and his nation.

We learn from Gideon's story that when we feel estranged from God, perhaps we should ask whether God is giving us space to argue with him, or whether we have betrayed him. Perhaps we should check if he has really abandoned us, or if we have abandoned him. Sometimes God makes himself a stranger because he wants to give us a genuine choice as to whether or not we will put him first. It is not too late to make sure that God has the rightful place in our lives.

NAOMI AND
THE STRANGER

The God who doesn't turn up at all

In which a widowed lady meets a stranger who
turns her world upside down, and we ask:
if God is out of sight, are we out of mind?

W ell technically, chemistry is the study of matter. But I
prefer to see it as the study of change."[1]

With these opening words a beleaguered chemistry teacher
introduces his new class to the essence of their subject, and in
so doing also introduces himself as the central character of the
hugely successful TV series *Breaking Bad*. Poor Walter White has
had a difficult life. Cheated out of the monetary rewards from
his groundbreaking chemical research, he is resigned to life as
a schoolteacher, moonlighting after school as a cashier in a car
wash to make ends meet. The intense financial pressure he is
under, trying to support his heavily pregnant wife and disabled

teenage son, is exacerbated when he is diagnosed with inoperable lung cancer. He just cannot catch a break. Walter's biography seems like a commentary on the second law of thermodynamics, that the entropy of an isolated system always increases over time; or, perhaps more simply put, things tend to a maximum state of disorder; or, to summarize, chaos rules. Almost everything that can go wrong, goes wrong. So Walter decides to gamble his life on one last chance. He redeploys his knowledge of chemistry and teams up with a former student to produce a new and highly addictive form of the drug crystal meth. Over the next five seasons, the TV series presents a "study of change"—the disintegration of a man's life alongside the creation of a new drug kingpin.

Breaking Bad currently has an entry in the *Guinness Book of World Records* as the most highly acclaimed television program of all time. My social media feed would go crazy the day a new entire series launched on Netflix—coinciding, apparently, with a disproportionate rise in sick leave. The unraveling of Walter White's life and his slow-burn onscreen mutation was compulsive viewing. Perhaps as viewers we identify with the mundanity of the domestic treadmill and are drawn to this dark-Cinderella transformation, from a near-enough nobody to a kickass drug lord undermining cartels, innovating leading-edge chemical research, and earning millions. Perhaps we are intrigued by the bonding of the two protagonists, equal but opposite. Perhaps we know something of the ever-increasing cascade of crises during which God seems to be nowhere to be found.

Over the past four chapters we have been exploring our sense of alienation from a God who is to us both absent and present. Adam, Abraham, Jacob, and Gideon all struggled with different physical and spiritual experiences of home and exile. In strange ways and offbeat circumstances, each of our leading characters met God in the form of a stranger. In inhospitable times and places, each of them experienced something of God's welcome or hospitality. But at the end of Gideon's story we are left with a problem. Just like Walter White in *Breaking Bad*, there is a disconnect between his public life and his private life. Gideon's reputation is built on following the one true Lord, but he ends up leading the people astray.

Maybe we can empathize a little with Gideon's and Walter's disconnected lives. Maybe we spend a lot of time keeping up appearances to disguise the things going on beneath the surface that we do not want others to see. Maybe outwardly we claim to have confidence in God, but inwardly we struggle with doubts, a sense of dullness, or growing disillusionment. Or maybe deep down we do believe in a loving, powerful God, but to anyone looking on, our lives look like a mess, just one disaster after another. We long for God to marry the two for us—a strong, secure faith with a steady, sorted life. We long for God to change our hearts and our situations. But when God doesn't turn up for us, and we are left by ourselves to struggle and suffer, our biggest disconnect is from God himself.

The book of Ruth is a bit like *Breaking Bad*, with very different results: two strangers of very different ages and backgrounds, and with nothing left to lose, are transformed and united as they struggle together against all odds. They encounter a series of crises and tragedies and come through to a truly happy ending— but perhaps the strangest thing is that throughout this entire book of the Bible God seems completely absent. There are no divine visitations, no prophecies, no priests, no visions, no dreams, no angels, no thunderbolt miracles. This is rather peculiar since the events of this story will end up shaping the whole future of humanity. Usually when the Bible tells of something revolutionary, God has appeared somewhere on the scene, even if—as we have seen—it may be in the guise of a stranger. But perhaps the book of Ruth is closer to how most of us actually experience life. Perhaps for us, whether on the daily treadmill or in the midst of a crisis, we have come to expect that there will be no divine visitations, no prophecies, no priests, no visions, no dreams, no angels, no thunderbolt miracles. Perhaps bitter experience has taught us that just when we need God most, he feels most absent. For those of us who struggle with God being so much of a stranger that he doesn't turn up at all, there may be something in the book of Ruth, and the story of Naomi in particular, that can help us.

Like time-lapse photography capturing moments from a violent chemical reaction, the short book of Ruth begins with the unfolding of domestic tragedy that with each snapped moment seems to go from bad to worse. Yet the bigger story of the book is a dramatic metamorphosis that takes place over six scenes and will end up changing the whole world.

The first scene takes us rapidly down into the pits of despair, and is set in dark and desperate days that force a family to flee across the border as refugees.

In the days when the judges ruled, there was a famine in the land. So a man from Bethlehem in Judah, together with his wife and two sons, went to live for a while in the country of Moab. The man's name was Elimelek, his wife's name was Naomi, and the names of his two sons were Mahlon and Kilion. They were Ephrathites from Bethlehem, Judah. And they went to Moab and lived there.

Now Elimelek, Naomi's husband, died, and she was left with her two sons. They married Moabite women, one named Orpah and the other Ruth. After they had lived there about ten years, both Mahlon and Kilion also died, and Naomi was left without her two sons and her husband. (Ruth 1:1-5)

These events take place around the time of Gideon, when we have already heard that for most people life is about doing "as they saw fit" (Judges 21:25). Their moral, spiritual, practical, and political decisions are being made without reference to God at all. It is not because God hasn't been turning up; they just don't feel the need for him. Then a famine breaks out in the land. For all we know, it could be the same famine that drove Gideon to thresh what little grain he had in a winepress to feed his hungry family. We know that the famine caused many Israelites to leave their homes. But for one couple at least, things had become so bad they felt they had no other choice but to move to the land of Moab.

Naomi and Elimelek must have thought long and hard before even considering Moab as a place of safety. There had been bad blood between the two nations of Israel and Moab ever since the conception of Moab, when Abraham's nephew Lot, after being rescued by angels from Sodom, fathered children through incestuous intercourse with his own daughters. It could not have been easy for any Israelites to consider starting a new life in Moab. Not only were there simmering disputes between the countries, but as famines do not respect borders, quite likely supplies were stretched there too. In fact, however, there is no indication that the pagan Moabites resented the arrival of these particular refugees, or showed them any animosity.

This Israelite family may have had an inbuilt resistance to the whole idea of relocating to Moab, and the Moabites as a nation may well have had a distaste for Israelites, but nevertheless Naomi and Elimelek seem to have been welcomed and integrated well into everyday life there. Sometimes our prejudices are dismantled when we actually meet people from the groups we fear or resent most. We can end up recognizing our common humanity, even the image of God that is in all of us, in our new neighbor.

From my own experience of talking to refugees, forced to leave all they have known and loved as they flee for their lives, most want to return to their homes—they just need to be sure that life would be safe for them and their children. It seems the same is true for Naomi and Elimelek; the Hebrew word for their status indicates they were more like asylum seekers applying for temporary protection visas rather than economic migrants seeking permanent citizenship. They were considered "resident aliens" or "sojourners," as opposed to naturalized immigrants.[2] Their real allegiance still lay back in Bethlehem. The name "Bethlehem" is a bit of a name-drop at this point in the story. Just as referencing the planet Krypton or the city of Gotham conjures up far more than a location in popular culture today, so by mentioning Elimelek's hometown Bethlehem, this book's original readers would have made the connection to that Old Testament superhero, King David. We know from the end of the book that Ruth was written down after the birth of David, since his name is included in the genealogy. This reference makes clear the deliberate connection of this story with that of Israel's greatest king. As we track through the book, we will see hints of David's story. And those of us in the know will see it also as a prequel for the gospel story that begins in Bethlehem in a manger. The name "Bethlehem" literally means "House of Bread," but at this moment in history, ironically, the bread house was empty—closed until further notice. Its name presumably indicated a heritage of plentiful provision in Bethlehem's history, and along with the significance of its role in the future, the current desperation of the displaced family at the center of this story is highlighted.

The disparity we so often see between the promise of God's presence and his apparent absence, his past provision and his current withholding, is a difficult no-man's-land for faith. Many of us find ourselves stuck in just the state of spiritual uncertainty Naomi must have found herself in. God fed the nation with manna in the desert, yet has left her family starving. The God who brought his people to the Promised Land, a land "flowing with milk and honey," forces Naomi to leave the Promised Land because of the lack of bread and water. She flees her homeland in order to protect her children and escape death—but tragedy follows her. Soon she is an exile, a widow, and a single parent.

Five hundred miles north of Bethlehem, the city of Kobani was also once a peaceful and productive place to live. It was renowned for its ethnic diversity and its production of olive oil. But when ISIS arrived in 2014, the problems began. It was besieged, thousands of citizens were slaughtered, and then came the airstrikes. Abdullah Kurdi felt he had no choice but to flee for his life, together with his wife and two sons. They made it across land to Turkey, and then in the middle of the night they boarded a boat at Bodrum and headed for the safety of Kos in Greece, just fourteen miles (twenty-two kilometers) away across the Mediterranean Sea. After just a few minutes, however, the boat capsized. In the water, Abdullah tried desperately to hold on to his family, but the waves washed them away and claimed their lives. The body of one of his sons washed up on a Turkish beach the next day. Many of us will have seen the heart-rending picture of Aylan on the front page of our newspapers, and this image changed our collective perspective on the refugee crisis. To lose a child in any circumstance is terrible; for Abdullah and indeed for thousands of other unnamed refugee families, the unnecessary and cruel loss is even more devastating.

Naomi's risky journey seeking safety also ended in her losing the people she loved. After the death of her husband, her two sons marry local women, and both seem to struggle with child-lessness. At that time in the Middle East, with no birth control and a strong drive to have children, a couple would have expected to get on and have children immediately, but ten years later there are still no grandchildren for Naomi. The pain and shame of infertility would have been something the whole family wrestled with. She left her homeland in search of a fruitful life elsewhere, and though her sons find wives, they remain barren. And then, abruptly, her two sons die.

Quite suddenly, all the male characters have disappeared from the drama in inexplicable, tragic circumstances.[3] In patriarchal societies where there was nothing approaching a welfare state, widows and the fatherless were exceptionally vulnerable. So Naomi is left dealing with the multiple tragedy of displacement, childlessness, bereavement, and poverty. She is a grieving, vul-nerable, isolated stranger. Naomi has lost everything, including her very sense of self, and even her faith. In her darkest hour, God, it seems, has failed to turn up when she needed him most.

God is not portrayed as a friend to Naomi, or a Savior to her family. His voice is not heard in consolation. He sends no re-assuring dreams or prophets. God is invisible, and whatever he may be saying is inaudible in the midst of this tragedy. Perhaps we can relate to Naomi at this point. Without guidance or comfort

or any form of miraculous intervention, we are forced to just
get on and do the best we can on our own. So when Naomi hears
that her homeland is finally on the brink of a successful harvest,
she makes the difficult decision to return to Israel and seek
refuge there.

※※✕※※

Scene Two takes place on an unmarked part of the road between Moab and Bethlehem.

> With her two daughters-in-law she left the place where she
> had been living and set out on the road that would take
> them back to the land of Judah.
>
> Then Naomi said to her two daughters-in-law, "Go back,
> each of you, to your mother's home. May the LORD show
> you kindness, as you have shown kindness to your dead
> husbands and to me. May the LORD grant that each of you
> will find rest in the home of another husband."
>
> Then she kissed them goodbye and they wept aloud and
> said to her, "We will go back with you to your people."
>
> But Naomi said, "Return home, my daughters. Why would
> you come with me? Am I going to have any more sons, who
> could become your husbands? Return home, my daughters;
> I am too old to have another husband. Even if I thought
> there was still hope for me—even if I had a husband tonight
> and then gave birth to sons—would you wait until they
> grew up? Would you remain unmarried for them? No, my
> daughters. It is more bitter for me than for you, because
> the LORD's hand has turned against me!" (Ruth 1:7-13)

Unlike Jacob's experience at Peniel or Abraham's encounter
at Mamre, we are given no landmark to commemorate where
this turning point in the story takes place. But sometimes history

is changed unexpectedly and by unlikely people in inconsequential places. Sometimes what we do in private is more significant than what we do in public. Sometimes it is those conversations and decisions that cannot be caught on camera, shared on social media, or even spoken about in church that end up being of crucial importance to the kingdom of God. Naomi's two surviving daughters-in-law have helped her move out of her home in Moab and accompanied her part of the way on her journey. In an indicator that Naomi certainly has a remnant of faith left in her shattered life, she prays God's blessing on them as they return to their mothers and begin their lives over (Ruth 1:8-9).

We learned in chapter two that traveling in the ancient world was a hazardous occupation that most people would never dream of undertaking without absolute necessity. The journey from Moab to Bethlehem would have been particularly dangerous for three unaccompanied women, carrying all their possessions, even if there was a caravan of fellow travelers to join. For one woman alone it must have been nearly unthinkable. But Naomi, despite her grief, her status as head of the family, and her own physical vulnerability, nevertheless releases her daughters-in-law from any kind of legal or moral obligation that they may have felt toward her. She generously commends them for the kindness they have shown her and the departed men in their lives, and sends them back to Moab, where they have the greatest chance of finding security and fulfillment.[4] She will complete the rest of the journey alone, or die trying. After all, she has nothing left to lose. Orpah reluctantly heads home to Moab, but Ruth remains, undeterred. Clinging on to her mother-in-law, she utters these words, which have inspired deep feelings of sorority throughout the centuries:

Don't urge me to leave you or to turn back from you. Where you go I will go, and where you stay I will stay. Your people will be my people and your God my God. Where you die I will die, and there I will be buried. May the LORD deal with me, be it ever so severely, if even death separates you and me. (Ruth 1:16-17)

This confession marks a turning point in world history, as we will see, and we should note that the exchange takes place between two refugees at a dusty border crossing. There is a parallel here with Abraham's faith-filled trust in journeying to an unknown land with no heir on the horizon to make the journey worthwhile. There is another parallel, perhaps, with Jacob's divine encounters as he traveled away from home to stay with Laban. But unlike Abraham's and Jacob's experiences, God has not turned up, even as an unknown stranger, in Naomi's hour of greatest need. However, this stranger, this foreigner Ruth, will turn out to bring God to Naomi, and indeed the world, in a way that they could not even have begun to imagine.

They say blood is thicker than water, but Ruth's words and life say love is stronger still. Ruth is not only making a commitment to Naomi; she is also committing herself to Naomi's God. To the strange invisible God who has allowed one of his own to suffer grief upon grief. Her conversion declaration on the Bethlehem road will prove to be of defining significance. We will see how Ruth the Moabitess is included not only in Naomi's family but in the family of God. Nobody could have guessed the far-reaching spiritual consequences of Ruth's kindness to a widow in her distress.

Here, in the no-man's-land between their two countries, in the no-man's-land between their tragic history and their uncertain future, Ruth commits totally to lifelong love, friendship, and support of Naomi, whatever the cost, until death parts them. But also, Naomi accepts Ruth into her life and home. Just as Abraham is blessed after his welcome of strangers, just as Jacob is blessed after his wrestling with a stranger, so Naomi will be blessed through the company of a girl who willingly takes on the status of being a stranger in a strange land.

Here, at this threshold moment, we are drawn into the beautiful personal relationship between two refugee women. Whatever our stance on the political reasons or solutions for the problem of mass migration, recognizing the humanity at the heart of the thousands upon thousands of stories of real tragedy may well cause us to think hard about our own response. When I spent time in the refugee camps of Lebanon, I found myself asking how I would react if civil war broke out in my country and I needed to get my family away from ISIS death squads or the government-supporting military. What would I do if the roads were closed and public transport inoperative? What would I do if the only way to escape violence was to trust black-market people-smugglers, making extortionate charges to desperate people because they have a monopoly on hope? What would I pack if I was told my luggage was restricted to two plastic bags?

Each and every one of the refugees I met had faced the same heartbreaking decisions.

When I saw the welcome that Lebanese Christians, themselves facing challenges and living in a volatile situation, gave to Muslim refugees, I was radically challenged to rethink my definition of hospitality. Lebanese churches have not just been caring for refugees on a special Sunday once a year, or during a Lent volunteering drive. The Lebanese Christians I met had been caring for refugees day in, day out, for four years. They were not just donating some old clothes that they were going to throw out anyway, and calling it generosity. They were not just liking a Facebook post, changing their profile picture, or retweeting an update on Twitter. They were not just wearing a ribbon, writing a check, or sacrificing a blanket. Although all these things can be helpful, we kid ourselves if we think that by doing any of them we have fulfilled our responsibility to live justly in the world. Too often all we do is only conscience alleviation. The Lebanese believers showed me another level of compassionate service that went above and beyond. They had changed their own lifestyles in order to welcome these distressed and vulnerable women, men, and children. They knew them by name; they listened to the stories that had brought them to Lebanon; they were teaching their children and eating meals together.

Ruth's commitment to Naomi proved not to be just lip service. Ruth left her own blood relatives, the possibility of safety and security, her hopes of remarriage and of children, in order to be with Naomi. Ruth raises the bar of hospitality, compassion, and love.

Yet despite Ruth's incredible lovingkindness toward her, Naomi feels broken and alone. The third scene in the story takes place back in Bethlehem. Despite the imminent hope of the barley harvest, Naomi enters into a time of emotional and spiritual famine. Compared to Ruth's amazing declaration of faith in a God previously not her own, so far from her home, Naomi's words on arriving home to the women she grew up with could not be less faith filled or inspirational: "Don't call me Naomi. . . . Call me Mara, because the Almighty has made my life very bitter. I went away full, but the LORD has brought me back empty. Why call me Naomi? The LORD has afflicted me; the Almighty has brought misfortune upon me" (Ruth 1:20-21).

This journey has brought home to Naomi the extent of her inner transformation over the last ten years of hardship. "Naomi," which means "pleasant one," no longer fits—and she says she should instead be called "Mara," which means "bitter one." Naomi offers us a type of a female Job.[5] Just as he was stripped of his wealth and his family by God himself, so Naomi knows this same affliction, and it cuts so deeply that even the implication of her name feels like an insult.

Here is someone wrestling with deep dissatisfaction. Here is a woman so defeated by death and disaster that she has lost her very sense of herself, wanting now to be defined by the bitterness that she feels. Her physical journey has come full circle—the refugee has returned—but, unlike the story of the prodigal son that Jesus will tell centuries later, coming home seems to have left her further away from God than when she started out.

Such feelings are not unusual. A similar story could be heard in many foster homes, women's refuges, or refugee camps. Whether you have been forced out of your home country by war, disaster, or civil unrest, or out of your home by domestic violence, illness, or family breakdown, the problem is not just one of physical location, and the solution is not just one of resettlement or return. There are huge questions of integration, identity, and purpose that remain a long-term struggle. Displacement can continue to define people's lives long after the event. Instead of providing comfort to those of us in this situation, faith can itself be an uncomfortable reminder of all we've faced, with the nagging feeling that God has failed us because through all the difficulties he just didn't seem to turn up.

However, this is not the end of Naomi's story—in fact, we are only halfway through. From this point onward we will start to see glimmers of hope that will stretch far into the future. But this will come from a perhaps unexpected source. Most stories, so it often seems, need a man to come and rescue damsels in distress. Except in the Bible. Thanks to women like Deborah, Esther, Jael, and Ruth, we can counter this norm as we see strong women doing the rescuing. At this lowest point of Naomi's life, Ruth, in a foreign country with no means of income and no men to fix things, does not sit around waiting to be rescued. Instead she takes the initiative to provide for her mother-in-law by going out to harvest in the fields. This was a brave move. A young, single, foreign woman could have been extremely vulnerable among male workers in the fields of Bethlehem.

"As it turned out" (Ruth 2:3) is the phrase that the Bible uses to explain the coincidence of where Ruth ended up harvesting. She "just happened" across a field and it "just turned out" to belong to a distant relative of her late father-in-law. Once, in the book of Exodus, Pharaoh's daughter "just happened" to be bathing in a river where baby Moses was crying in a reed basket. Once, in the book of Esther, King Xerxes will "just happen" to be reading about how his life had been saved by a man due to be executed the next day. God's interventions may be inconspicuous, but these coincidences suggest that maybe he is not so very far away after all.

※※※※

Finally, this drama is ready for a new male character. As Scene Four begins, Boaz enters with a greeting, "The Lord be with you!" to which the workers in the field reply, "The Lord bless you." Boaz wants his employees to enjoy the presence of God while they work. They do not need to be in the temple or enjoying the day of rest in order to sense God's presence. They can find him even while toiling at the very ground that God cursed with thistles and thorns. For Boaz, the challenge of farming stubborn ground does not take away the potential of God drawing close.

Abraham taught us that in providing food for unexpected strangers, a dining table can be holy place. Jacob showed us that the toughest journey can be an opportunity to meet God. Gideon taught us that God can turn up in the most mundane of places. Now Boaz's words hint that our workplace can become sacred space. And he is about to find out that entertaining strangers can be a spiritual exercise that is more than it seems.

Boaz asked the overseer of his harvesters, "Who does that young woman belong to?"

The overseer replied, "She is the Moabite who came back from Moab with Naomi. She said, 'Please let me glean and gather among the sheaves behind the harvesters.' She came into the field and has remained here from morning till now, except for a short rest in the shelter."

So Boaz said to Ruth, "My daughter, listen to me. Don't go and glean in another field and don't go away from here. Stay here with the women who work for me. Watch the field where the men are harvesting, and follow along after the women. I have told the men not to lay a hand on you. And whenever you are thirsty, go and get a drink from the water jars the men have filled."

At this, she bowed down with her face to the ground. She asked him, "Why have I found such favor in your eyes that you notice me—a foreigner?"

Boaz replied, "I've been told all about what you have done for your mother-in-law since the death of your husband—how you left your father and mother and your

homeland and came to live with a people you did not know
before. May the LORD repay you for what you have done.
May you be richly rewarded by the LORD, the God of Israel,
under whose wings you have come to take refuge."
(Ruth 2:5-12)

Boaz spots Ruth working in the field and, for the third time in
a row, she is introduced as a Moabitess. I was born and brought
up in England, so it is particularly grating for me when people
make too big a deal of my Asian family heritage. Whether it was
the boys at school calling me "Paki," or a Christian friend imper-
sonating an Indian accent whenever he spoke to me, constant
reference to my otherness is unsettling. It implies that I do not
belong, and makes me feel excluded. I have some sympathy for
Ruth as her background must have seemed to follow her like her
shadow. Being known as a Moabitess must have made it doubly
hard to feel at home in her new country. But it turns out that
this is not the only thing she is known for: she is also tagged for
her loyalty to Naomi, which has become a greater part of her
identity. When the overseer describes Ruth to Boaz, he acknowledges
the circumstances that bring her harvesting in a field in Bethlehem,
and he pays tribute to her devotion to her mother-in-law, and to
her diligence in working from daybreak with barely a moment's
rest (Ruth 2:6-7). All this has made an impression on the men
around her, and it captures Boaz's attention.

Boaz, the wealthy landowner, greets the refugee woman
foraging in his field as "daughter." This is generous in itself, but
it is even more remarkable in an Israelite man, a member of
God's chosen people, when addressing a Moabitess. Usually reminded constantly that she is a stranger, now she is given a
greeting from the other end of the spectrum—as a family member.

Ruth's willingness to be a good daughter to Naomi, even in a foreign land, prompts Boaz to accept the foreigner Ruth as a daughter too. Ruth's kindness goes viral: her compassion to Naomi draws compassion from Boaz, and it takes Ruth by surprise.

Ruth and Boaz had something else in common: a willingness to bless the poor, the outcast, and the stranger. In Ruth it came out in the mercy she showed to Naomi. In Boaz it became clear in the mercy he was showing to Ruth. For both Ruth and Boaz, kindness to those in need of it was more than just lip service. For Ruth it meant a dedication to hard manual labor for long hours in a country she was unfamiliar with. For Boaz it meant a wholehearted commitment to the gleaning laws, given by God way back when his people were living as refugees themselves:

> When you are harvesting in your field and you overlook a sheaf, do not go back to get it. Leave it for the foreigner, the fatherless and the widow, so that the LORD your God may bless you in all the work of your hands. When you beat the olives from your trees, do not go over the branches a second time. Leave what remains for the foreigner, the fatherless and the widow. When you harvest the grapes in your vineyard, do not go over the vines again. Leave what remains for the foreigner, the fatherless and the widow. Remember that you were slaves in Egypt. That is why I command you to do this. (Deuteronomy 24:19-22)

This is a visionary and yet immensely practical command, looking ahead from the people of Israel's time in the desert to when they will be established in the land. In the busyness and urgency of the season of harvest, God commands his people not to harvest too intensively. They should deliberately leave behind enough of the crop to make it possible for the vulnerable to collect enough food to eat. Why not collect the harvest and deliver a proportion of it to those in need? That was something they were supposed to do too, but the practice of gleaning is not charity; rather it is an aspect of hospitality, framed by three important principles: dignity, proximity, and memory. The gleaning principle underlines the intrinsic value of work and the intrinsic dignity of those made in God's image, ensuring that the poor and the marginalized still have a sense of agency and poise in their lives. Encouraging the poor to work alongside the harvesters ensures there is personal contact between the haves and the have-nots. God knew this proximity would help to establish empathy, community, and relationship, which is fundamental to integrating the poor into, rather than isolating them from, wider society. Lastly, the motivation for this benevolent attitude is their history of oppression and marginalization as former slaves, the lowest of the low in a foreign land, and their memory of God's presence with them at that time.

The book of Ruth offers us a worked example of the Deuteronomic law and helps us to consider how, in our very different contexts today, we should express the same commitment to the economically vulnerable. We do not all have fields that we can make available to glean, but we can all live out the same principles of hospitality—memory, proximity, and dignity. The Bible teaches that we too were once homeless, exiles, pilgrims, and refugees, far from God, displaced, oppressed, and excluded from his family. Remembering our spiritual origins helps us remain humble before the God who cares about such things and retain a soft heart toward those who are in need. Distributing food and clothing may be necessary at the emergency relief level, but should not be the sum total of the church's work with the poor. We need to find ways to enhance people's dignity and respect their personhood, enabling all who can to find meaningful work and take care of their families.[6] There is a temptation to take the charity approach, for example, in the church's refugee engagement, to stay removed by throwing money at a problem, rather than building relationship with a person—after all, we may say, we can help more people more easily that way. But hospitality is a powerful way for us to get close enough to people in need to develop meaningful relationships of trust and mutual respect that promote integration into our communities and churches. Boaz's recognition that this refugee is a "daughter"— a member of his family—challenges us to a countercultural attitude and action toward refugees in our world today.

Though keeping it at a suitable arms-length level, Boaz shows real hospitality to Ruth, this woman who had been a stranger to him. When Ruth returns home day after day with a sizeable amount of barley, something begins to change in Naomi. For a woman who had rebranded herself as bitterness incarnate, some sweetness enters her life as she spontaneously praises God for the compassion of Boaz toward her and her late family. Could it be that two strangers in her life, Ruth and Boaz, are enabling Naomi to draw close again to the God who has for so long been a stranger to her?

This is a beautiful story—but Scene Five is about to get rather strange. Boaz and Ruth end up happily married, but not without what looks like some serious manipulation, on a number of fronts. There seems to be a shadow side of the story here. Does Naomi manipulate her daughter-in-law into doing something underhand? Does Ruth entrap Boaz, putting him in a position where he had to marry her? Is Boaz effectively cheating the man who should have first refusal on marrying Ruth?

We don't see God at work here in a declared way, so in the silence of the Almighty, are we simply observing people taking things into their own hands to secure their future prosperity? We may say, how is this different to Walter White gambling everything on the chance that crystal meth would be his salvation?

> One day Ruth's mother-in-law Naomi said to her, "My daughter, I must find a home for you, where you will be well provided for. Now Boaz, with whose women you have worked, is a relative of ours. Tonight he will be winnowing barley on the threshing floor. Wash, put on perfume, and get dressed in your best clothes. Then go down to the threshing floor, but don't let him know you are there until he has finished eating and drinking. When he lies down, note the place where he is lying. Then go and uncover his feet and lie down. He will tell you what to do." (Ruth 3:1-4)

This strange rendezvous takes place on the threshing floor. Now, we have already seen God appearing to Gideon on a makeshift threshing floor, but setting that aside, it seems an unlikely place for God to be at work. Yet this love story at the heart of the book of Ruth is directly responsible for a lineage that will bring us to Jesus himself, when God finally turns up in the flesh. So whatever our concerns, God is clearly at work in this marriage proposal.

It was Ruth who took the initiative to secure food for the family, whereas it was a newly reanimated Naomi who took the lead in securing a husband for Ruth. On discovering Boaz's identity, she recognizes that this is a match made in heaven. He is already under some level of obligation to meet the legal requirements to ensure the future well-being of the family, and he has already shown a particular interest in her daughter-in-law. Naomi coaches Ruth in the culturally appropriate etiquette: she is to bathe, apply perfume, and dress up. So far, so good. Then she is to hide in his sleeping quarters, and in the pitch black, when he is asleep, she is to expose his feet and lie there under the corner of his blanket. For this much detail to be included, it was obviously as strange a dating ritual to a Moabitess as it is to us today. When Boaz wakes to discover Ruth at his feet, she follows Naomi's script to effectively ask him to marry her. It is a risky moment. Will he be offended, even outraged, that this refugee woman he has been generous toward is now asking for so much more?

We are not left wondering for long before Boaz replies, "The LORD bless you, my daughter. . . . This kindness is greater than that which you showed earlier: You have not run after the younger men, whether rich or poor. And now, my daughter, don't be afraid. I will do for you all you ask. All the people of my town know that you are a woman of noble character" (Ruth 3:10-11). In this spontaneous outburst Boaz reveals something of his character. Boaz seems to disregard his own generosity to Ruth, and sees only her generosity to him. He sees the opportunity to care for her needs not as a burden upon him but as a privilege Ruth has afforded him. Interestingly, this was also how Abraham expressed his service toward his three visitors. For Boaz, genuine loving hospitality is not seen as a chore, but as a blessing. And in this Ruth and Boaz have something in common that far outweighs the significant differences between them in wealth, age, and nationality.

The dramatic moment of choice for Boaz on the threshing floor echoes the dramatic moment of choice for Ruth on the road from Moab. Both of them reveal themselves to be decisively compassionate, willing to make tough decisions in favor of others—and to pay whatever cost is necessary to do the right thing.[7]

However, it appears that as much as Boaz would like to take Ruth as his wife, he needs to follow due process, which involves first offering Ruth to a male relative who is in line to be her "kinsman redeemer." Ruth returns to Naomi and tells her the good news and the bad news. In the face of this turnaround of events, Naomi is quietly calm, confident that with a little patience all will be resolved. It is interesting to note this major change in Naomi's disposition. To me this change demonstrates not fickleness in Naomi's relationship to God, but rather her devotion. Those who are willing to wrestle honestly with doubt, despair, and the dissonance between what God promises and what God delivers are not those with the least faith, but those with the most. Those who are unwilling to just let things slide with God but rather seek to resolve them, show how important God is to them.

Now it is Boaz's turn to take action and resolve matters: can he find a way to honor God, honor Ruth, and honor his relative? As we leave him puzzling over a way to settle things, we are left on tenterhooks to see how this love story will unfold. In the final scene we find a prenuptial arrangement taking place at the city gate. The book of Ruth has given us a glimpse of what trusting God looks like in exile, on the road, in the workplace, in the bedroom, and now we are in the ancient world's equivalent to the courtroom.[8] Boaz heads to the city gate to fight for the legal right to marry Ruth. This was the place where legalities and assets were discussed, and Boaz has done his homework. Not only has he located the relevant relative; he also brings up a hitherto unmentioned field belonging to Naomi. This is strange. First, because it was unusual in the ancient world for a widow to be named as the owner of property. Perhaps it was just a forgotten part of Elimelek's inheritance—and Naomi is now the only living family member. Second, it is strange as not even Naomi seemed to know about this particular asset. And third, why would this affect who gets to marry Ruth? Boaz explains it like a two-for-one deal—buy a field, get a dependent free. The romantic in me sees Boaz being strategic in his rhetoric so that the other relative goes along with the idea that the land is not worth the hassle of another mouth to feed. Boaz, though, sees things very differently. He has his heart set on winning Ruth, so for him it is the field that is the irrelevant extra. Whatever Boaz's plan, things turn out for the best, and he announces to the town his intention to both redeem the field and marry Ruth.

His shrewdness in sealing the deal and his unheralded betrothal somehow elicit worship to God from the elders of the town, who also offer the following unexpected blessing on Ruth the refugee: "We are witnesses. May the LORD make the woman who is coming into your home like Rachel and Leah, who together built up the family of Israel. May you have standing in Ephrathah and be famous in Bethlehem. Through the offspring the LORD gives you by this young woman, may your family be like that of Perez, whom Tamar bore to Judah" (Ruth 4:11-12). What is it that makes the elders so honor Ruth as to place her up there with the standing of Jacob's wives, who gave birth to the twelve tribes of Israel? That the names of these women of national renown should be invoked on behalf of a Moabitess is a sign of the degree of acceptance the community has given Ruth. The elders also pray that Ruth and Boaz together will be like Tamar and Judah. Theirs is the only other occurrence of this kind of "levirate" marriage in the story of Israel—where a man marries the widow of a family member to care for her and preserve the family name, as set out in the Law. It must be said that the incident with Tamar and Judah goes to a whole other level of strange that deserves a chapter of its own someday. Suffice to say here that it involves a fake prostitute and a honey-trap seduction. Nevertheless, this bizarre episode in Israel's history is not so embarrassing that it cannot be part of this celebratory wedding blessing for Ruth and Boaz. Indeed, Tamar and Judah's son Perez was an important ancestor of Boaz, and therefore his name was likely highly regarded in the region.

The scene ends with Boaz and Ruth wed and conceiving a child together, her previous decade of infertility notwithstanding. Following this unlooked-for birth in Bethlehem, we see people gathering to worship. The women who barely recognized Naomi when she arrived back from Moab now sing to her again, underlining Naomi's significance in this story:

> "Praise be to the Lord, who this day has not left you without a guardian-redeemer. May he become famous throughout Israel! He will renew your life and sustain you in your old age. For your daughter-in-law, who loves you and who is better to you than seven sons, has given him birth."
>
> Then Naomi took the child in her arms and cared for him. The women living there said, "Naomi has a son!" And they named him Obed. He was the father of Jesse, the father of David. (Ruth 4:14-17)

Why does the song celebrate the birth of a child as if to Naomi? Does this mean Ruth has become irrelevant now she's borne a child? Maybe the townsfolk realize the importance of a new generation to the family that Elimelek left behind? Perhaps it is because Boaz is the kinsman redeemer and so the genetic connection with Naomi has been upheld. Or perhaps Naomi will adopt this boy as if he were her own son, to make up for the sons she lost. Whatever the reason, this baby in some way symbolizes Naomi's rehabilitation, guarantees her welfare, and revives her spirit, although it is Ruth who gets mentioned in the genealogy. Yet God still has not turned up in this story, at least not in the way he turned up right in front of Adam and Eve, Abraham, and Jacob. However, nobody now seems to be in any doubt that God was there all along: "He has not left you." Naomi has gone through quite a transformation, and it is fitting that the story ends with a song of celebration of this fact. God is given the credit for filling up the emptiness and restoring the sweetness to the one formerly known as Mara.

Perhaps asking "Where is God?" while looking at the book of Ruth is a little like a tourist wandering around Oxford looking for the university. Where is it? It is both nowhere and everywhere. Because the Oxford colleges are spread out across the city, there is no single location for the university—yet at the same time, the university is "all around you, in it you live and breathe and have your being" (see Acts 17:28). God was present in Israel when the famine came; in fact, perhaps the famine was God-ordained, to help Israel remember their need for him. God was still sustaining the universe when Elimelek, Mahon, and Kilion were dying. God was showing his mercy through the refugee girl Ruth, when she chose to stick by her grieving mother-in-law on the Bethlehem road. God was in fact taking special care of the widows and the strangers in this story, not only blessing them, but blessing others through them. God was in the detail when Ruth "just happened" to find herself in Boaz's field. God was at work in Ruth's care shown to Naomi, in Boaz's generosity to his employees and to Ruth, and in the town's hospitality toward this new family unit. God is even at work in the final genealogy—overruling circumstances to connect the characters of the story to himself, not just through his mercy in leading them to find temporary refuge in hard times, but to connect them to David, and as the New Testament genealogy shows us, ultimately to Jesus, the one whose act of merciful hospitality would also guarantee their eternal security. So it is right and fitting that the story concludes with the acknowledgment that God is to be glorified as the ultimate provider. God may have been out of sight, but we were never out of mind. God does not need to turn up when he is there all along.

When life lurches from sweet to bitter or from bitter to sweet again; when we long to conceive a child, or mourn the death of a child, or celebrate the birth of a child; when our once-full cupboards become bare, or once-bare cupboards become full; when our faith is strong or when our faith is shattered; when the harvest is lost or when the harvest is gathered; when our neighbors become strangers or when strangers become family; when our past is full of tragedy or our future is uncertain; when we face challenges in our personal life or in our public life—this is the testimony of Naomi: God does not need to "turn up" when he has been there all along. What happens when bad things collide with good people?

Walter White's misfortune in *Breaking Bad* transforms him from an upstanding citizen to a corrupt criminal, leading him eventually to embody everything he initially despised. His motivation and morality are compromised, and he leaves chaos and destruction in his wake. Naomi's misfortune, on the other hand, leads to a very different transformation. God, although appearing utterly absent from her life, reveals himself as the architect of positive transformation for Naomi, Ruth, and Boaz, a transformation that spans their lifetimes and reaches far beyond. Naomi's transformation is catalyzed by the kindness of strangers—it is the surprising grace of God shown to her by others that presents her with hope and heals her soul.

Henri Nouwen described hospitality as "the creation of free space where the stranger can enter and become a friend instead of an enemy. Hospitality is not to change people, but to offer them space where change can take place."[9] Naomi's testimony about the transformational hospitality of a refugee and stranger has been not only a study in change, but a study in the welcome, the unusual hospitality of God himself. There is a sweetness to God's grace even through the bitterness of human suffering.

DAVID AND THE STRANGER

The God who used to turn up

In which an angry king calls out to a stranger,
because there are more giants to slay,
and we judge how hard it is to love our enemies.

I lose control and, without understanding why, I sense the car tipping over the embankment and into the river. As the cold water pours in through door seals and windows, it soaks my body and I begin struggling with the seatbelt to escape. It is as the water is about to cover my mouth that I begin to scream, and that is usually the point where I wake up, perspiring and panicking. There are a few potential variations on this recurring dream. Sometimes I am in the sea with land nowhere in sight and no boats or help anywhere near, just endless wide-open ocean. Sometimes I escape the car and am trying to tread water but failing, slipping down under the water, struggling to get to the surface as my lungs feel like they are about to explode. Sometimes I wake up and I have numb hands because in my sleep my arms have been crossed over my body, as if I had been clinging to a flotation device all night. Apparently this is quite a common night terror, and it definitely turns up when I am at my most anxious or busy. Just as my laptop keeps whirring away after I have shut it down, my subconscious sometimes needs to work overtime to fan those anxieties away, deal with unfinished business of the day, and prevent a real-world meltdown.

The images from our underwater nightmares not only give us a nighttime release from the buildup of anxiety, but also supply a few idioms to explain to others how we can feel overwhelmed by circumstances beyond our control. "I'm up to here," someone may admit as they struggle with the ever-harder job of caring for elderly relatives on top of other commitments. Then they draw an imaginary line in the air with their finger way over their heads. "I'm struggling to keep my head above water," confesses someone else who has lost their job to new technologies or government cuts. "I'm out of my depth," sighs someone else who has taken on a challenging new responsibility they were not really prepared for.

For those of us who regularly feel as if we are drowning under the weight of circumstances, our anxieties, or successive crises, there is much encouragement to be taken from one of the all-time major heroes in the Bible—who puts it so much better than I can. Naomi's great-great-grandson David poetically explains that all-too-common sinking feeling.

> Save me, O God,
>   for the waters have come up to my neck.
> I sink in the miry depths,
>   where there is no foothold.

I have come into the deep waters;
>   the floods engulf me.
I am worn out calling for help;
>   my throat is parched.
My eyes fail,
>   looking for my God. (Psalm 69:1-3)

Just like in my nightmares, David is unable to tread water or feel the security of firm ground beneath his feet, and he fears he is about to go under. He has shouted himself hoarse trying to get God's attention. His strained eyes are now failing. God is a stranger to him—not only out of sight, but also out of earshot and out of reach. Sadly, there is nothing strange about suffering, and both life and the Bible are full of it, especially in the book of Psalms. We have plenty of hymn books on offer, but in this, the only official, divinely endorsed collection of worship songs on the planet, it may seem strange to hear David speaking like this, expressing ever more desperate feelings. David is one of the legends of faith. Every child who has ever been to Sunday school knows his story.

Time for a "flashback" look at David's life, to see how it is possible to go from a faith-filled hero where no trouble was too hard to handle, to a quivering wreck, apparently deserted by God, and angry as hell.

Many years previously, Ruth's grandson Jesse sent his older sons to the front line to guard against an attack from neighboring Philistia. His younger sons, including the youngest, David, didn't go—perhaps David was considered too much of a runt to make the cut. Anyhow, his job was to stay home to tend the sheep. This had the added advantage for Jesse of having an errand boy on his doorstep. He would send David on the odd food-delivery run to keep his older boys well fed, and the unit commander well oiled too, to keep them in his good books. As a side benefit, it meant Jesse could also satisfy his own hunger for news of how his boys were faring in battle. On one occasion, David left his sheep and set off, laden with bread and cheeses, and with no idea of the surprising turn of events that was about to take place. Singer-songwriter Rich Mullins puts it well: "David didn't kill Goliath because he set out to slay giants. He set out to give sandwiches to his brothers, and Goliath got in the way."[1] Remember Eve's fruit, Abraham's veal, Jacob's soup, Gideon's handfuls of wheat, and Ruth's unexpected armfuls of barley? The sharing of food can be a dangerous and life-changing occupation. David's packed lunch delivery is about to give him, and us, some serious food for thought.

On hearing Goliath's taunts, the young shepherd boy becomes incensed. He cannot let the offense of the larger-than-life Philistine's ultimatum go by, and knows he has to do something. Goliath had been coming out of the ranks to mock the Israelites for forty days before David turned up, and the thousands of Israelite soldiers were getting used to him shouting "his usual defiance" (1 Samuel 17:23). But turning up fresh from the fields, David simply could not let this outrage pass. David's reaction puts him at odds with his family, and with his eldest brother in particular. Eliab is livid at what he sees as David's conceited presumption. Eliab even doubts David's reason for being at the front line, knowing apparently "how wicked your heart is" (1 Samuel 17:28), and accusing his little brother of the voyeuristic interest in war zones known today as dark tourism. But Eliab's fierce words chiding him for skiving off his duties with the sheep do not weaken David's resolve. Despite the lack of blessing from his family and ignoring the shortage of XXS-sized armor, David finds a way to face down Goliath—with well-known results.

What is it that makes David, possibly the youngest person there to hear Goliath's taunt, react so differently to the rest? Why is it that while everyone else is "dismayed and terrified" (1 Samuel 17:11), David, faced with the near-impossible challenge of dispatching a giant, is the only one to see that with the might of God himself on their side (and his God-given transferable skills) anything is possible? Goliath sneers at the puny champion that Israel has sent against him, but David declares, "You come against me with sword and spear and javelin, but I come against you in the name of the LORD Almighty, the God of the armies of Israel, whom you have defied" (1 Samuel 17:45).

We are not given much access to David's inner life during the events of this auspicious day. Perhaps it was his big brother's taunts as much as those of exceedingly tall Philistines that sharpened his anger. We know only of the great confidence in God that young David shows: "The LORD who rescued me from the paw of the lion and the paw of the bear will rescue me from the hand of this Philistine" (1 Samuel 17:37). And we know how five smooth stones become divinely guided missiles in his sling.

David's giant-killing exploits were not restricted to the initial Goliath showdown. Over the course of his life, with God's help he led huge military and strategic victories, defeating the Philistines on countless occasions and capturing the city of Jerusalem from the Jebusites for his own capital. But David was also faced with numerous other battles—with himself. Sometimes, on those occasions, God's help was not so forthcoming.

This brings us to the question at the heart of this chapter. What do we do with a God who used to turn up and now doesn't?

With a God who used to show up and save us but now feels more like a stranger? Perhaps we remember times when we heard God's voice, saw God's power at work in our lives and through our prayers, or felt God use us for his purposes—yet now all that feels like memories of a dim and distant past. Where has that God gone? We strain to see him, to hear his voice, to grasp his saving power, but the ground is sinking beneath our feet. What used to be the solid foundation of our lives has turned to miry uncertainty, and we just cannot gain a foothold.

Once David had stood boldly in the name of the Lord Almighty, against a giant no less. In fact, whether he faced a giant or an irate, spear-throwing father-in-law (see 1 Samuel 18:11), David had always operated with exemplary confidence, trusting in God's protection and blessing. Even when he had committed adultery and murder and God sent a prophet to confront him, David knew a very real sense of God's forgiveness. Even when he was on the run, a refugee of sorts, hiding in the caves to escape Saul's murderous threats, David could sing of God's great love. The Lord was his refuge and his strength in the very toughest times. David went into battle against the Philistines time and again relying on a God who was real to him.

But scattered among David's psalms of confident dependence on God, there are many psalms penned by David that express his doubts and despair. Although it is liberating to learn from this example that God is OK with us expressing these feelings, it is frustrating to know that God doesn't always step in to buoy David up, whether emotionally or in practical terms. If David, the great chosen king and anointed savior-shepherd-songwriter of the Israelites, cannot keep it together, what hope have we got?

Beneath David's tough exterior, the hardened warrior wrestled with internal battles that were more relentless than the Philistine army. Why did the God who enabled David to overcome taunts, trouble, and terror in the Goliath story appear to desert him when it came to this inner turmoil, later in his life, after he had become king? Why did the David who in his youth was willing to go up against a giant with some stones and a sling wind up doubting God's interest in his life at all?

We will wrestle with these questions as we dive deeper into Psalm 69, because there is a chance that understanding something of David's experience can help those of us who feel God has recently become more of a stranger to us than ever before.

> I am worn out calling for help;
>> my throat is parched.
> My eyes fail,
>> looking for my God.
> Those who hate me without reason
>> outnumber the hairs of my head;
> many are my enemies without cause,
>> those who seek to destroy me.
> I am forced to restore
>> what I did not steal.
> You, God, know my folly;
>> my guilt is not hidden from you. (Psalm 69:3-5)

Apparently this particular psalm was set to music. We may never know what that tune sounded like, but the name "The Tune of Lilies" conjures up a far more serene mood than the jarring, discordant lyrics of the psalm warrant. David is really not in a good place. Not only does he feel like a man overboard, drowning in a violent sea, hopelessly out of his depth; he is facing real danger from the enemies around him. He feels isolated and victimized. He cannot understand why so many people hate him and want to do him harm.

To top that off, David knows that morally, spiritually, he has put distance between himself and God too. Those of us who have been through difficult times may know how suddenly attacks can seem to come on all fronts. We face some sort of crisis, and simultaneously it seems our immune system crashes, we miss a payment, we crash the car, family and church are otherwise engaged with no time to help us; we can't see a way out through all the obstacles, and we lose sight of God. It is a sadly common story.

In these crises of life, we can experience the weight of all four degrees of separation we looked at in chapter one when Adam and Eve were exiled from Eden. Spiritually, socially, geographically, and emotionally, David feels displaced from the life he should be in, and struggling. He feels he has become a stranger to his family. He feels he is estranged from the God who used to turn up to help him out, but now is nowhere to be seen. In the midst of all this, perhaps because of all this, he cries out in desperation:

Lord, the LORD Almighty,
    may those who hope in you
    not be disgraced because of me;
God of Israel,
    may those who seek you
    not be put to shame because of me.
For I endure scorn for your sake,
    and shame covers my face.
I am a foreigner to my own family,
    a stranger to my own mother's children;

for zeal for your house consumes me,
    and the insults of those who insult you fall on me.
        (Psalm 69:6-9)

Despite feeling out of his depth, abandoned, and attacked on all fronts, David does not stop crying out to God. And he does not stop worrying about the impact of his situation on others. He fears the difficulties he is facing will cause other people to stumble in their faith and lives. Even though it may be those very people who are causing him to stumble.

I have spoken with many Christians facing all sorts of tough situations, and they commonly reflect on how their difficulties have been exacerbated by others. Perhaps in your leadership at work, at home, or in the church you have known the pain of suffering and the added misery that comes from dissenting factions, vociferous critics, or unsupportive friends and family. Feeling kicked when you are down can be the last straw. Maybe you have felt such a sense of isolation and intimidation that you have been tempted to just throw in the towel and walk away, shaking the dust off your feet in the hope of moving on. But even when others have let you down, you still feel a responsibility not to let *them* down. Maybe you have been fortunate enough to experience something of the presence of God especially keenly at this point, or maybe, like David, you have noted what seems to be God's conspicuous absence.

David's concern for those around him fuels his anger. His complaint against God is that having endured scorn and ridicule for God's sake, it has led not to his vindication but to vilification, not to public praise but to public shame. And not any old public, but the public that counts the most—his own family. When we are estranged from our closest relatives, something fundamental is lost. Just like Jacob, the tragedy of being an outcast from his family forces David to call out to God. But for David it is not just his lies and cheating that have got him into trouble, he says, but also his very passion and zeal for God.

There are a couple of episodes in David's life that may help to illustrate this powerful zeal for God—and how it sometimes seemed to cause more trouble than it was worth. One of David's major projects as king was to capture and develop the city of Jerusalem. David was so passionate about building Jerusalem as a city for God that he decided he would install there that most holy of relics, the Ark of the Covenant containing the stone tablets God had given to Moses. David took all his men with him to ensure a full parade of honor to mark the occasion. But then something very strange happened.

> They set the ark of God on a new cart and brought it from the house of Abinadab, which was on the hill. Uzzah and Ahio, sons of Abinadab, were guiding the new cart with the ark of God on it, and Ahio was walking in front of it. David and all Israel were celebrating with all their might before the LORD, with castanets, harps, lyres, timbrels, sistrums and cymbals.
>
> When they came to the threshing floor of Nakon, Uzzah reached out and took hold of the ark of God, because the oxen stumbled. The Lord's anger burned against Uzzah because of his irreverent act; therefore God struck him down, and he died there beside the ark of God.
>
> Then David was angry because the LORD's wrath had broken out against Uzzah. (2 Samuel 6:3-8)

The God who patiently called Gideon away from a threshing floor, and who brought Ruth and Boaz together on one, now appears again on a different threshing floor. But this time it is to strike Uzzah dead. This story is hard to swallow. Surely God should intervene to stop a terrorist who commandeers a nineteen-ton truck to deliberately mow down a crowd of people out for an evening stroll in the south of France, not a man steadying God's gold box on a cart to save it from falling? Uzzah, as far as we know, was simply trying his best to protect God's honor, but in return only received an immediate execution at the hands of God himself. I find David's response to God's actions completely understandable: he is afraid and he is angry. This is not the God he thought he knew. How could he trust a God like this? God doesn't present any rationale, any apology, any explanation. So we too are left with the question hanging: why does the God who has the power to strike Uzzah dead for his accidental irreverence, or to kill Ananias and Sapphira in the New Testament for their dishonesty in apparent generosity, not strike dead the perpetrators of far worse atrocities today? David needs a cooling-off period for his anger at God to simmer down, or possibly for God's anger with him to be assuaged. So he puts his plans to move the Ark on hold for three months.

This side of eternity, we may not get to see what God is ultimately doing about the injustice in our world. We may never fully comprehend why God acts or doesn't act in certain circumstances. In fact, it may be arrogant of us to think that our minds are able to grasp the intricacies and interwoven causal connections in our universe. Perhaps one day it will be explained to us. Somehow, David is able to move on in his relationship with God, and this incident does not become a permanent barrier. Three months later, David feels confident that God would bless his decision to relocate the Ark. And when it finally arrives safely in Jerusalem, he is so relieved that he hosts a party. It includes a ceremony of sacrifice, a generous distribution of bread and fruitcake to everyone, and an exuberant dance from David, exchanging his elaborate royal robes for a simple priestly vest: "Wearing a linen ephod, David was dancing before the LORD with all his might, while he and all Israel were bringing up the ark of the LORD with shouts and the sound of trumpets" (2 Samuel 6:14-15).

However, David's accomplishments, worship, hospitality, and passion meet with brutal criticism from his own wife, who accuses him of being undignified: "How the king of Israel has distinguished himself today, going around half-naked in full view of the slave girls of his servants as any vulgar fellow would!" (2 Samuel 6:20). Perhaps her indignation was the tip of the iceberg compared to that of his greater critics. Perhaps this was the context for David losing his footing and feeling out of his depth, surrounded by enemies that were once friends, and strangers who are family. All because he felt so passionate for God's honor that he couldn't resist a party with his people.

Jesus himself would experience something not too dissimilar. The one who brought the wine to the party, blessed all who came to him in need, and fed the crowds in their thousands, saw people unreasonably and viciously turn against him. The Jewish leaders said it was undignified of him to eat with sinners, heal on the sabbath, and preach liberation in the temple. Jesus says that although they had seen the miracles, nevertheless, "They have hated both me and my Father. But this is to fulfill what is written in their Law: 'They hated me without reason'" (John 15:24-25).

Jesus is directly quoting the very same psalm of David we have been exploring in this chapter. None of its verses would make a great piece of wall art, it is rarely quoted in greeting cards, and it certainly has not met with the approval of my highlighter pen. Yet it is one of the most frequently quoted psalms in the New

Testament. Somehow what David is experiencing is a foreshadowing of what Christ would experience. Like David, Jesus too showed a zeal for God that would alienate him from his family. On another occasion this psalm is recalled by the disciples when they see Jesus enraged by moneymakers desecrating the temple courts and preventing non-Jews from worshiping God there.[2] His disciples, we are told, "remembered that it is written: 'Zeal for your house will consume me'" (John 2:17).

In referencing David's "angry psalm," Jesus shows us how there can be a place for pure, holy anger. He is not defending his own rights, angry that he is being mistreated. Rather, he is defending the honor of God his Father and the right of Gentiles to come and worship. Out of his sense of justice, Jesus is willing to raise a whip of cords to drive animals and marketers out of the temple, but later he will not raise a finger to defend himself against the injustice of the Roman plot to execute him. Jesus is not cruel, but he is forceful.[3] He cannot remain quiet faced with the injustice he sees around him on this occasion. With courage and passion he breaks with decorum and takes immediate and effective action. The Jesus who is gentle, meek, and mild when being tortured and killed is also forceful, angry, and riled when necessary, to ensure the tables are turned on injustice and people are liberated to worship.

It is Jesus again who is in view when Paul cites the same psalm in the book of Romans: "Each of us should please our neighbors for their good, to build them up. For even Christ did not please himself but, as it is written: 'The insults of those who insult you have fallen on me'" (Romans 15:2-3). This time it is not Jesus' zeal for God's place of worship that is recognized, but Jesus' zeal for God's right to be worshiped. Biblical scholar and Christian statesman John Stott helpfully observes that Paul is asserting that "Christ so completely identified himself with the name, will, cause and glory of the Father that insults intended for God fell upon him."[4] Paul wants Jesus' passion for God despite criticisms and insults to become a model for us. In seeking the good of our neighbors, we too may experience alienation.

Many of us know the truth of this from experience. Nighttime street pastors, who voluntarily serve their communities at the most unsociable of times and places, are not always kindly received, and receive the most uncensored of insults. Children's workers often go home with complaints ringing in their ears, rather than compliments. Even a neighborly offer of help and hospitality can be met with suspicion or thinly disguised sneers. These insults can torment us. They can keep us awake at night. They can make us wonder if following God is worth it. They can rob us of our faith and sense of assurance. David, facing the cruel thanklessness of those nearest to him, was desperate to feel affirmed and supported by his God:

> But I pray to you, LORD,
>   in the time of your favor;
> in your great love, O God,
>   answer me with your sure salvation.
> Rescue me from the mire,
>   do not let me sink;
> deliver me from those who hate me,
>   from the deep waters.
> Do not let the floodwaters engulf me
>   or the depths swallow me up
>   or the pit close its mouth over me. (Psalm 69:13-15)

David asks for four things in the final sections of this psalm: rescue, reconciliation, retribution, and redemption. Asking first for rescue, he returns to the watery lexicon that he used at the beginning of the psalm. He asks God to intervene in his circumstances so that his head can be lifted above the water. He asks God not to let him sink or be swallowed up or swept away in the flood. Some of us may have a problem with these kinds of words; they seem self-centered and personally preoccupied. Where is David's concern for others now? Why can't he be more like Paul on death row, who prayed not for rescue, but for blessing on those around him? But Jesus, in the same position, prayed more like David than Paul. His personal anguish was so intense that he sweated blood as he asked God to save him from his suffering—yet we could hardly dare accuse Jesus of not caring about those around him or putting their needs first, as indeed his final conclusion showed. What are we to make of this variety of responses? What Paul, David, and Jesus have in common is that they all exhibit moments of great courage, and yet also all exhibit times of real humanity and utter weakness. We should not try to iron out but to appreciate the honesty of the Bible that shows us authentic humanity across the spectrum of human experience and emotion.

The 150 psalms in our Bibles offer us great variety in this respect. There are calls for justice, confessions of guilt, celebrations of creation, conversations with God about wisdom and insight, and complaints about doubt, pain, or abandonment. Here in Psalm 69 we see a cry to God for rescue, and we can be assured from Jesus' example, too, that this expression can be a legitimate form of prayer.

The problem for many of us is not that we are afraid to pray like this, but that we are too prone to do so. Too often our prayers are rescue prayers, treating God like a recovery service, not just there for the extreme breakdowns, but to fix every flashing light on the dashboard, and whenever and wherever we struggle to get started in the morning, for whatever reason. Our prayer life can become so self-serving that we lose sight of God and others. Maybe it's not that God makes himself a stranger by failing to intervene every time we ask for help. Perhaps we make God a stranger by ignoring the things he cares about. While being encouraged by David that even when our relationship with God feels distant, we can freely bring our rescue prayers to him, at the same time, this psalm challenges us to return often in reflection on God's honor and God's concerns.

Second, David asks for reconciliation with God:

Answer me, LORD, out of the goodness of your love;
    in your great mercy turn to me.
Do not hide your face from your servant;
    answer me quickly, for I am in trouble.
Come near and rescue me;
    deliver me because of my foes.
You know how I am scorned, disgraced and shamed;
    all my enemies are before you.
Scorn has broken my heart
    and has left me helpless;
I looked for sympathy, but there was none,
    for comforters, but I found none.
They put gall in my food
    and gave me vinegar for my thirst. (Psalm 69:16-21)

David feels the threat of being barred from fellowship with God, just as Adam and Eve were barred from the garden because of their betrayal. For David this leads to a recognition of his need for reconciliation, and he appeals to God's goodness and mercy. These two characteristics remind us of Psalm 23, David's most famous of psalms, which assures us of God's presence through the darkest of valleys and ends with the great declaration, "Surely your goodness and love will follow me all the days of my life, and I will dwell in the house of the LORD forever." That one man was inspired to write both psalms is telling. Sometimes we are confident of God's love and grace, and sometimes we are not. Sometimes we sense God's presence, and sometimes we sense his absence.

Goodness and mercy are synonymous with grace and forgiveness, which brings us on to another of David's psalms.[5] This recognition that his own sin has caused God to hide his face occurs again in Psalm 51, where David asks God, "Do not cast me from your presence" (Psalm 51:11), after he has been caught in a grievous spiral of sin involving adultery, deception, and ultimately murder. However, David also prays the opposite in Psalm 51:9, asking God to "hide your face from my sins." This paradox of guilt that both drives us away from God and drives us to him is probably strangely familiar to many of us. It is part and parcel of the problem of God as stranger.

What we have in David is a vivid example of someone forced to recognize the moral distance between themselves and God, yet also recognizing that there is nowhere else to go with that moral guilt than back to God himself. David desperately needs divine reconciliation, because everything in his life is falling apart. When he says that his food has been contaminated with gall or bile and his drink poisoned with vinegar or acid, David is using metaphorical language to describe the effect that the stress is having on every aspect of his life. He cannot even gain comfort and pleasure from his food. The only thing that can nourish and sustain him now is reconciliation with God. Just like Naomi, only God can transform the bitterness in David's life.

We cannot read this part of the psalm without reflecting on Jesus' death on the cross. At the beginning of the crucifixion they offered Jesus "wine to drink, mixed with gall; but after tasting it, he refused to drink it" (Matthew 27:34). Some understand this drink as a form of narcotic to deaden the pain of the crucifixion. Jesus refuses to drink it, perhaps to show that he was determined to face all the horrors ahead of him in full consciousness.[6] Later, suffering the slow, agonizing torture of hanging on the cross, Jesus cried that he was thirsty, and someone fetched him wine vinegar and lifted it up to him on the stalk of a hyssop plant (Matthew 27:48). Jesus, the one who said that his blood would be poured out like the wine of the Passover meal, is the one who drinks the bitter cup of God's wrath so that we can be transformed and welcomed with the new wine of the coming kingdom of God. Like David, Jesus is looking to God for reconciliation—of the whole world to the Father.

Third, David asks for retribution, and this is where things get very strange, especially in the light of this connection with Jesus.

> May the table set before them become a snare;
>   may it become retribution and a trap.
> May their eyes be darkened so that they cannot see,
>   and their backs be bent forever.
> Pour out your wrath on them;
>   let your fierce anger overtake them.
> May their place be deserted;
>   let there be no one to dwell in their tents.
> For they persecute those you wound

and talk about the pain of those you hurt.
Charge them with crime upon crime;
    do not let them share in your salvation.
May they be blotted out of the book of life
    and not be listed with the righteous.
But as for me, afflicted and in pain—
    may your salvation, God, protect me. (Psalm 69:22-29)

We need to spend a little more time here because these words are violent and dark and may seem to us totally inappropriate even to think, let alone pray, far less record as part of the inspired word of God and include as an exemplary prayer for God's people.

There are a number of difficult psalms like this, psalms that call for divine vengeance (Psalms 58; 68:21-23; 69:23-29; 109:5-19; 137:7-9). Technically speaking, these "imprecatory" psalms involve what J. C. Laney categorizes as "an invocation of judgment, calamity, or curse uttered against one's enemies, or the enemies of God."[7] In most of our sermons and our churches, even those like the Church of England that have a tradition of reading or singing psalms in public worship, these are often omitted or edited.[8] Laney goes on to explain:

> Perhaps there is no part of the Bible that gives more perplexity and pain to its readers than this; perhaps nothing that constitutes a more plausible objection to the belief that the psalms are the productions of inspired men than the spirit of revenge which they sometimes seem to breathe and the spirit of cherished malice and implacableness which the writers seem to manifest.[9]

However, what if these strange psalms, which God inspired and included in Scripture, can be especially useful to us precisely because they express ideas that we find difficult and unpalatable? This reversal of expectation is not out of place here. David wants to turn some tables of his own. Here he expresses it literally, wishing to switch places so his own poisoned food is fed to his enemies, while he feasts on their mouthwatering banquets. As David vents his anger, he provides a brutal level of detail of what he wants God to do to his enemies that indeed sounds like Laney's "cherished malice."

He wants them to become entrapped as they eat dinner—*and* blinded, *and* permanently disabled. He wants God to make them homeless—*and* to wipe out their entire households. He asks God to fully charge them with the extent of their crimes *and* to refuse them entry to eternal life. After pouring all that vitriol on the bad guys, David, as a self-confessed bad guy himself, then asks to be treated very differently: he wants God's salvation to protect him. How can David ask for mercy for himself but be unwilling to show mercy, even in his prayers, to his enemies?

It is easy to see why churches would choose to omit these difficult words from their public worship. Surely these passages are too controversial for our pulpits, too morally ambiguous for our worship songs, too violent for Sunday school? So why has God allowed them to be included here?

Perhaps, in our violent, morally ambivalent, and controversial times, we need to park our preconceptions briefly and hear the raw, uncompromising starkness of these psalms once more. There is a major challenge for us here in these verses, but some observations from Walter Brueggemann may offer some helpful insights as to how we might navigate the difficult ideas in this psalm.[10] He notes that many of us are offended by these psalms because we think that believers should not feel this way. But his question is, what if you *do* feel this way? What if you have been so cruelly wronged that you feel your abusers *should* suffer the consequences of their actions? What if you are so incensed about a crime that you *would* be happy to hear that the perpetrators had died of food poisoning or been blinded? What if you feel like poking their eyes out yourself? He suggests we have three options with our natural thirst for vengeance. Option one, of course, is to act on such feelings, although Scripture tells us that vengeance belongs to God alone, quite apart from legal limitations on our actions. Option two is to deny the feelings or bury them, but strong emotions like this often tend to come out somewhere else in your life, and often when and where you least expect. Certainly deep-seated anger in abused children we have fostered often causes them to "act out" in problematic ways, especially if they have been unable or unwilling to "speak out." Option three is to "place the situation in the hands of God."[11] This third option, rightly understood, recognizes the emotional need to express our anger, along with our spiritual need to rely on the perfectly just God to judge as he sees fit. What it does not mean is simply bottling it up or papering it over in the belief that it is un-Christian to have those feelings in the first place.

These imprecatory psalms model a realistic acknowledgment of our darkest feelings, while not only recognizing God's unique role as Judge and Ruler, but offering a kind of cathartic and necessary transference of vengeful feelings over to God. In other words, they allow us to express the inexpressible, to think the unthinkable, and yet still retain hold of our faith in God. Viktor Frankl was a Jewish psychiatrist who was captured by the Nazis and put into a concentration camp. He set up a care unit within the camp to help newcomers try to adjust to the horrors of camp life. He also set up a suicide watch for prisoners. Frankl survived three years living in the camp and then, after he was liberated, went on to have an important career lecturing and researching in psychological healing. One of Frankl's most famous observations was that "between stimulus and response there is a space. In that space is our power to choose our response. In our response lies our growth and our freedom."[12] The breadth of the psalms—from the darkest of the imprecatory psalms to the most uplifting of the celebratory psalms—contains resources to help us work through how we are going to respond to even the most difficult aspects of whatever life may throw at us. By ignoring them we may inadvertently be robbing ourselves of help to live and reflect well in a complex and broken world.

Notice that David does not say that he is going to wreck the lives of those who have hurt him—he asks that God should do it. God forbade us vengeance not because vengeance is wrong, but because vengeance is his alone. God knows that, as creatures in his image, we instinctively want to put things right, but that as fallen creatures, we cannot safely make those judgments. Aristotle once said, "Anybody can become angry—that is the easy part, but to be angry with . . . the right person, and to the right amount, and at the right time and for the right purpose, and in the right way—this is not within everybody's power."[13] I would suggest it is only fully in God's power. In this instance it appears that David knows the dark side of himself well enough that he entrusts his yearning for vengeance to God to take action rather than trying to do it himself. Or, as Brueggemann puts it for the benefit of those of us feeling wronged, "Vengeance is transferred from the heart of the speaker to the heart of God."[14]

The apostle Paul states this very clearly when he writes to the church in Rome, warning them about how to handle the injustice of opposition and persecution: "Do not take revenge, my dear friends, but leave room for God's wrath, for it is written: 'It is mine to avenge; I will repay,' says the Lord. On the contrary: 'If your enemy is hungry, feed him; if he is thirsty, give him something to drink. In doing this, you will heap burning coals on his head.' Do not be overcome by evil, but overcome evil with good" (Romans 12:19-21). Is this a strange passive-aggressive form of vengeance? Far from it. In our next chapter we will see how burning coals in the Bible often symbolize holiness, atonement, repentance, and transformation. John Stott observes, "Recent commentators draw attention to an ancient Egyptian ritual in which a penitent would carry burning coals on his head as evidence of the reality of his repentance. In this case the coals are 'a dynamic symbol of change of mind which takes place as a result of a deed of love.'"[15] Paul urges kindness that will engage the offender and offer a positive, practical way forward—not only leaving ultimate vengeance for God, but encouraging hospitality that will work to bring God's kingdom about. This hospitality somehow has the power to turn the tables, overcoming evil with good and turning enemies into penitents.

I have seen firsthand that the open, loving, and unconditional welcome offered to children who have experienced neglect, sexual abuse, and physical violence can make a huge difference to a child's future. Recently I was invited to talk about the transforming power of hospitality given through foster care. Across the table was a woman who was clearly angry and hostile. She explained that she had been treated very badly by her foster parents as a teenager—she believed they had "stolen her childhood." As a foster parent myself, I could only apologize for the terrible things that had been done to her and validate her anger by agreeing that they should not have happened. Nothing I could do would make amends for the terrible experience she had suffered. All I could do was go on to tell story after story of the children I knew whose foster parents had gone above and beyond for them, dramatically illustrating different ways I had seen that hospitality brought healing. At the end of the seminar, the woman came up to me. Somewhat more open this time, she said, "OK, not all foster parents are scum." I believe good will ultimately overcome evil, but it is a long process that we are all engaged in.

Another way we can view these imprecatory psalms is to understand the way that hyperbole is used throughout the Scriptures. Jesus tells his disciples that if their eye causes them to sin, they should gouge it out, or if their hand causes them to sin, they should cut if off. Yet physical self-dismemberment has never been a recognized spiritual discipline or a part of regular Christian liturgical practice. It has always been understood that this is exaggerated speech. When we are passionate about something, it is natural for us to overstate our feelings. When you haven't eaten for a while, you may declare yourself to be so starving you could eat a horse. Or when your teenager has stayed out past midnight again, you might use some strong language about what violence he will be met with when he finally walks through the door. Yet despite your vivid and terrible threats, it is understood by anyone listening that you have no intention of carrying them out. David's expressions of vengeance could be a similar kind of hyperbole, a means of venting his anger with no genuine intention of harm at all.

We know that God is not oblivious or passive to the suffering and injustice in the world. We have seen God intervene both at a personal level and at a national level. We have seen God rescue Lot's daughters and destroy Lot's city. We have seen him wrestle with Jacob to help fix a family feud and recruit Gideon to help restore the nation of Israel. God, we are promised, will not turn his face away from the injustice and suffering of the world. He will deal with the evil we see around us. When God repeatedly claims that vengeance belongs to him (Deuteronomy 32:35; Psalm 94:1; Isaiah 63:4), we are not to think of someone who has lost their temper exhibiting indiscriminate anger but rather, as Brueggemann states, a righteous Judge who takes his time to pass appropriate sentence on each crime.[16] David's psalm, which is clearly messianic in that it points to Jesus' death, is also prophetic in that it reflects something of God's anger at the injustice in the world.

For such a difficult psalm, it certainly gets a lot of air time from Jesus and the early church. We have already looked at three occasions where it is referenced. A further occasion is when Judas Iscariot feels such remorse at his role in the betrayal and execution of Jesus that he takes his own life. The field where his suicide takes place became known as the "field of blood" and for obvious reasons was blacklisted by the property developers of the time. The apostle Peter claims that these events were somehow a fulfillment of the line in the psalm, "May his place be deserted; let there be no one to dwell in it" (Acts 1:20). If David is declaring that those who oppose God's anointed King will suffer, and Judas is illustrative of this, then we should also read in this psalm a terrible warning. The grotesque word-pictures of David's anger give us a glimpse into the implications of what it means to stand against Jesus, God's chosen King. We cannot afford to sentimentalize Jesus, choosing only the attributes that make us feel safe. For those of us who are tempted to do this or who are struck by this angry, just, passionate side of God for the first time, it is a necessary challenge to meet the stranger God of David here. Aware of the consequences of opposing Jesus, we can implore the all-powerful God to save us too.

So how does the prophetic link to Jesus' death affect our understanding of this call for retribution? Perhaps these verses of vengeance can reveal something powerful by way of contrast. David pours out his hot anger to God, and asks him to rain down terror on those who stand against him. But faced with an even worse experience of betrayal, suffering, and physical pain, Jesus does not respond like this. The true Messiah's magnificence overshadows that of his predecessor David, even at the height of his power. When Jesus is betrayed and opposed, bruised and beaten, crucified and then offered vinegar instead of wine, he who had no sin, who had every right to cast stones in judgment against the rest of us, cried out to God in a very different way. He did not ask that God would hold these people accountable for every crime, or that God would turn the tables on them and pour out his wrath on the world. Instead, Jesus cried out to God to forgive them. At the cross, God's justice and his mercy meet perfectly. A God of vengeance goes with a God of forgiveness. But while David prayed that God would forgive him and smite his enemies, Jesus prayed that God would smite him and forgive his enemies.

In a work context we may be urged to smile for the customers, be nice to the boss, make a good impression, schmooze the clients. Part of being professional, it seems, is to distance our public persona from the complexity of our personal feelings. I would quickly lose confidence in a surgeon who tells me all about his failing marriage and his inability to concentrate during a pre-op. Bored salespeople are unlikely to meet their targets, and nervous pilots should probably be grounded. But the dissonance between the person we present to the world and our authentic self can be very tiring to maintain. Especially for those of us who find we cannot let our guard down even with our friends and church family. Where can we go to express ourselves freely, without barriers, pretense, facades, or maintained or curated public images? This psalm, the place where David admits to the world that he can't find God, is, paradoxically, a place where God makes room for us to come and express our worst and darkest feelings to him. Desperation, doubt, and anger are all given legitimacy here. The God we complain against, and argue with, and despair of, invites us to nothing less than an authentic relationship with him.

David seems to switch tactics completely as he comes to the end of the psalm. He looks to the future and declares that he will praise God, recognizing that this will be honoring to God and helpful to the poor.

> I will praise God's name in song
>   and glorify him with thanksgiving.
> This will please the LORD more than an ox,
>   more than a bull with its horns and hooves.
> The poor will see and be glad—
>   you who seek God, may your hearts live!
> The LORD hears the needy
>   and does not despise his captive people.
> Let heaven and earth praise him,
>   the seas and all that move in them,
> for God will save Zion
>   and rebuild the cities of Judah.
> Then people will settle there and possess it;
>   the children of his servants will inherit it,
>   and those who love his name will dwell there. (Psalm 69:30-36)

This is a dramatic volte-face. Is this just a bolt-on happy ending, added by David because he feels bad that the psalm has been so dark up until now? Or does it mark a true turnaround—is this release of praise the goal of David's cathartic cries to God? David has accumulated anger against his enemies that is, on the one hand, ugly and brutal and unrelenting. But on the other hand, he is angry because he knows this is not life as it should be. He knows that God has promised so much more. He retains a confidence that God will yet redeem his people and there will be liberty and joy. Even if he is not saved yet, his final hope is that there will be this grand finale to the story. A finale when the offering of true praise means God will no longer need sacrifice. A finale that will overcome poverty and captivity, because God will make everything right. This is the rescue that he looks forward to, even if no immediate rescue is forthcoming. Prophetically, he hints at a rescue for everybody and everything, everywhere. David's memory of a God who turned up in previous days will carry him through to a hope in a God who will one day turn up again.

We have come a long way from a young boy serving lunch to his brothers at the battlefront. David's anger at the injustice done to God's people by Goliath was not a fifteen-minutes-of-fame thing. Those early God encounters shaped his whole life, even though that life took him to some dark places. It took him into war zones to fight on behalf of (and against) God's people. It took him to dark caves, hiding and waiting for God's timing to be right and to bring peace to the kingdom. It took him through the shame of repentance and the grief of losing a child. And it took him through the darkest inner turmoil as he wrestled with his own sense of estrangement, and with God becoming stranger.

Nevertheless, David remained committed to battling the giants that stand in opposition to the God he knew, whatever forms they took. He would never give up waiting for God's presence to return. Because when God's name, God's place, and God's people are wronged, even giants need to be afraid.

ISAIAH AND
THE STRANGER

The God who turns life upside down

In which a mourner meets a stranger and is given
an impossible task, and we discover what
we should do when worship is a waste of time.

Let me put some things straight. No, I am not related to Hare Krishna. No, my dad has never run a corner shop. No, I don't eat curry for breakfast.

It drives me mad when people assume things about me. I resent that surprised expression on people's faces when I walk into a room and speak English. Equally, it annoys me that people think that just because I am over forty, I must prefer golf to ten-pin bowling or red wine to Coca-Cola. Just because I am evangelical, it does not mean I hate gay people. Just because I have children with additional needs, it does not mean I think I got a raw deal when it comes to parenting. I hate it when I attend a school

meeting and the teacher only gives my wife eye contact, as though
I as a dad have no personal interest in my child's education. Or
when I am in a meeting with social workers and a supposedly
professional child expert tells me that all Christians exorcise
demons as a response to misbehavior and brainwash their children.
The point is, just because you know something about me, it does
not mean you know everything about me. Being judged or labeled
or stereotyped has a paradoxical effect: people who think they
know me don't know me at all. I am even more of a stranger to
them than they realize. What if we have treated God the same
way? What if we have made assumptions about God based on
what we think we know, and misled ourselves along the way?
What if all those assumptions and prejudices have actually made
God more of a stranger to us without us even realizing?

Do we assume that, because we know God is compassionate,
he is not that concerned about sin? Do we assume that, because
God is holy, we will never be good enough for him? Do we assume
that, because God calls himself our Father, he is going to be like
whatever our experience of human fathering has been? Do we
assume that because God loves Christians, he cannot love Muslims
or atheists? Do we assume that because we attend church, we
are somehow guaranteed a place in God's good books? It is very
hard for us to identify our own assumptions. We need the Holy
Spirit—and some very discerning and honest friends or strangers—
to help point them out.

When it comes to allowing our prejudices to shape our picture
of God, we are in august company. For generations, God's own
chosen people made a series of fateful, and sometimes literally
fatal, mistakes along the same lines. Through lazy thinking or
willful ignorance, when it comes to understanding God, misinformation and misjudgment have been rife throughout history.

Sometimes God needs to challenge our prejudices and assumptions, and we see this happen a lot during the time of the Old Testament prophets. When God turns up in the book of Isaiah, he is forced to show how far removed he is from them and their expectations of his preferences, by turning things they took for granted totally upside down.

━━━━

Before entering the Promised Land the Israelites were specifically told that if they turned their backs on the true and living God, then he would turn them out of the land. But, as we saw in Gideon's story, they ignored this warning and began to worship idols. Some thought the main cause of the troubles in Israel had been the (lack of) leadership structure and having a king would sort everything out. But King Saul ended up morally and spiritually compromised, as did David, the giant-killing shepherd-boy-turned-singer-songwriter-turned-warrior-turned-king. His son Solomon, despite the gift of divine wisdom, struggled to apply this to his own appetites and ended up abusing his power and privilege, worshiping false gods and acquiring a hard-to-imagine 700 wives and 300 concubines (1 Kings 11:3). God sent prophet after prophet to warn king after king and call them back to the covenant promises they had made to him under Moses' leadership. They continued in their idolatry, however, acting as though God was a soft touch, so slow to anger and abounding in grace that they could get away with anything and everything. But sadly, they had misjudged God; their prejudice had clouded their perception, to their great shame and imminent danger. Eventually they pushed things too far, and things turned ugly.

When we get to the book of Isaiah, we can find the writings very confusing. Its sixty-six chapters relate to such a long period of time that for centuries there has been a debate about whether there was one author or three, and where exactly it fits into a historical timeline. Some chapters of Isaiah describe events in the life of Jesus with pinpoint accuracy, which for some readers has set the expectation that the whole book acts like a script for the future. Yet so much of the book is daunting and difficult to understand that it is rare for Christians to be truly familiar with more than a handful of verses. Nonetheless, Isaiah's prophecies are vital for the church today because the whole book speaks to a people who are comfortable in their knowledge of God and yet profoundly mistaken about him. We ignore its message at our peril. The devastating opening chapter sets the tone for the rest of the prophecy.

> Hear the word of the LORD,
>   you rulers of Sodom;
> listen to the instruction of our God,
>   you people of Gomorrah!
> "The multitude of your sacrifices—
>   what are they to me?" says the LORD.
> "I have more than enough of burnt offerings,
>   of rams and the fat of fattened animals;
> I have no pleasure
>   in the blood of bulls and lambs and goats.
> When you come to appear before me,
>   who has asked this of you,
>   this trampling of my courts?
> Stop bringing meaningless offerings!
>   Your incense is detestable to me.
> New Moons, Sabbaths and convocations—
>   I cannot bear your worthless assemblies.
> Your New Moon feasts and your appointed festivals

I hate with all my being.
They have become a burden to me;
    I am weary of bearing them.
When you spread out your hands in prayer,
    I hide my eyes from you;
even when you offer many prayers,
    I am not listening." (Isaiah 1:10-15)

We can tell Israel is in trouble as soon as we hear the comparison with Sodom and Gomorrah. We saw in chapter two how endemic sin and injustice were in those cities and the fiery consequences that followed. The people of Israel may well have made free with the names of those cities in calling down God's judgment on their pagan neighbors—but surely didn't expect to be compared to them themselves. The litany of complaints that follows is a wake-up call for this complacent people. God sees through the pretense that is their worship. Their offerings are meaningless, their rituals are detestable, their festivals are hateful, their gatherings unbearable and worthless. Fake worship is no better than idol worship—both involve substituting something meaningless for something true. And so God declares himself a stranger to them. He hides his eyes from them. He will not listen to their prayers.

These words at the beginning of Isaiah are disturbing. What if the very worship we are offering to God, week in, week out, in an attempt to draw close to him, is actually pushing him away? What if God makes himself a stranger to us because our worship itself is not just a bit tired, but actually repugnant to him? What if he is closing his ears to our prayers and shutting his eyes to all the sacrifices we are making for him? What if all our efforts to enjoy his presence are instead the very cause of his absence?

These questions cut to the very heart not only of our Sunday practices but of our faith itself. The problem for Israel is not really what they have been doing when they gather for corporate worship, but what they haven't been doing when they're not gathered to worship. God's challenge to his people is that they have substituted ritualistic worship for the living of a worshipful life. Israel, like so many of us today, tried to keep God happy through ceremony and sacrament and failed to please God with lives of faithful service.

This chapter reminds me a little of a conversation that invariably occurs in my house on Father's Day. After showering me with gifts at breakfast, it is as though my children think I must be so pleased with them, they can get away with anything. It may start out as a minor bicker, but invariably by midafternoon there comes a time when enough is enough. And then comes my annual reproof: "I love that you wanted to give me presents this morning, but I would gladly return them all for a few hours of family harmony. I would enjoy seeing kids who respected each other far more than a bar of chocolate any day. If you really want to show me some appreciation for being your dad, then ditch the attitude and show some cooperation and compassion to each other."

If we want to show our appreciation for God, says the book of Isaiah, no amount of singing and praying can substitute for what is really important to him: showing compassion to the needy, seeking justice for the oppressed, or defending the orphan and the widow. For many Christians, worship is synonymous with singing songs on a Sunday—we often talk about "worship leaders," "worship songs," and "worship times." But that is precisely the type of wrong idea God refutes here in Isaiah. God clearly explains the worship he enjoys from his people: stop

doing wrong. Learn to do right; seek justice. Defend the oppressed. Take up the cause of the fatherless; plead the case of
the widow (Isaiah 1:17).

This first chapter of Isaiah is so important that it has been
placed chronologically out of sequence. Just like a flash forward,
this message is recorded first, even though Isaiah's call to be a
prophet does not take place until chapter six. This opener acts
as a literary prologue, introducing themes that will recur
throughout this vast prophetic book. The difference between
true and fake worship is so critical that whoever arranged the
material of Isaiah's words in written form wanted to make sure
that we didn't miss it.

As we consider which of our assumptions and prejudices may
be estranging God from us, we get the privilege of watching
Isaiah come face-to-face with exactly this same challenge, as he
comes face-to-face with God himself.

> In the year that King Uzziah died, I saw the Lord, high and
> exalted, seated on a throne; and the train of his robe filled
> the temple. Above him were seraphim, each with six wings:
> With two wings they covered their faces, with two they
> covered their feet, and with two they were flying. And they
> were calling to one another:
>
>> "Holy, holy, holy is the LORD Almighty;
>> the whole earth is full of his glory."
>
> At the sound of their voices the doorposts and thresholds
> shook and the temple was filled with smoke.
>
> "Woe to me!" I cried. "I am ruined! For I am a man of
> unclean lips, and I live among a people of unclean lips, and
> my eyes have seen the King, the LORD Almighty."

Then one of the seraphim flew to me with a live coal in his hand, which he had taken with tongs from the altar. With it he touched my mouth and said, "See, this has touched your lips; your guilt is taken away and your sin atoned for." (Isaiah 6:1-7)

There is something profoundly satisfying about confounding people's expectations. Recently I was in a restaurant and, picking up where the waiter was from, I greeted him in (rusty) Albanian. He nearly jumped out of his skin. He had never met a foreigner who could speak his language before, and definitely not someone with brown skin. Once he got over his shock, I think I made his day—far from his homeland, he unexpectedly found someone who valued his country and his culture. I like to think something similar is going on in this passage. God has seen Isaiah in the temple and is going to surprise him, shock him, confound his expectations, and turn his world upside down. Because here God has found someone who is prepared to try and speak his language.

Isaiah's call reads like the photographic negative of Gideon's. By comparing these two "theophanies," we already see something of the foolishness of making assumptions about God and confining him to our expectations. The God who appeared to Gideon in the workplace appears to Isaiah in the temple. Gideon was in private. Isaiah was in public. Gideon's people were under the oppressive rule of the merciless Midianites, while Isaiah's people were mourning the death of their good King Uzziah. God hid his glory from Gideon by appearing as a stranger; Isaiah is left in no doubt whatsoever that God has turned up. Gideon saw God in his humility, while Isaiah saw God in his majesty. Reluctant Gideon is conscripted by God into national service, while repentant Isaiah is worried about his own worthiness, but freely volunteers to serve God among the nations. Despite these differences, what is clear is that both felt completely inadequate for the task, and God commissions them anyway.

I wonder how you would react if God turned up at church. Not the sort of turning up we might talk about in the normal course of things—a comforting-thought or warm-sensation kind of turning up. Not incognito, in the guise of a stranger. I'm talking visible manifestation of his glory. The fall-on-the-floor, prepare-to-die kind of turning up. What would that be like? How would you react? Why does God appear like this to Isaiah, and what does it teach him, and so us, about a God who is stranger than we know?

First, God wants Isaiah to grasp something of his glory, dangerous though it is. For all the power and magnificence displayed before him, Isaiah knew he was seeing just a minuscule fraction of God's glory, but even that was enough for him to feel completely undone by the encounter. It was God himself who explained to Moses, "No one may see me and live" (Exodus 33:20). God nonetheless allowed Moses to catch a glimpse of his dangerous glory. Moses was told to hide for protection in the cleft of a rock, only momentarily seeing God from behind. Hundreds of years later in the New Testament, John, whose Gospel cites Isaiah's prophecies four times, writes, "No one has ever seen God, but the one and only Son, who is himself God" (John 1:18). So John clearly sees Isaiah's vision as in some way a dialed-down, veiled expression, more like Moses' glimpse of glory, than Jesus' full-on exposure of the unfiltered glory of the Father.

Second, God wants Isaiah not only to grasp something of his glory, but to grasp something of the deep anguish he is experiencing. Isaiah, like Abraham before him, gets a behind-the-scenes insight into the conversation of divine counsel.[1] He overhears the deliberation of God about his next move in response to Israel's sin. In this way, something of God's broken heart for his sinful people is transmitted to Isaiah. In parenting we use a similar tactic sometimes with our children. Instead of chastising them to their face again, we allow them to overhear us weighing up what we should do to help them break a bad habit, and explaining how we feel. It helps them hear not just the anger, but also the anguish they have caused. Isaiah immediately sinks under the weight of his own guilt and the guilt of his community: "Woe to me! I am ruined! For I am a man of unclean lips, and I live among a people of unclean lips" (Isiah 6:5). Already in mourning because of the death of his earthly king, Isaiah now grieves at an entirely new level as he grasps the unclean, unworthy lip service his people have been giving to the King of Kings.

Third, God wants to deal with Isaiah's sin. This is graphically illustrated by the touching of Isaiah's lips with a burning coal. The coal is so hot that even the resplendent angel of God needs tongs to hold it. Alec Motyer, a lifelong scholar of Isaiah's prophecy, explains that here "fire is not a cleansing agent but the expression of the active, even hostile, holiness of God."[2] As the coal touches Isaiah at the place of his newly self-recognized sin, Isaiah's lips, one of the most sensitive parts of the body, do not burn. The coal is not there to wound or deform. Rather, it signals that God's sublime holiness is capable of dealing with the very things that would preclude Isaiah from being near him and also of atoning for the overwhelming guilt he is feeling (Isaiah 6:7). Motyer explains that atoning here means "cover," in a similar way that we might offer to "cover" a friend's debt. God finds a way to meet the exact requirements for our forgiveness, and cancel the penalty.[3] The payment is so perfect that although Isaiah identifies his lips as the part of his body most in need of cleansing, they are not only cleansed but redeemed. They become the instrument through which God will use Isaiah most clearly, as Isaiah speaks out God's prophetic word to his rebellious nation. This is a beautiful picture of the grace of God. Isaiah did not clean himself up—he confessed his sin, and then God forgave him, cleansed him, and repurposed what had been used improperly, to be used for good.

Fourth, God wants to transform Isaiah. Moments earlier Isaiah felt unworthy, inconsolably so. Now he is unstoppable! Isaiah hears something of God's concerns, and immediately accepts them as an invitation. God asks himself, "Whom shall I send? And who will go for us?" (Isaiah 6:8), and Isaiah steps forward for this divine commission, his sin dealt with and his confidence restored, and is instantly appointed by God as a prophet. It is interesting how often in the Bible being reconciled with God is intricately tied in to participating in God's plans. God chose and blessed Abraham and in the same breath made him a blessing to the world. God blessed Jacob, who then went and made peace with Esau. God blessed Gideon and then appointed him to go and save his people. So now Isaiah, in a single encounter, is first convicted by God, then atoned for by God, then commissioned by God. The repeating pattern in the Bible seems to show that repentance transforms and reorients our life such that we become willing recruits for God's service. Sadly today, we too often separate out the two elements. We are prone to offer people salvation without service, rescue without recruitment, a Messiah yet no mission, and cleansing without a calling. But we cannot separate becoming a Christian and living for God. God's redemption comes with an invitation. We are given the privilege of accepting this invitation and offering ourselves up to God's purposes: "Here am I. Send me!" (Isaiah 6:8).

The call to Christian discipleship is an integral part of coming to faith—not a bolt-on extra for the people who are most keen. But true following is costly and difficult. Just as our relationship with the God who often seems like a stranger to us will be frustrating and challenging, so pursuing service for God will also be frustrating and challenging. It does not come naturally to do right, seek justice, and defend the oppressed, the fatherless, and the widow, in the name of the God who has saved us and called us. Isaiah is warned about these frustrations from the outset. Things are not going to be straightforward. The surprisingly difficult message that Isaiah is commissioned to deliver is that God is going to be a stranger to his people:

> He said, "Go and tell this people:
>   'Be ever hearing, but never understanding;
>   be ever seeing, but never perceiving.'
> Make the heart of this people calloused;
>   make their ears dull
>   and close their eyes." (Isaiah 6:9-10)

In this passage we see again the essence of what we have been discovering in this book. God draws close to us, he surprises us with a taste of his glory, he commissions us to surprising service to others—and yet he is still a stranger to us.

〰〰〰

Isaiah's challenge reminds me of those geometrically impossible line drawings produced by the Dutch artist M. C. Escher. One of my favorites is his lithograph *Ascending and Descending*, which borrows from a depiction of an impossible object by psychologist Lionel Penrose and his mathematician son Roger Penrose. No matter how many steps you go up you never reach the top, because somehow the top of one staircase becomes the bottom of another, and on and on in an infinite loop. Frankly, a lot of people feel this way about their daily work and life. Just when we reach the bottom of the ironing basket or our email inbox, it strangely seems full again. Just when we manage to achieve one deadline, others loom up before us out of nowhere. Just as one class of children have been taught to read and write, along come another thirty who don't know their alphabets. Isaiah is called to reveal to God's people that they are going to be unreceptive to God's revelation. Why on earth would God give him such a strangely fruitless job?

Many Christians can relate to Isaiah's impossible task. I have sat with many men and women who feel they are getting nowhere with what they are sure God has called them to do. I have listened as people have opened up about a seemingly irrefutable call on their lives and the sacrifices they have made personally and financially in order to obey it, only to see all their effort come to nothing. Whether by inner conviction, prophetic vision, or in obedience to their understanding of Scripture, they have sought to honor God's call but have seen only fruitlessness. Some have tears in their eyes as they explain how confused they have felt. Some are filled with anger that is far from the holy kind we considered in the last chapter. One person explained to me that he felt like a small child whose dad had given him a model plane to build, and after much patience and diligence he finally puts the last piece in place. As he proudly hands it over, his father smashes it to pieces in front of him. What father would cause his son such distress? Like David in the last chapter, whose zeal for God left him feeling as though God had abandoned him to sink in the flood, perhaps you too can relate to the frustration of performing apparently thankless and fruitless tasks out of service to God, leaving you humiliated and heartbroken.

Why would God give his newly commissioned prophet such a
disheartening and depressing job? Why set someone up to fail
like this? Be a prophet to a people who will never understand,
no matter how often they hear the message? This impossible
commission God gives Isaiah seems like the archetypal fool's
errand. But what if Isaiah's heartbreak at the failure to pass on
this message could in fact be the best possible means of knowing
better a God who is heartbroken?

Isaiah's terrible prophetic message was not to be delivered to
a hated enemy, but to his own hometown. It was not a message
of impending revival but imminent resettlement. God's people
are going to have the Promised Land snatched away from under
them, and they will be exiled and forced to live as slaves and
refugees in a foreign country that worships pagan idols. Not only
is God allowing their world to be turned upside down; he is
orchestrating it, and doing so as part of his covenant promise.
The historical marker we are given for the beginning of Isaiah's
prophetic ministry was the death of King Uzziah, in the year
743 BC. The end of Uzziah's reign marked the end of around five
decades of peace and prosperity. God had forewarned his people
in Deuteronomy that it was going to be hard to keep trusting
him when things were going well and they were no longer a
nomadic people depending on God daily for bread from heaven.
Moses too had warned them that familiarity would breed con-
tempt and prosperity would breed idolatry (Deuteronomy 6:10-12).
And so God's gift of the Promised Land came with an official
health warning. Because it is easier to trust God as a wandering
refugee than as a secure resident, God issued a warning in Leviticus: "If you defile the land, it will vomit you out as it vomited
out the nations that were before you" (Leviticus 18:28). God is
dedicated to the spiritual well-being of his people above their

transient physical security; if they stray, they will have to go through the sickening pain of displacement and exile in order to come back to a right understanding.

Perhaps you can see something of this in your own experience. With security often comes the myth of self-reliance: we congratulate ourselves on our prudence and diligence, and forget God's providence, letting our relationship with him become distant. However, with insecurity and displacement often comes the recognition of our need of God and the desire for him to draw close to us. Our faith can be strangely stronger in times of difficulty. In retrospect, we may see that short-term gain brings long-term pain, whereas short-term pain can bring long-term gain.

Isaiah and his prophetess wife acknowledge this in the naming of their two sons: Maher-Shalal-Hash-Baz means "quick to the plunder" (Isaiah 8:3), and Shear-Jashub means "a remnant will return" (Isaiah 7:3). Isaiah surrenders his home and family to the illustration of this tension between the temptations of the imminent and God's overriding plans for the ultimate. It is not dissimilar to the contrast Jesus will teach on in Matthew's Gospel: "For wide is the gate and broad is the road that leads to destruction, and many enter through it. But small is the gate and narrow the road that leads to life, and only a few find it" (Matthew 7:13-14). The names of Isaiah's own sons illustrate this unlikely paradox of finding God where one might think him hardest to be found. He is greater and yet stranger than we expect; there is hope, but only some will find it. In a reiteration of his call, Isaiah includes his family saying, "Here am I, and the children the LORD has given me. We are signs and symbols in Israel from the LORD Almighty, who dwells on Mount Zion" (Isaiah 8:18).

What would it mean for us today, for our family to be signs, symbols, visual aids, or pointers to the coming reign of God? How could we publicly reflect God's purposes and priorities in the very identity of our family? How can we make visible to the world the values that define us as a family set apart for God? How will people who come into our homes recognize our devotion to God? How will they see that we follow God's agenda to do right, seek justice, and defend the oppressed, fatherless, and widow? Do we help to point people toward the narrow path to life?

Captain Susan Hillis works for the Center for Disease Control in the United States. She speaks Spanish, Russian, and German, holds a PhD in Epidemiology, and was the US government's lead in the response to the Ebola virus outbreak in West Africa. Her work is worship to God as she seeks to defend the oppressed peoples of the world. But what stunned me about Susan when I met her was how she worshiped and witnessed through her home life. Fifteen years earlier, she was out on a family bike ride when her son was run over and killed on the eve of his tenth birthday. In the wake of the tragedy, the family's grief inspired in her a passion to care for children who had lost their parents. Up to now the Hillises have adopted eight children, and you cannot visit their home without being struck by their living testimony to a God who is a father to the fatherless and protector of widows and orphans. Just as we cannot all have such an impressive résumé as Susan, so not every Christian can or should adopt so many children as she has, but we do all have a responsibility to actively care for the vulnerable at a personal level and in ways that are clear to be seen.

The people of Israel's failure to act in this way is the reason why God cannot stand their worship, and why he cannot allow them to stay in the land he has given them. They are going to be taught a tough and terrible lesson—they are going to be attacked, overrun, plundered, and forcibly repatriated to Babylon. God is going to turn his nation out to turn their understanding of him upside down. Perhaps in exile, when they will experience firsthand what it means to be the oppressed, the victims, and the vulnerable, they will begin to understand why it is so important to understand how much God identifies with the "other," the stranger. Perhaps they will learn finally the true meaning of worship.

Jesus summarized the whole of the Old Testament Law in a single combined commandment: to love God and love your neighbor. This is why Abraham's hospitality toward and honoring of God were shown to be inseparable. This is why Ruth's commitment to a widow in distress and dedication to Naomi's God went hand in hand. This is why David's psalm combines his zeal for God with concern for his people. This is why true worship must always be about both welcoming God who is stranger and welcoming God in the stranger. But even in exile, and toward the end of the book of Isaiah, the Israelites need God to remind them again that these two facets come together as the key to acceptable worship.

> Shout it aloud, do not hold back.
>   Raise your voice like a trumpet.
> Declare to my people their rebellion
>   and to the descendants of Jacob their sins.
> For day after day they seek me out;
>   they seem eager to know my ways,
> as if they were a nation that does what is right
>   and has not forsaken the commands of its God.
> They ask me for just decisions

and seem eager for God to come near them.
"Why have we fasted," they say,
  "and you have not seen it?
Why have we humbled ourselves,
  and you have not noticed?" (Isaiah 58:1-3)

At first glance, there seem to be signs of good spiritual health here. The people are fasting. In this respect they are doing better than most Western Christians I know, who struggle to take fasting seriously. In a culture obsessed with consuming, body image, and diets, food is difficult to put out of our thoughts, even between meals. God, who is quick to provide food—whether it be the abundance of Eden or manna in the desert—nevertheless recommends fasting to his people. He knows that it can mark the depth of our devotion, and that literal hunger is good for developing a spiritual hunger. These Israelites are overtly serious about God, publicly dedicated to this most severe of spiritual disciplines.

Isaiah, however, needs to raise the alarm. God interrupts with an announcement: these fasting worshipers are nothing but tricksters. Isn't this too harsh a judgment? Here they are, living as literal aliens and strangers in a foreign land, yet still holding to a fast—and God declares it despicable! What are they doing wrong? Why won't God listen to them and do as they ask?

The next part of the passage makes it clear:

Yet on the day of your fasting, you do as you please
  and exploit all your workers.
Your fasting ends in quarreling and strife,
  and in striking each other with wicked fists.
You cannot fast as you do today
  and expect your voice to be heard on high.
Is this the kind of fast I have chosen,

only a day for people to humble themselves?
Is it only for bowing one's head like a reed
    and for lying in sackcloth and ashes?
Is that what you call a fast,
    a day acceptable to the LORD? (Isaiah 58:4-5)

So why is God so incensed? For one thing, the physical hard-ships of this "worship," far from helping them focus on God, are only making their treatment of others more unthinking, less caring. It is not only a means of trying to manipulate God; it is also a cover for their manipulation and mistreatment of others. While they may be fasting, they are also playing fast and loose with justice, exploiting their workers and treating one another with violence. They seem to think that taking one day out to fast—and letting everyone know about it as they vent the frus-trations a bit of hunger heightens—is going to pull the wool over God's eyes and incline him toward them.

This disconnect between personal religiosity and public ethics, as Brueggemann describes it, is a serious one.[4] God sees through the charade that is formal compliance to accepted religious behavior. Fasting is supposed to indicate a broken spirit and a contrite heart, but it is just an illusion. God could see that there was no heartbreak, no contrition, no compassion, and no repen-tance, as demonstrated not only in their attitude toward God, but in their treatment of others. They used God as if he was a genie, duty bound to grant them wishes if they just rubbed enough ashes on their hungry bodies. They treated others with immorality and injustice and thought God would not even notice, let alone care.

It is easy to criticize God's people for their foolishness here, until we reflect on our own lives. There are plenty of us who believe that so long as we have good theology, it doesn't matter what we do in our home or workplace or community or nation or world. There are plenty of us who believe that as long as we attend church, it doesn't really matter what happens in and around our bank account, how we treat our spouse or colleagues, or which Internet sites we visit. There are plenty of us who pray and tithe and even fast, but who do practically nothing for those who are suffering around us. It is no wonder that people accuse Christians of being judgmental hypocrites, "holier than thou"— because often that is exactly what we are. Religion is too often used to provide a thin veneer of respectability covering over a corrupt reality; when it comes to seeking justice, we have a long way to go.

God makes it crystal clear that he cannot stand hypocrisy. His logic is clear: if our worship has no connection with his heart for justice in this world, then it has no connection with him (Isaiah 58:4). If we do not listen to the cries of the poor, God will not listen to our cries in prayer. As Proverbs puts it: "Whoever shuts their ears to the cry of the poor will also cry out and not be answered" (Proverbs 21:13).

The things that count for nothing as worship in God's eyes, according to Isaiah, are perilously similar to the very things we still most easily count as worship today: turning up for services, singing, praying, fasting, making other spiritual-type "sacrifices" for God. In the New Testament Paul comes up with a similar list of potentially worthless worship: speaking in tongues, prophecy, knowledge, faith, giving to the poor, persecution, and suffering (1 Corinthians 13:1-3). Paul says they are empty rituals unless they are fueled by the essential element that is love. And by love, Paul does not mean a private inner feeling only, but an integrated expression that comes out in our disposition toward others.

His fourteen characteristics of love in 1 Corinthians 13 include patience—tolerance *of others' failings*; and kindness—an active response *to others' needs*. Love, he says, does not envy but wants the best *for others*. Love does not self-promote at the expense *of others*. Love is not proud, but treats *others* with equal importance. Love will not shame or humiliate *others*. Love does not lose its temper with *others*—love holds no grudges against *others*. Rather, love puts the needs of *others* first; it encourages *others*. And love always defends *others* who are vulnerable, builds *others* up, never giving up, but keeps on helping *others* get back on their feet (1 Corinthians 13).

These are the attributes and attitudes that will authenticate our worship. In a world where passive tolerance seems often to be held up as the highest virtue in the way we relate to one another, these active and interactive virtues upheld by Paul are truly revolutionary. Tolerance is the willingness to accept others from a distance, but love is a hospitality that welcomes others, up close and personal. While tolerance is devoid of emotional transaction, love is full of emotional investment. Well-known apologist Josh McDowell asserts, "Tolerance costs nothing. Love costs everything."[5]

Who are these "others," though? It is not just our friends and family, where these things should come more easily. Isaiah and Paul—not to mention Jesus—are united in asserting that a godly love must mean responsiveness to strangers, wanting the best for strangers, treating strangers with equal importance. Emotional investment on behalf of strangers is truly countercultural, but it lies at the heart of God's call to love our neighbor—to keep loving as we go beyond the bounds of what comes easily.

The late Alec Motyer calls Isaiah the "Paul" of the Old Testament,[6] because he has given us such a rich theology and has a very strong emphasis on faith. Both the prophet and the apostle teach that unless our worship and love for God translates into loving service *to others, to strangers*, then it is useless, or "I am nothing . . . I gain nothing," as Paul puts it (1 Corinthians 13:2-3). Isaiah is now ready to explain to us what true fasting looks like:

> Is not this the kind of fasting I have chosen:
> to loose the chains of injustice
>   and untie the cords of the yoke,
> to set the oppressed free
>   and break every yoke?
> Is it not to share your food with the hungry
>   and to provide the poor wanderer with shelter—
> when you see the naked, to clothe them,
>   and not to turn away from your own flesh and blood?
>   (Isaiah 58:6-7)

Temporary abstinence from food may help boost our appetite for God temporarily, but continual life habits, connecting with God through serving the poor, will give us continual opportunity to know God better. Old Testament scholar Brevard Childs writes, "The ritual of fasting is not rejected out of hand, but redefined by enlarging its parameters."[7] This expansive view of worship overlays what we as Christians may tend to keep separate: intimacy with God and activism for God. The prophet outlines two distinct but intricately related kinds of activities that God requires from his people as a means of intimacy with him. The first involves structural change in society, and the second involves personal change. The first involves smashing, and the second involves sharing.

First, Isaiah calls God's people to be involved in bringing liberation, loosing chains, untying cords, and breaking yokes. In other words, there are oppressive social structures and systems disadvantaging people, and these need to be broken down. The kind of worship God wants must involve that deconstructive task of undoing the inequalities that keep people poor.

It took eighteen years of campaigning, fighting, laboring, and advocacy by the Clapham Sect, led by the irrepressible William Wilberforce MP, before slavery was finally abolished on August 28, 1833. The next day the *Christian Observer* newspaper rightly made the connection with Isaiah 58: "Now indeed we may indulge in the hope that God will regard our fasts, for is this not the kind of fast that he has chosen? To loose the bands of wickedness."[8] Two days later, Wilberforce died. His legacy was the liberation that comes from loosing and smashing structural chains. Political and social engagement at local, national, and international levels is a fundamental part of our Christian worship, as this is where we can tackle the root causes and systems behind poverty.

Second, Isaiah makes it clear that worship is worthless unless it welcomes the needy, poor, and unworthy. Brueggemann helpfully summarizes Isaiah's acceptable fasting as "shared food, shared home, shared clothes."[9] If you think it is difficult not to have food for a day, then this may seem an even harder discipline. God is calling us not just to go without food for a while, but to share our food with those who are in need. You could argue that fasting is half of an equation, our going without. The other half of the equation is actually doing something to meet someone else's need. Can you think of people who have no food choices, and invite them in to share yours? Can you extend that to sharing daily not only your food, but your privacy, your stuff, your homes, your habits, your hearts?

Isaiah's redefinition of fasting is intended as a reenvisioning of Israel's worship of God. It is not so much about the difference between outward observance and inner attitudes—though that is important—as a fundamental shift in who we are. This is a shift that the Israelites ultimately failed to make. It took the traumatic dislocation of God's people to captivity in Babylon, God turning their world upside down, to help them see that they had their whole attitude to God and what he wants upside down in the first place. Their experience in Babylon was like the emergency adrenaline shot applied straight to the heart when someone has suffered a drug overdose. It may be an extreme and painful intervention, but it is motivated by love. God wants to shock us with the life-bringing truth that worship is not one type of thing we do, but a way we do everything.

If we want our relationship with God transformed, we must take heed of Isaiah's words. We must be involved both in smashing down barriers that divide us and others, and that divide people from freedom through injustice in all its forms, and in sharing what we have been given to rebuild connections and draw people back to God. We must be involved in speaking the message and *being* the message. This affects our lips and our lives, our politics and our families. Pursuing justice for the marginalized and welcoming the vulnerable into our homes need to be integral parts of our lives that signpost all to God. Hospitality is not to be a hobby; it needs to be at the heart of who we are.

Many of us treat our homes as our places of refuge and recuperation, where we can relax, unwind, and leave all the troubles of the day behind us. Some might say that this is the heart of what it means to be English: "An Englishman's home is his castle." But Christians need to have a totally different approach to our hearts and our homes: "A Christian's home is God's hospital."

We turn expectations upside down when we see our homes as places of refuge and recuperation *for others*, not just for ourselves.

This really hit home for me when we became foster parents. Up until then I'd had only sporadic interaction with poverty and inequality in my life. I had volunteered at a soup kitchen and even spent one Christmas Day serving the elderly. But days and months would go by where I would basically forget about the needy. It was like sorting out my car insurance; it was something I knew I needed to do, but it became sidelined because it was not an ongoing part of my daily life. Becoming a foster parent changed all that. Suddenly our whole family was confronted 24/7 with children carrying scars from neglect and abuse. As we interacted with social workers, police officers, lawyers, and birth parents, these children's lives became entwined with our own. Without any conscious decision on our part, issues of disability access, special educational-needs provision, immigration and asylum, domestic abuse, poverty, and addiction became forefront issues because together we were caught up in the middle of these things. These were not just newspaper headlines, infographics, or campaigns—this was my family.

In the midst of all the chaos and heartache that is part and parcel of fostering, I glimpsed a little of what Isaiah was teaching centuries earlier: intimacy with those suffering injustice leads to intimacy with God. It is a common discovery for those involved in these types of ministries. Those who open their homes to strangers find that somehow God has walked through the front door with them and has made himself at home too. Susan Hillis puts it like this: "The path had its glories and trials . . . jail sentences, addictions, teen pregnancy, and valedictorian, missionary, sculptor, state wrestling champion. And through it all, my eyes are on Him and it is well, it is well with my soul. We have all learned about unfailing love. It always multiplies."[10] Isaiah records it in the form of a promise: to those who say, "Here am I, send me," to God, God will say right back to them, "Here am I."

> Then your light will break forth like the dawn,
>   and your healing will quickly appear;
> then your righteousness will go before you,
>   and the glory of the LORD will be your rear guard.
> Then you will call, and the LORD will answer;
>   you will cry for help, and he will say: Here am I.
> If you do away with the yoke of oppression,
>   with the pointing finger and malicious talk,
> and if you spend yourselves in behalf of the hungry
>   and satisfy the needs of the oppressed,
> then your light will rise in the darkness,
>   and your night will become like the noonday. (Isaiah 58:8-10)

Bono, the lead singer of U2, one of the world's most successful rock bands, used his signature poetic gifts to express this truth:

> God is in the slums, in the cardboard boxes where the poor play house. God is in the silence of a mother who has infected her child with a virus that will end both their lives. God is in the cries heard under the rubble of war. God is in the debris of wasted opportunity and lives, and God is with us if we are with them.[11]

The renowned spiritual writer Henri Nouwen explains that the Scriptures show us that "hospitality is an important virtue, but even more than that, in the context of hospitality guest and host can reveal their most precious gifts and bring new life to each other."[12] Where do we find the God who is distant, elusive, mysterious? We have already discovered some strange and un-likely places in Scripture where God turned up.

What if prime among those unexpected places where we can enjoy God's presence is in our very homes? Giving radical hos-pitality does not just change the lives of the people we seek to help—it changes us. And it is not just that our worship of God is expressed through our concern for and hospitality toward the vulnerable. These acts and attitudes display God's character to a watching world and bring other people to worship God too. True hospitality is a virtuous circle. As we open our hearts and homes up to strangers, we open our hearts and homes to God. As strangers find God, we find God.

EZEKIEL AND THE STRANGER

The God who turns up the volume

In which a young refugee meets a stranger
far from home and discovers
why there is hope in exclusion.

I am walking through the Apple headquarters in Cupertino, California, half a world away from home—and it feels like it. It feels as if I am in a shrine to Steve Jobs. His words adorn the walls of the building, and his high-design ethos shapes everything from the huge trees inside the lobby area to the clean lines of the hallways and the minimalist chic of the dining areas. There are no candles to light, so in the Apple store I buy a black T-shirt—a medium-sized homage to the man with a penchant for wearing black turtlenecks. On the front it has just three words, in a simple, clean font: "the crazy ones." This is a reference to a famous marketing campaign that Apple used in

1997, which won many awards, including an Emmy. Many saw
it as the renaissance of Apple as a technology powerhouse, after
years of losing out to Microsoft and Intel. It set the stage for
the iMac range of computers, and a revolution in approachable
personal computing.

The ad featured images of major figures from the history of
the twentieth century such as Albert Einstein and Martin Luther
King, with actor Richard Dreyfus reading the following words in
the background:

> Here's to the crazy ones. The misfits. The rebels. The trouble-
> makers. The round pegs in the square holes. The ones who
> see things differently . . . the people who are crazy enough
> to think they can change the world, are the ones who do.[1]

In this advertisement Apple boldly positions itself as a natural
partner with the outliers in society—the radicals, the creatives,
the innovators, the nonconformists who are willing to ask the
difficult questions and challenge authority. Apple is praising
those who don't fit in, elevating the geeks, asking consumers to
associate with those who are on the margins—and join a coun-
terculture, a revolution.

The print campaign that went along with the Apple television
ads had the grammatically dubious construction "Think Different."
It was a bold campaign. Apple did not feel bound by conventional
rules, and certainly not by syntax. At a time when most technology firms used a picture of their product and added an
explanation of what it did, Apple instead created a feeling, a
brand association that suggested that by choosing Apple products,
however oddball, however marginalized we were in making that
choice, they—and therefore we—were in the same category as
such world-changing leaders.

The campaign appealed to my ego at the time. I wanted to use my creativity and skill to, as Jobs said, "make a dent in the universe."[2]

The idea of making a difference connected with what I was reading in my Bible about making my mark on the world. My peers and I firmly believed that each short-term mission, each new prayer initiative, each festival, conference, and course was potentially world changing. We wanted to be those history makers, game changers.

Over the years I have stayed loyal to both Apple and my faith. Apple has managed to convince me to upgrade my MacBook or my iPhone on numerous occasions, each time promising a technology upshift that I can't live without. Similarly, the church has promised a series of life-changing blessings, faith-revitalizing events, and thought-changing books. Remember that special prayer everyone was talking about that would give you everything you needed? Remember that experience you just had to go to North America to pick up? Remember that new translation of the Bible that would totally fix your doctrine? Remember that course that would save your marriage? All of these things may have had their strengths, but in the longer term too many turned out ultimately to be big talk that delivered little.

To be honest, these days I find it harder to believe the hype on both fronts. In this respect I feel like an Isaiah, who, as we saw in the last chapter, faithfully stuck to his ministry even though he knew it wouldn't, couldn't, change the hearts of God's people. Sometimes I think if I were to talk to my younger self, I might well tell him not to be so foolish and naive, to change his expectations and accept life's limitations. I would tell him that, despite what my new T-shirt may say, shutting up and blending in is a much safer option. I could give him all sorts of tips and pointers about how best to get through life under the radar, safe from any accusation of being "crazy." At other times, however, I still want to be one of those crazy ones who can change the world. That's when I need a good shot of Ezekiel.

Of all the strange Old Testament prophets, Ezekiel is the best fit for my "crazy ones" T-shirt. His message and his methods were edgy, to say the least. But he was used by God in his time, and he has something important to teach us today about understanding the God-who-is-stranger. Not only that, we will zoom in on a particularly unsettling allegory that God gives to Ezekiel in a vision—and which raises some serious questions about how God relates to strangers.

Ezekiel was a refugee. Unlike Isaiah, who received his vision of God on home territory in the temple in Jerusalem, a bit of basic deduction suggests that Ezekiel was forcibly resettled to Babylon around 597 BC, at the age of twenty-five.[3] At the moment Middle Eastern, male, twenty-something refugees have a major public relations problem on a scale that even Apple would struggle to turn around. I meet many people willing to show kindness to unaccompanied refugee children, and a good number who care about the women, the disabled, and the elderly. But when they find out that most of the refugees fleeing from places like Afghanistan, Eritrea, and Syria are young men, their attitudes become significantly less benevolent and much more fearful and suspicious.

Disaffected young men, who are not able or not allowed to work in the profession they may have trained for and are pumped full of frustration, are particularly susceptible to ideological recruitment and radicalization. Like me when I was first captured by Apple's branding, they are still young enough to believe they can change the world, but not old enough to discern hype from hope. Ezekiel fits that age, stage, and rage category perfectly. He would have grown up with the dominant expectation of serving in the temple of Jerusalem, but forcible removal shattered those dreams. This young, bearded refugee would not be picked for a "Refugees Welcome" poster campaign. Instead he would be a prime candidate for a security watch list. Nonetheless, he was at the top of God's recruitment list.

We have seen how the accounts of the calling of Abraham, Jacob, Gideon, and Isaiah each set the tone for the different mission God recruits them to. Each one of them has a very different encounter with strangers—who just turn out to be God himself. Unfolding in a similar vein to Isaiah's, the calling of Ezekiel takes place with a visual encounter (Ezekiel 1:3-28) and then a spoken call (Ezekiel 2:1–3:9). But whereas Isaiah's vision was dominated by the omnipotence of the Lord, his power and glory, Ezekiel's vision focuses on the omnipresence of the Lord—on his ability to appear wherever he wishes, and his mobility. A long way from his hometown of Jerusalem and well outside the boundaries of the temple, far away from Israel, Ezekiel meets with God:

> I looked, and I saw a windstorm coming out of the north—an immense cloud with flashing lightning and surrounded by brilliant light. The center of the fire looked like glowing metal, and in the fire was what looked like four living creatures. In appearance their form was human, but each of them had four faces and four wings. Their legs were straight; their feet were like those of a calf and gleamed like burnished bronze. Under their wings on their four sides they had human hands. All four of them had faces and wings, and

the wings of one touched the wings of another. Each one went straight ahead; they did not turn as they moved. . . .

As I looked at the living creatures, I saw a wheel on the ground beside each creature with its four faces. This was the appearance and structure of the wheels: They sparkled like topaz, and all four looked alike. Each appeared to be made like a wheel intersecting a wheel. As they moved, they would go in any one of the four directions the creatures faced; the wheels did not change direction as the creatures went. Their rims were high and awesome, and all four rims were full of eyes all around. . . .

Then there came a voice from above the vault over their heads as they stood with lowered wings. Above the vault over their heads was what looked like a throne of lapis lazuli, and high above on the throne was a figure like that of a man. I saw that from what appeared to be his waist up he looked like glowing metal, as if full of fire, and that from there down he looked like fire; and brilliant light surrounded him. Like the appearance of a rainbow in the clouds on a rainy day, so was the radiance around him.

This was the appearance of the likeness of the glory of the LORD. When I saw it, I fell facedown, and I heard the voice of one speaking. (Ezekiel 1:4-9, 15-18, 25-28)

Imagine trying to provide a running commentary of a fireworks display for someone who is visually impaired. Imagine how difficult it would be to try to capture all the colors, patterns, and explosions in words. Ezekiel has the task of trying to do something similar as he puts in words the sensory extravaganza of his vision. Ezekiel cannot provide us with a blueprint or a technical diagram, so instead he paints an impressionistic word picture of what he has seen. He uses words a bit like J. M. W. Turner used brush strokes to express flames in his painting *The Burning of the Houses of Parliament* in 1834, or a volcanic eruption on the island of St. Vincent in *The Eruption of the Souffrier Mountains* from 1812. It would be impossible to work out the cause of the fire or the exact scale of the volcano from Turner's paintings, but that is not the painter's purpose. Turner aims to recreate the mood and emotions of the experience, as does Ezekiel here. He successfully gives us a startling sense of the majesty and magnificence of God. There seems to be a deliberate sharing of imagery between the callings of these two prophets, Isaiah and Ezekiel, so a direct comparison will render some interesting insights.

First, both visions include angelic beings and a magnificent throne. Just as this was an amazing reassurance to Isaiah of God's overarching control even after the death of the king, so it was to Ezekiel, even in the light of the loss of his homeland. Second, there are burning coals in both accounts: it is the same holy God who has the power to wound and heal, convict and forgive, destroy and atone. But Ezekiel alone sees wings that meet and wheels that intersect. Unlike the idols of other nations, fixed and immovable, God is not static. He is on the move, unhindered by geographical boundaries.

Feeling far away from home and destabilized in his faith, Ezekiel needed this reassurance that God was with him in exile just as he had been in Jerusalem. However, only a few chapters later Ezekiel witnesses similar imagery of a fiery heavenly chariot in thundering clouds used to depict God storming out of Jerusalem (Ezekiel 10). The wheeled throne is no longer an escort vehicle, showing that God can be elsewhere than the temple, but a getaway vehicle, indicating God's intention of being anywhere but the temple. It is revved up and ready to remove God's presence from the Holy of Holies. This is devastating news. The temple, which had been essential to Ezekiel's life and faith and sense of community, is about to be deserted by the one who commanded its creation for his glory.

This is difficult teaching for us too. Christian memorabilia—posters, pens, and the like—reminds us that God is "an ever-present help in trouble" (Psalm 46:1) or, as Jesus promised to his disciples, "I am with you always" (Matthew 28:20). Yet the Bible teaches not only the reality of God's presence, but also the real risk of his absence, as we have seen in each chapter of this book so far. Adam was created for and then cast out of God's perfect presence. Sodom was visited then destroyed by God's angels. Gideon, Naomi, and David all knew God's presence and his absence, as did God's people in exile in the time of Isaiah and Ezekiel. We know from our own experience both God's drawing close and his drawing back. God may be ever present, yet he is often absent. How can this be, that he is both friend and stranger? And how can we stay faithful to God through these different seasons?

Ezekiel has to face the challenge of being an outsider both to the Babylonians and to his own people. To be honest, Christians pretty often find themselves in the same position. In writing this book I found myself identifying a bit with Ezekiel. His message does not sit easily with the way that Western culture is currently going. The call to welcome the stranger is politically unpopular. I have been on radio phone-ins where people argued with me on air that refugees should not be accepted into our nation, that they are part of a secret Islamic takeover, that our country is full and we have no obligation to help even the children caught up in the crisis. Advocating for compassion, grace, and hospitality does not always receive a warm welcome. Equally, this message may not be any more welcome in the church. Some

Christians argue that all this compassion is a distraction from gospel ministry. Others argue that the church should not be welcoming refugee children when we don't have enough foster parents to care for "our own children." It is difficult and disheartening to face criticisms from all sides!

Maybe you have tasted something similar to this, of being different from those "out there" yet not accepted "in here" either. Whether they were called to a change of career, to take a stand for Bible-based teaching and values in their children's schools, or to speak out for the rights of adults with learning difficulties or of families in financial crisis, I have met Christians whose calling and efforts to bring inclusion for all have led to them experiencing exclusion from both within and outside church circles. Perhaps Ezekiel can help and encourage us all. Just like Isaiah, he has to speak to a people who will not listen, but this time God wants to metaphorically turn up the volume, giving them opportunities to watch and learn as well as listen. First of all, we may as well dispel from the start the idea that as Christians we can or should blend in to our culture. Ezekiel has absolutely no hope of fitting in, because God asks him to do some pretty strange things. On one occasion Ezekiel was put into a trance-like state for a week (Ezekiel 3:15). Another time he was struck mute to symbolize God's people's inability to hear and respond to God's word (Ezekiel 3:24-27). He had to make a scale model of Jerusalem, with siege works lined up against it (Ezekiel 4:1-3). He lay on his left side for 390 days and his right side for forty days to symbolize the duration of God's punishment on the northern and southern kingdoms (Ezekiel 4:4-8). He reluctantly performed a public cooking demonstration roasting barley cakes over cow dung (Ezekiel 4:9-15). He shaved his beard off with a sword and divided the trimmings into three sections, burning a third, throwing a third to the wind, and scattering the rest around the city while striking it with a sword, to symbolize the various fates of death or exile for those proportions of God's people (Ezekiel 5:1-6). We can only imagine how foolish Ezekiel must have felt undertaking these odd assignments. And though the distance of history helps us to keep them at arm's length, these stories do not seem much less strange and embarrassing today. It is little wonder churches avoid preaching the book of Ezekiel.

Yet the book of Ezekiel is surprisingly relevant. We do feel at odds with the world around us. Many of us feel that the things God asks us to do are frankly embarrassing in an increasingly secularized society. Being seen praying, singing, and associating with uncool people is not the done thing. Talking about matters of life and death and good and evil as if they matter is politically incorrect and can be socially isolating. It seems weird to prioritize God's kingdom in our careers and with our ambitions instead of making money, spending it, and looking forward to retirement. It is not easy to go against the flow and stand up for justice and the rights of the widows and fatherless. In professional life it is much easier to divorce our faith from our work than to be a living parable like Ezekiel. Publicly following God's ways leaves us open to accusations of being weird, foolish, deviant, eccentric, and strange.

At his Stanford commencement address, back in 2005, having already come clean about some very serious health conditions, Steve Jobs implored the students:

> Your time is limited, so don't waste it living someone else's life. Don't be trapped by dogma—which is living with the results of other people's thinking. Don't let the noise of others' opinions drown out your own inner voice.[4]

This speech, which included input from veteran screenwriter Aaron Sorkin, was described by Jobs's biographer Walter Isaacson as one of the best speeches ever delivered to graduating students.[5] It was certainly inspirational, encouraging us not to be afraid to separate ourselves from the crowd. But listening to our inner voice—with its mix of ego, personal desire, and self-interest alongside good intentions and God-given wisdom can be fraught with problems too. The Bible tells us not to be trapped by either, but to tune in to the voice of God leading us. Just as Ezekiel the prophet heard and obeyed God's voice while far away from home, so we, in our spiritual identity as strangers in a strange land, need to listen attentively to the voice of God. We need to pay attention when he speaks if we want to make the most of our time on the planet.

But what the voice of God asked Ezekiel to do is not really what we want to hear. What if he asks us to do or say things that will only alienate us further from those he has sent us to reach? How can we understand a God who makes the Christian faith so hard to live out, promote, and defend? To help us see not only why God is a stranger to us, but also why he may make us seem strangers to those around us, Ezekiel contains a very disturbing story. It is so shocking that at first glance it is difficult to reconcile with what we think we know of the grace and compassion of God.

We need to hold on to the idea that wrestling with the stranger, more difficult parts of the Bible can help us come to the most profound understanding of God. This dark parable of Ezekiel will take some wrangling as it gets stranger and stranger, each scene more disturbing than the one before. The violence it portrays is tragically all too relevant to the horrors of our world today:

This is what the Sovereign LORD says to Jerusalem: Your
ancestry and birth were in the land of the Canaanites; your
father was an Amorite and your mother a Hittite. On the
day you were born your cord was not cut, nor were you
washed with water to make you clean, nor were you rubbed
with salt or wrapped in cloths. No one looked on you with
pity or had compassion enough to do any of these things
for you. Rather, you were thrown out into the open field,
for on the day you were born you were despised.

Then I passed by and saw you kicking about in your blood,
and as you lay there in your blood I said to you, "Live!" I
made you grow like a plant of the field. (Ezekiel 16:3-7)

The story begins by depicting Jerusalem as an abandoned baby
girl, left naked in a field in a pool of blood, with her umbilical
cord still attached, tiny legs kicking against seemingly inevitable
exposure and death. But the baby is found and fostered by God
himself, who nurtures her and enables her to flourish and thrive.
It is a brutal and yet beautiful beginning.

The rejection of female babies is sadly not relegated to history,
and can begin even before birth. Horrific evidence has been
discovered in India of illegal sex-selective abortions, including
the bodies of dozens of female fetuses whose bodies had been
melted with acid, their bones crushed and buried.[6] Dr. Sabu
George, who has spent the last twenty-five years campaigning
against what he articulates as a "genocide" of baby girls in Delhi,
states that in India the first few months in the womb are the
riskiest part of a woman's life.[7] In a culture where boys can earn
money to support the parents but girls are deemed too expensive
to keep and require a dowry when they get married, gender-based
abortion has been seen as the ultimate solution. For those who

can't afford abortion, there is a horrific alternative—killing baby girls after birth, through poisoning, throat-slitting, starvation, smothering, or drowning; or, as is more commonplace, disposing of them by abandonment—the practice that is described here, and was certainly commonplace in the Roman Empire, and no doubt earlier too.[8] These daily atrocities do not make daily news now any more than they did then. But perhaps it is time for Christians to make some noise about these clear violations of God's commands. It is not just India where these tragedies are taking place. Baby girls have also been abandoned en masse in China, casualties of their one-child policy. Back in 1990 it was estimated that 100 million girls were "missing," largely in these two countries, based on a statistical analysis of population figures—through neglect, lack of health care, and deliberate "gendercide."[9] There is also disturbing evidence in the UK and elsewhere that some unscrupulous doctors may be offering gender-based abortion in the West too. And of course the girls who make it through will still be statistically far less likely to be educated, paid an equal wage, be allowed to inherit property, or be taken seriously in public life.

Perhaps less has changed since Ezekiel's day than we might hope. The patriarchal society that put men's names in genealogies and dismissed girl babies as an economic burden is perhaps as dominant in many places in the world today as it was back then in the Middle East.[10] God is not afraid to take a wholly different stance to that of his creation. He sees this baby girl not as a burden but as a person; not as worthless, but so valuable that he would step in and rescue her.

God's concern for vulnerable children is evident throughout the Bible. He consistently describes himself as a "father to the fatherless" and a "protector of widows and orphans." This aspect of God's character has inspired believers around the world to engage in a radical interpretation of hospitality that rescues abandoned babies, fosters and adopts children deemed unwanted, campaigns against neglect and cruelty to children, and fights for the equality and dignity of all people. God's loving rescue of the most vulnerable in this story illustrates his depth of compassion and mercy for Jerusalem, once a pagan city with a dubious history, now taken under God's wing and cared for. It challenges us, as it was to challenge Ezekiel's listeners, to remember our rescue by God and the pride he takes in us despite what we have come from, and therefore not to be embarrassed to make a stand for him against injustice. It challenges us to emulate him, opening up our hearts and homes to those who are most vulnerable.

This story has not finished, however.

I made you grow like a plant of the field. You grew and developed and entered puberty. Your breasts had formed and your hair had grown, yet you were stark naked.

Later I passed by, and when I looked at you and saw that you were old enough for love, I spread the corner of my garment over you and covered your naked body. I gave you my solemn oath and entered into a covenant with you, declares the Sovereign LORD, and you became mine.

I bathed you with water and washed the blood from you and put ointments on you. I clothed you with an embroidered dress and put sandals of fine leather on you. I dressed you in fine linen and covered you with costly garments. I adorned you with jewelry: I put bracelets on your arms and a necklace around your neck, and I put a ring on your nose, earrings on your ears and a beautiful crown on your head.

So you were adorned with gold and silver; your clothes were of fine linen and costly fabric and embroidered cloth. Your food was honey, olive oil and the finest flour. You became very beautiful and rose to be a queen. And your fame spread among the nations on account of your beauty, because the splendor I had given you made your beauty perfect, declares the Sovereign LORD. (Ezekiel 16:7-14)

The second scene takes place many years later when the baby girl has been nurtured by God into a grown woman and is "old enough for love" (Ezekiel 16:8); therefore they marry. This is quite a disturbing image: a foster father marrying the very foundling baby he raised. The parent-child relationship here, as well as the presumed large age gap, must raise concerns of abuse and exploitation. Reading this today in the light of the tragically all-too-familiar headlines of sexually abusive foster parents and grooming pedophiles, as well as growing awareness of forced child marriages,[11] might make us think this story is advocating an abhorrent form of child abuse. But Ezekiel's audience would have heard this very differently. The relationship between a woman rescued from a foreign background and a much older male relative would have reminded them of the celebrated romance of Ruth and Boaz. Just as in that story, God says that he "spread the corner of my garment over you." This symbolic gesture, not dissimilar to the giving of an engagement ring, indicated a promise of eternal love and protection. Ruth was no powerless, abused damsel in distress, but a strong, independent, generous, noble female character who took the initiative to choose a man whom she not only loved and respected, but who would help her in providing the security for her wider family. Boaz the father-figure becomes a husband-helper.

This double metaphor recurs elsewhere through the Bible. As Christians we love the picture of God as our Father who has rescued us and adopted us into his family, making us his children and coheirs with Jesus. We also treasure the verses that speak of a God who has loved us with an everlasting love, that tell us that our Maker is our husband, and that the church is the bride of Christ heading for the ultimate wedding party. These two themes infuse many of our most loved worship songs for good reason.

With that in mind, we see a whole new spin on Ezekiel's story. This is an incredible rags-to-riches love story that illustrates God's merciful dealing with his lost people. From the bloody nakedness of her abandonment, this young woman is now being bathed, and clothed in finery. Once a baby left in the field to starve to death, now she is being offered choice foods. Not only has she been rescued; she is recognized and admired in her own right. Jerusalem has come a long way since God first chose her for his holy city. Now she has not only become the capital of the nation but is privileged with hosting God's temple; her place of honor is shown by the very presence of God on earth in her midst. The allegory is poignant: by personifying his city Jerusalem, not only does this powerfully set the scene for the betrayal that is to come, but hints at the time when God's presence will be personally experienced by believers through the Holy Spirit living inside us. Paul says exactly this in his first letter to the Corinthians: "Do you not know that your bodies are temples of the Holy Spirit, who is in you, whom you have received from God? You are not your own; you were bought at a price. Therefore honor God with your bodies" (1 Corinthians 6:19-20).

Do we recognize something here of our own incredible rescue by God from hopelessness and death? Do we understand something of the beauty and honor of being part of God's love story? Do we grasp something of the wonderful privilege of God's presence in our lives? Therefore, Paul tells us, we are to honor God with our bodies however strange it may seem to the world around us. Paul's theology of the body as a temple is exactly what leads him to highlight the implications of sexual immorality, the same issue that frames the next part of the Ezekiel story. Having been transformed from a helpless, naked baby to a beautiful bride, the third scene tells us about another transformation: the beautiful bride becomes a profligate prostitute.

> But you trusted in your beauty and used your fame to become a prostitute. You lavished your favors on anyone who passed by and your beauty became his. You took some of your garments to make gaudy high places, where you carried on your prostitution. You went to him, and he possessed your beauty. You also took the fine jewelry I gave you, the jewelry made of my gold and silver, and you made for yourself male idols and engaged in prostitution with them. And you took your embroidered clothes to put on them, and you offered my oil and incense before them. Also the food I provided for you—the flour, olive oil and honey I gave you to eat—you offered as fragrant incense before them. That is what happened, declares the Sovereign LORD. (Ezekiel 16:15-19)

Issues surrounding sexual promiscuity regularly make headlines. Whether it is the urgent appeal to intervene in the refugee crisis before more girls are lost to the sex trade, or public figures betraying their families for an affair, abusing their positions and suppressing the evidence, this choice of allegorical comparison is as relevant now as it was then.

The sexual exploitation of women has been an abominable scar across humanity for generations.[12] But this particular account makes it very clear that this woman's prostitution is a freely chosen personal decision on her part. Unlike so many, she is not under financial pressure so desperate that she has no other option in order to feed her children. She is not in such a vulnerable situation that she is at the mercy of the men who exploit her. There are no indications of grooming or pimping. If there is any coercion involved, it is on her part: she entices, seduces, and pays her new lovers with the gifts she had received from her husband.

Worse is to come. She sacrifices the lives of their children in pursuit of her own pleasures:

> And you took your sons and daughters whom you bore to me and sacrificed them as food to the idols. Was your prostitution not enough? You slaughtered my children and sacrificed them to the idols. In all your detestable practices and your prostitution you did not remember the days of your youth, when you were naked and bare, kicking about in your blood. . . .
>
> I am filled with fury against you, declares the Sovereign LORD, when you do all these things, acting like a brazen prostitute! When you built your mounds at every street corner and made your lofty shrines in every public square, you were unlike a prostitute, because you scorned payment.
>
> You adulterous wife! You prefer strangers to your own husband! All prostitutes receive gifts, but you give gifts to all your lovers, bribing them to come to you from everywhere for your illicit favors. So in your prostitution you are the opposite of others; no one runs after you for your

favors. You are the very opposite, for you give payment and none is given to you.

Therefore, you prostitute, hear the word of the LORD! This is what the Sovereign LORD says: Because you poured out your lust and exposed your naked body in your promiscuity with your lovers, and because of all your detestable idols, and because you gave them your children's blood, therefore I am going to gather all your lovers, with whom you found pleasure, those you loved as well as those you hated. I will gather them against you from all around and will strip you in front of them, and they will see you stark naked. I will sentence you to the punishment of women who commit adultery and who shed blood; I will bring on you the blood vengeance of my wrath and jealous anger. Then I will deliver you into the hands of your lovers, and they will tear down your mounds and destroy your lofty shrines. They will strip you of your clothes and take your fine jewelry and leave you stark naked. They will bring a mob against you, who will stone you and hack you to pieces with their swords. They will burn down your houses and inflict punishment on you in the sight of many women. I will put a stop to your prostitution, and you will no longer pay your lovers. Then my wrath against you will subside and my jealous anger will turn away from you; I will be calm and no longer angry. (Ezekiel 16:20-42)

The husband has not only lost his wife, but his children too. How could someone who knew what it meant to be tossed aside as a helpless child and left to die just turn around and slaughter her own children? Her husband confronts her with her behavior and in his rage threatens her with terrible consequences. What would happen if he were to gather together all her lovers—the Babylonians, Egyptians, Philistines, and Assyrians? He can just imagine the scene. In their anger and jealousy of each other they would surely strip her naked, steal her riches, and stone her to death. In the frenzy, perhaps they would even dismember her corpse and burn down her house. This is not a historical event that is being recorded, of course, like the attempted rape of Lot's guests or Lot offering his virgin daughters to the mob. This is a vision that is invoked by God, in order to convey something of his fury at the pain, betrayal, and senseless evil outcomes of spiritual adultery.

Nonetheless, it seems a strange way to elicit sympathy for a wronged party. Why would God identify himself as wanting to exact a vengeance even worse than that in David's imprecatory prayer? Why would he want to be seen as a threatening husband, throwing his weight around? There is a global pandemic of violence against women—one in three women will be subjected to physical attack or abuse in her lifetime.[13] In that light, what are we to make of this scene, of a woman about to be violently assaulted and killed? We may applaud a fitting punishment for a male sexual predator; can we really feel the same way about such brutality toward a female, even though she too is presented as a sexual predator?[14] Why are her ex-lovers involved in the inflicting of the punishment, by abusing and violating the woman? Is the Bible promoting a misogynist line—"She asked for it; she deserves what she gets"? This dark story jeopardizes our understanding of a God of justice and compassion, love, and forgiveness. Here we come face to face with a stranger God we find hard to recognize.

There are four different angles from which we can come at this, to get some clues about what is going on here.

First, it may be helpful to consider the uses of allegory. As an extreme form of metaphor, allegories are often deliberately provocative; they are designed to elicit an emotional response from us. They are not meant to give a balanced, factual account, but rather a passionate, one-sided view to capture our imaginations in a way that makes an impact. If I tell you that my teenager's room is a disaster zone, I am not suggesting you announce a national state of emergency or add it to the World Risk Index. I use the phrase to shock you into a level of sympathy for me in my efforts to persuade her to clear it up. Similarly, just because God is described as a warrior in the Old Testament does not mean that he endorses military violence and wartime cruelty willy-nilly. When allegory is used in the Bible, we are supposed to take on the challenge and try to discern which elements are divinely mandated, not swallow the story whole. Just because God is using a domestic violence metaphor does not mean that God is in any way endorsing such behavior. In fact, with this allegory God shows clearly that he does not think such attitudes are acceptable. He begins by ensuring that we are clear about why he is choosing it—to illustrate his anger at his people's infidelity: "I am filled with fury against you . . . acting like a brazen prostitute!" (Ezekiel 16:30). Sadly, it seems as if the description portrays behavior that women and men in 700 BC would have connected with. Perhaps this language is necessary to communicate as much as possible the pain of a patient and forgiving husband whose straying wife has cost him his family and his reputation. Perhaps the damage of such marital disharmony is what the story is primarily about, not a lesson in gender relations or an endorsement of domestic abuse.

Second, we know that elsewhere in the Bible, women who were either victims of sexual violence, or considered sexually deviant in their communities according to cultural mores, are treated by God in a way that is counterculturally gracious. Rahab, Hagar, Tamar, and Bathsheba, for example, instead of being shamed or cut out of the Bible, are all affirmed by God. Jesus was born of a virgin, despite the accusations that would inevitably ensue and the shadow of illegitimacy that would be cast over him. Jesus makes space for a Samaritan woman who may not be given a name but certainly had a reputation (John 4), and he allows a woman, who lived a sinful life, to pour her perfume on his feet as an act of worship (Luke 7:37). When Jesus comes across a woman caught in adultery (John 8), he protects her from the vengeance of the mob and offers her forgiveness and a fresh start. Although there are plenty of declared attitudes in the Bible that seem misogynistic and backward, looking at the roles women actually played in this long history tells a different story.

Third, in Christian theology there are what are called *communicable* and *incommunicable* attributes of God.[15] The incommunicable attributes are characteristics that God alone can possess—his self-existence, omnipotence, omniscience, self-sufficiency, and transcendence, for example.[16] The communicable attributes are ones that we as his people can emulate, such as his mercy, love, creativity, and justice. Because God speaks, and we speak, for example, we recognize that there is a parallel between us. But no one would claim that our speech is as pure, holy, accurate, effective, or infallible as God's. Similarly, although we can understand something of the anger at the betrayal that God is expressing in this allegory, we cannot even begin to imagine or grasp the extent of the pain that a perfect and loving God feels when his beloved people are unfaithful. In communicating with us, therefore, God has to accommodate to our limited understanding by using language and emotions we understand.

Just as a parent telling a toddler not to touch the electric sockets will exaggerate tone of voice and facial expression because no amount of words explaining the dangers or effects of electrocution would be understood, so it may be that here God has to exaggerate the brutality of the story because that is the only way to communicate his pain at his people's unfaithfulness. God turns up the volume on the issue so we can't miss it. John Calvin, the sixteenth-century Reformed theologian, describes it this way: "Because our weakness cannot reach [God's] height, any description which we receive of him must be lowered to our capacity in order to be intelligible. And the mode of lowering to represent him not as he really is, but as we conceive of him."[17] Our upset at the imagery, the whole tone of the story, is precisely the point: this *is* a shocking circumstance.

Finally, this brings us on to the other literary devices used here, of hyperbole and personification. Ezekiel's picture of extreme vengeance reminds us of the hyperbole in David's angry psalm, when he asks God to wreak all sorts of atrocities on his enemies. Like David, the verbal diatribe replaces the acting out of the violence in reality. If God describes verbally what could happen should he unleash the full weight of his fury, but actually withholds that fatal blow, then by way of contrast his right and power to judge and his patient and compassionate mercy are powerfully portrayed. Ultimately, this prophetic allegory is a personification of God's holy city. Through metaphorical language, God is warning Jerusalem that their insatiable idolatry and toleration of injustice have torn apart the relationship between them, and that God will eventually have to allow this center of worship to be destroyed and burned down.

In the middle of a litany of terrible deeds that Jerusalem has committed against God, we get a glimpse of divine mercy.

There is a ray of hope that another transformation may be possible, but this takes form via a most unexpected detour. God says, "I will restore the fortunes of Sodom" (Ezekiel 16:53). Just when we thought Sodom had been dealt a final blow, we learn that God can bring restoration even out of those abominable ashes, the place where sexual hostility not hospitality defined their treatment of strangers. If that is true, then there is hope for the ashes of Jerusalem too. Through Ezekiel God promises, "Yet I will remember the covenant I made with you in the days of your youth, and I will establish an everlasting covenant with you . . . and you will know that I am the Lord" (Ezekiel 16:60, 62). Yes, God has been a stranger to his people, hiding his face from their sin and threatening them with terrible consequences. But they have been a stranger to him too, not returning his love, shaming him, dishonoring his name, and treating him worse than they would a stranger. Yet at the heart of this apparently total relational breakdown, God promises a future reconciliation.

Ezekiel's strange prophecy is just as relevant today as it was in his time. Are we being faithful to our gracious Father God, the one who loves us? Or have we forgotten our own sorry state before God intervened in our lives? Have we, like Jerusalem of old, betrayed our Rescuer and Redeemer? Or do we remember God's grace to us as vulnerable children and seek to demonstrate this same grace to others in need? In a world where children are still abandoned, promiscuity is still rampant, and domestic violence still wrecks lives, there is hope. Ezekiel's brutal, stark, and emotional allegory gives us a fresh glimpse of a God who is deeply pained by the unfaithfulness of his people and the injustice in the world.

Centuries later, outside Jerusalem, another stranger was accused of treacherous betrayal. Mirroring the threats against the woman in Ezekiel's story, this stranger, once a helpless babe, was stripped naked, mobbed, pierced with a sword, and torn apart "in the sight of many women" (Ezekiel 16:41)—and God turned his face away. The physical death of Jesus as the representative of God's people everywhere is the antithesis of the pictorial death of the prostitute representing God's people of Jerusalem. Jesus was innocent not guilty, the betrayed not the betrayer, the faithful one not the faithless one. He cried out to God not for the destruction of the city that had rejected him, but for its salvation. How he longed to gather the people there to himself as a hen gathers her chicks.

Just as the death of Jesus resonates with some of these stories in Ezekiel, so too does his resurrection. In a vision, Ezekiel is transported to a mass grave, lying open, perhaps not unlike the macabre resting place of the bones of those unborn girls discovered in India. God tells Ezekiel to prophesy life to this valley of the dead, and with a rattling and scraping the dry bones realign, and reassemble themselves into skeletons. Tendons and ligaments appear, followed by flesh and then skin. To the inanimate pile of corpses Ezekiel speaks the words God has given him: in effect, "Let there be life." Suddenly a mighty army appears, living and breathing.

> Then he said to me: "Son of man, these bones are the people of Israel. They say, 'Our bones are dried up and our hope is gone; we are cut off.' Therefore prophesy and say to them: 'This is what the Sovereign LORD says: My people, I am going to open your graves and bring you up from them; I will bring you back to the land of Israel.'" (Ezekiel 37:11-12)

This is not hype. This is the resurrection hope for our broken world. New life comes from dry bones. Cities are raised from the ashes. Temporary exclusion leads to permanent inclusion. Not only can we dare to dream big; we can dare to dream the impossible, because with God all things are possible. Although we may stand out in the world for his sake, we can stay faithful to the message he has given us, because ultimately he will bring us home. Although our sense of God's presence may fluctuate, we can stay faithful to him, because ultimately he will bring us home.

Abdul Fattah Jandali was a Syrian immigrant. Because of his refugee status and his Muslim religion, he was deemed not good enough to marry the girl he loved or raise the child he fathered. His son was put up for adoption. Paul and Clara Jobs accepted the child as their own. If Steve Jobs had read the prophecy of Ezekiel, I am sure he would have found a lot to connect with—an abandoned child who was taken in and enabled to thrive, a misfit who changed the world. The following quote is too long for a gift-shop T-shirt, but in it Jobs grasped something about how we are supposed to interface with our world:

> That's maybe the most important thing. It's to shake off this erroneous notion that life is there and you're just gonna live in it, versus embrace it, change it, improve it, make your mark upon it. I think that's very important and however you learn that, once you learn it, you'll want to change life and make it better, cause it's kind of messed up, in a lot of ways. Once you learn that, you'll never be the same again.[18]

MARY AND THE STRANGER

The God who turns up in all the wrong places

In which a pregnant homeless woman meets
a string of strangers, and we meet a baby
who sparks generosity and genocide.

Saturday morning. Strike one: my alarm clock went off way too early, dragging me away from my bed and my family. Strike two: I had to speak at a Christian men's breakfast. For me there is something profoundly uncomfortable about an event that women are only allowed to come to if they are doing the cooking and not the eating, seen but not heard. Strike three: when I got there, the room turned out to be filled with predominantly retired men—unlikely candidates for my talk, aimed at recruiting adoptive dads for children in care. It was one of those mornings where I wondered how on earth I got to where I am. This breakfast event seemed to be the least useful

or enjoyable use either of my time or God's. My mood of re-
sentment probably showed, to be frank. I dismissed the room
as a lost cause. But as we have been discovering through this
book, sometimes God turns up in unexpected places and through
unexpected people. This was to be one of those days.

As I sat down to tuck into breakfast an elderly gentleman sat
next to me, full of enthusiasm for the work of my charity. As
the conversation developed I began to see why he cared so much.
Aged seven, John had found himself on a train full of children.
Just as the train was about to pull away from the platform, his
mother handed him a watch through the open window and then
stepped back and waved goodbye. They would never see each
other again. John's parents were among the 6 million Jews killed
in the Holocaust, shortly after he was evacuated on the Kinder-
transport program. They were among the 6 million people living
in the wrong place at the wrong time, caught on the wrong side
of Hitler's fanaticism. Seventy-six years later, John was able to
tell me of his tremendous gratitude for the love and commitment
of the family who not only sheltered him, but adopted him as
their own after it became clear that he no longer had a home to
return to.

I went home from that breakfast humbled and honored to
hear John's story of faith in the midst of such terrible tragedy.
As I read his book later that day, I discovered that years after
his evacuation, he and his brother Arthur received a moving
letter from his parents, written before they had died.

Dear Boys,

When you receive this letter the war will be over because
our friendly messenger won't be able to send it any earlier.
We want to say farewell to you who were our dearest

possession in the world, and only for a short time were we able to keep you. . . . We go bravely into the unknown with the hope that we shall yet see you again when God wills. Don't forget us, and be good. I too thank all the good people who have accepted you so nobly.[1]

One of those good people was Nicholas Winton. The previous Christmas he had planned to go on a skiing vacation, but a friend persuaded him instead to visit Prague. On that trip the twenty-eight-year-old stockbroker came across hundreds of refugees traveling across Europe, and he was particularly overwhelmed by the plight of the children. Back in his room in London he set up an office and orchestrated six trains to travel to Czechoslovakia with the express purpose of evacuating refugee children to safety. Winton secured homes and sponsorship for them. He also navigated the complex political system, even forging Home Office documents in order to get children out of Nazi-occupied territory. In all he organized eight trains carrying 669 children to safety. He did this secretly—apparently not even his wife knew about it. Fifty years later she discovered a scrapbook and passed it on to the media, who rightly fêted him. But Winton's memory was filled not with the children he saved, but with the children he failed to save. On September 1, 1939, a train with 250 children left Wilson Station in Prague, but that day Hitler invaded Poland and the Czech borders were closed. They never made it to Liverpool Street Station.

Nicholas and John were strangers to each other. Their paths crossed briefly in 1939, and again sixty years later, but Winton's open hospitality changed the whole of John's life. The story of Jesus is not dissimilar. Jesus was to dedicate himself to a rescue mission like no other. Strangers around the world now owe their lives to this man. But before we get to Jesus' identity as a rescuer like Winton, we must not forget that first he was a refugee like John, forced to flee his country under threat of genocide. As we explore the forgotten side of the Christmas story, we see something of what it means to find God in the wrong place at the wrong time.

From the moment he was conceived, Jesus was identified with the underclass of humanity. His parents lived in Roman-occupied territory during what Steve Holmes describes as a "brutal and repressive" period of history.[2] Apart from suffering the shame of being an occupied nation, the suffering Jews had to pay heavy taxes to the Roman overlords and live with the unpredictable ways in which Roman imperial whim made itself known in the far provinces—as well as the intermittent murders, terrorism, and insurgent uprisings that came from disillusioned Jewish factions.

Then, Jesus was born into a difficult family relationship. His parents were unmarried when the teenage Mary told her fiancé Joseph of her pregnancy by the Holy Spirit. Mary surely knew what was going through Joseph's mind—the betrayal, cheating, and lying he must be imagining of her. Was the girl he thought he knew just a stranger to him? Would he publicly accuse her of adultery, with its mandated punishment of stoning? Or would he look for another way to end the relationship quickly and quietly? How relieved Mary must have been when God visited Joseph and confirmed her story to him. Joseph enters this relationship knowing he would in effect be adopting a child that was not biologically his. Together they take on the humiliation, and set out on the uncertain path of pregnancy. Together they take it all on, even though they are impoverished. They knew their child to be the Son of God, yet they couldn't scrabble together enough money to pay the proper amount for a temple dedication ceremony, taking the poor man's option of offering pigeons instead.[3] Having seen throughout the Old Testament the consistency with which God works through displaced people and dysfunctional families, we should not be surprised that on top of all these challenges, this family is also pretty close to homeless when the baby is born, having traveled to Bethlehem for the census.

Jesus was born into a world of countrywide conflict, domestic discord, and personal poverty. From his very birth he was identified with the persecuted, the illegitimate, the homeless, and the marginalized.[4]

In Matthew's account of Joseph's encounter with God, when he discovers that Mary really is a divinely pregnant virgin, the Gospel writer links back to a prophecy from Isaiah: "All this took place to fulfill what the Lord had said through the prophet: 'The virgin will conceive and give birth to a son, and they will call him Immanuel'" (Matthew 1:22-23). Immanuel means "God with us."

We have seen that in the Old Testament God may be both absent and present by turns, both friend and stranger. How can we understand what it means to know God's presence without considering his absence? How can we appreciate God's presence unless we are frustrated at his absence? This tension is coming to a climax here. Adam's, Abraham's, Jacob's, Gideon's, Naomi's, David's, Isaiah's, and Ezekiel's elusive and brief encounters with the God who is a stranger were all insufficient to illustrate the paradox of how God wants to be with his people. Insufficient for them, insufficient for their communities, and insufficient for God. Now, finally, God has shown up, not for a momentary theophany, but for a lifetime, not fully incognito, but fully Immanuel. In Jesus, God lays aside his power and his glory and his kingly rights, to be truly with his people. Will God be recognized? Will he be welcomed? God turns up in the midst of military occupation, poverty, and oppression. Despite four hundred years of silence since the feeble return of God's people from a generation in exile, and six hundred years of almost continual occupation of Palestine, finally God declares himself present. God is no longer a stranger. God is not far away. God is not detached. God is not unconcerned. God has not rejected his suffering people. God has not disassociated from those who are troubled. He stands with them in solidarity.

Mind you, it is a strange kind of solidarity, this newborn sleeping on straw in a shed. And despite his arrival being heralded by astronomical phenomena and angel choirs, for the most part his birth and life will continue as it has begun, marked by the fact that he is a stranger, unrecognized and unwelcomed as the Son of God. Why does God choose to turn up in the middle of the night, in the middle of nowhere, to a couple of nobodies, in the middle of a census, to a country in conflict? Here is the news: God deliberately planned to turn up at the wrong time in the wrong place. God is Immanuel. God is present. God is with us. But God is also hidden, set apart, unassuming.

Despite Jesus' birth occurring outside the limelight of publicity, to people with no political clout, fame, or fortune; despite his arrival taking place in a tiny, forgotten corner of the Roman Empire, well-wishers arrive nonetheless. Not friends and family, but strangers. Nomadic shepherds, considered untrustworthy as they lived in the hills and were constantly on the move. They were regarded as unclean, too, carrying the stench of sheep and sleeping rough. But God sends angels to invite these homeless strangers to welcome his homeless son into the world.

Perhaps Mary had already begun to understand something of God's unusual habit of welcome and hospitality. Perhaps that understanding began when she realized that God had not thought it beneath him to invite himself into her life, and to become, as the carol says, "offspring of the Virgin's womb."[5] Or perhaps it was when they had run out of options and had nowhere to stay, and then by God's mercy a roof was offered them for the night. Perhaps it was a while before that, as she sang her worship to the God who had chosen her to host his Son:

> He has brought down rulers from their thrones
>> but has lifted up the humble.
> He has filled the hungry with good things
>> but has sent the rich away empty. (Luke 1:52-53)

Whenever it was that the penny dropped for Mary, by the time the shepherds arrived she knew that no unwashed outcast could be unwelcome under their roof. She draws them not only into her makeshift home but also into her affections. Luke explains that Mary treasured these moments in her heart (Luke 2:19).

Luke's Gospel continues to emphasize in chapter after chapter the significance of unexpected, risky hospitality when it came to being around Jesus. Right from the day he was born, strangers are welcomed into the most private of moments and amid the most meager of circumstances. In Luke's Gospel Jesus is the one who makes space for the sinners, the sick, and the separated to share food and fellowship with him, while the rich, the righteous, and the royals miss out or shun his offer of hospitality.

Matthew's retelling of Jesus' birth may focus more on the global reach of the good news message, but he does not overlook the significance of Jesus' first well-wishers either, and so he records the welcome given to the Magi. In contrast to the poor shepherds, these are rich, well-dressed dignitaries with social standing and expensive gifts,[6] but they too are traveling strangers. In fact, they were "from the East," an exotic description that would have sent a wave of fear and suspicion through most Jews at that time. The Magi were religious astrologers and had discerned from observing the stars that a great Jewish king had been born.[7] Naturally, they go to the palace first, in Jerusalem. But Jesus is going to be a different kind of king. He has begun his life among the poor and lowly for a reason. The Magi continue on their quest to find the King. Having been received by Herod, they are then deceived by him as he sends them on their way to find the baby with instructions to send news of its where-abouts, secretly plotting to kill the baby threatening his throne just as soon as he finds him.

By now the shepherds are long gone. The family is most probably living in a house, not a shed, and Jesus may not be a babe so much as a toddler. But Mary has not forgotten that God welcomes the least likely people. Like the shepherds, these strange visitors from the East receive a warm welcome from Mary. We are probably too familiar with the story to be shocked by Mary's response here. Jews would have been taught not even to associate with such people—unclean foreigners with strange religious beliefs—let alone accommodate them warmly. Matthew makes a point of including the welcome they receive, just as he makes a point of including the three non-Jews in the genealogy that starts his Gospel.[8] And those three are women at that, a doubly unusual inclusion in a Jewish family tree. We have intriguing hints here of God's hospitality to all people, despite the fact that Jesus' birth is seemingly ignoble and invisible.

Matthew does not say there were three Magi, as is often inferred from the number of gifts. Nevertheless, whether there were three or not, it is hard not to make the connection with Abraham, who welcomed into his temporary accommodation three strangers who announced a child who would grow up to bless the nations. It is hard not to make the connection between this story and that of King David, whose hometown of Bethlehem was again the scene for the demonstration of God's plan that people from all walks and nations are to be welcomed into his household. This Christ-child has turned up in the wrong place, and yet by doing so, from the outset he brings hope and peace as strangers come together from all sorts of backgrounds and places.

At the same time, the arrival of the Christ-child is also bringing division, destruction, and death. Herod's reaction to the news from the Magi that there was a new King in town was to order the extermination of all male children under two years old. It is understandable that the mass killing of small children does not feature in our popular yuletide celebrations. But why does the Bible itself not airbrush out the tragedy?

King Herod was a vicious and vindictive person. It was not out of character for him to order the killing of small children: we know that he ordered the execution of his own wife and at least two of his sons.[9] He is so determined to hold on to power that he is willing to murder any number of toddlers and babies. Herod's actions mirror those of Pharaoh at the time of Moses, who was so afraid of the growing immigrant community that he instructed the midwives to undertake gender-selective extermination to ensure no male babies survived. Herod just wants to get rid of one baby, but he sees infant deaths as mere collateral damage and unleashes military force against all boys under the age of two.

We have seen that Jesus' birth story sets him alongside the unwelcome, the poor, the outsider, the illegitimate, and the oppressed. If we thought a manger was bad, now there is nowhere in Israel where he is to be allowed to rest. If we thought homelessness was bad, now he is deemed an enemy of the state and Herod's death squads are combing the streets for him, committing mass infanticide as they go. But God has warned Joseph in a dream, and to escape the slaughter, he and his family go on the run. They cross the border into Egypt and seek asylum there.

Jesus was a refugee. The Son of God was an asylum seeker. The Prince of Peace went on the run from a brutal and merciless regime, crossing borders to find sanctuary. How can those of us who call ourselves Christians, who claim to belong to a Christian country, not welcome those who follow in Jesus' footsteps as a refugee? Even the UK's *Guardian* newspaper recognized the irony: "Some European politicians have framed their opposition to refugees as a defense of Christianity. That's ironic, since the Bible is full of refugees, and at times could be read as a 101 course on how to welcome them."[10] We prefer a civilized Jesus, a respectable establishment type who will comfort us, protect us, and promise that all our dreams will come true. The real Jesus, who identifies with the poor and the refugees, is a threat to our ambitions. Are we more like Herod than we like to admit? If there is no room for the outcast, vulnerable, poverty-stricken refugee Jesus in our lives, then we have to get rid of the other outcast, vulnerable, poverty-stricken refugees he associates with: collateral damage in our bid to protect a ruling position we are unwilling to budge from.

This issue is not going away. With one in every 122 human beings classed as refugees—well over 50 million people worldwide—we cannot ignore it. This tragic trend seems unlikely to be reversed in our lifetimes and is widely recognized as one of the defining humanitarian challenges of this century. Currently, wealthier Western nations are choosing to shun any responsibility to these vulnerable people. These are the very same nations where Christmas has become an increasingly significant, albeit consumer-oriented, public holiday. These are the same nations where secularism is on the rise and church attendance on the decline. There seems to me to be a strategic opportunity for a recovery of the Christmas story as a subversive text that must challenge the fear and xenophobia that is so often a society's first reaction to the mass movement of people. Jesus was a refugee.

Matthew describes what happens once the Magi have left:

> When they had gone, an angel of the Lord appeared to Joseph in a dream. "Get up," he said, "take the child and his mother and escape to Egypt. Stay there until I tell you, for Herod is going to search for the child to kill him."
>
> So he got up, took the child and his mother during the night and left for Egypt. (Matthew 2:13-14)

When Joseph hears God's voice in a dream and takes his family to seek refuge in Egypt, we are intended to make the connection with the wider story of the Bible. The most obvious parallel is with another dreamer, also called Joseph, whose family sought refuge in Egypt hundreds of years previously. Being refugees, and welcoming refugees, is critical to our understanding of our heritage, identity, and purpose as Christians.

Matthew draws attention to the parallels by quoting the prophecy of Hosea as he continues his biography of Jesus: "When Israel was a child, I loved him, and out of Egypt I called my son" (Hosea 11:1). Just like the people of Israel, Jesus lived as a refugee in Egypt, and just like Israel, Jesus is referred to as the Son of

God. The similarities keep coming. Just like the people of Israel, Jesus spent time in the desert being tempted. Just like the people of Israel, Jesus passed through the River Jordan. Jesus' baptism, like his birth, symbolizes his solidarity with others, says Dockery[11]—the willingness of God to identify with humanity. Jesus' baptism is an oddity for us looking back on it, as we know that he did not need to be made ceremonially clean and be given a fresh start; but Jesus wanted to introduce people to God's two-pronged version of hospitality. He gave grace as the receiver, not the deliverer of baptism. He reduced himself to be the guest, not the host. He became the servant, not the King. It is as Jesus is excluded, estranged, made an outsider and a refugee, that we can come to see two things. We see God's identification *with* the outsider, and we see his invitation *to* the outsider. God is a stranger, so that strangers can know God. If we know God, then we were once strangers, and we are to welcome strangers just as God welcomed us.

For the stranger that was Jesus, however, a warm welcome was rare. Jesus' exclusion and rejection in his early childhood, exemplified by Herod's pursuit and their flight to Egypt, was a pattern that would continue to mark his life. He was rejected by the people of his own hometown after preaching in their synagogue, where a sermon about God's concern for the poor and oppressed almost ended with him being thrown off a cliff by an angry mob. Jesus was rejected by the religious elite after healing the sick and disabled. Jesus was rejected for his choice of friends, food, and forgiveness. Jesus was rejected by his own brothers, betrayed by one of his own disciples, disowned by another, and turned on by the Jewish crowd when they called for his blood, demanding of the Romans, "Crucify him!"

The Gospel writer John puts it incredibly bluntly: "He came to that which was his own, but his own did not receive him" (John 1:11). He who came to teach us about being welcoming was time and again the least welcomed. Constantly on the receiving end of what we might call anti-hospitality, Jesus stood in solidarity with others in society who were rejected and marginalized. He fraternized with Roman collaborators, unclean foreigners, lepers, prostitutes, and the poor. He lived among the sick, the lonely, the bereaved, the morally outcast, and the extremists. He brought to them welcome, forgiveness, and hope. This is God's hospitality: Jesus welcomed the rejected despite being rejected for it himself. This is the God who is stranger: Jesus, who knew what it was like to be unwelcome in his own country, would die so that others could be welcomed into his own family. This is the God who turns up in the wrong places: Jesus is found with the least likely people, because he wants to make sure they are in the right place when it comes to their standing before God.

Christians love the Christmas story. But perhaps we need to turn the tables on the popular family-oriented celebration by demonstrating something of Jesus' flip-flop hospitality. We may not know many shepherds or traveling astrologers, but there are plenty of other unlikely people, people who are rejected and marginalized, whom we could invite into our homes and our hearts.

Under Nazism, one of the first groups of people to be picked out were children with learning difficulties. When the Netherlands was invaded, the Nazis banned the church services specifically for children with learning difficulties that were being run by a young girl named Corrie Ten Boom. For the Nazis, their treatment of these particularly vulnerable children was the starting point for the trajectory that would end in genocide. For Corrie, her treatment of these particularly vulnerable children was the starting point for the trajectory that would turn her humble kitchen table into a secret trapdoor, her home into a hiding place, and her protection of hundreds of Jews from Haarlem into an inspiration for Christians everywhere. Shortly after the services were shut down, she went to see her pastor, pleading with him to shield a Jewish baby she had rescued. He refused, for fear of losing his life, but at that moment Corrie's father appeared in the doorway. She credits his words as the turning point for her life:

> "Give the child to me, Corrie," he said. Father held the baby close, his white beard brushing its cheek, looking into the little face with eyes as blue and innocent as the baby's. "You say we could lose our lives for this child. I would consider that the greatest honor that could come to my family."[12]

Corrie and her father were not afraid to put themselves in harm's way for the sake of others, because they were driven by their faith in the Christ who had done the same for them. They followed a God who wrote himself into the pages of history at what seemed like an utterly wrong place and time: in the middle of a military occupation, and into a poverty-stricken family soon forced into being refugees. But for Jesus, this was *exactly* the right time and place to be in order to accomplish all that had been planned.

In the days before the Rwandan genocide, as ethnic tensions were rising, Christian students in the university tried to demonstrate Jesus' revolutionary hospitality, a hospitality of radical giving and willing receiving, and turned the tables around in their dining hall. It was normally divided with Hutu students at one end and Tutsi students at the other. Christians from both heritages deliberately moved the tables so they could sit together in the middle. They wanted to be a visible challenge to the tribal division they had previously gone along with. This was a very costly display of revolutionary hospitality. When the genocide broke out, these students were among the first to lose their lives. But nobody would forget the stand they took just by sitting together. Some will say those students were in the wrong place at the wrong time, but they followed a Christ who put himself in the wrong places to put things right.

If we want to know the God who is a stranger, we may have to start looking in all the wrong places. To do that we may have to start *being* in all the wrong places. If it wasn't beneath God himself to turn up in the lowly villages of ancient Israel or the refugee camps of Egypt, it cannot be beneath us. Where will our hospitality be most costly, most effective, and most appreciated?

YOU AND
THE STRANGER

The God who turns up the heat

In which you meet a stranger and learn that
your eternal destiny may well be based on something
you either forgot to do, or forgot you did.

There were once two strangers in an elevator. The first was busy adjusting his tie in the reflective surface of the elevator interior. He went on to brush down his suit, polish his shoes on the back of his trouser legs, and surreptitiously blow his nose. He was on his way to an interview, wanting to be suitably primed and preened. The second person was a young woman accompanying him to the room where the interview was to take place. She stood quietly, noting him gathering himself together, and as they exited through the elevator doors with time to spare, he asked her to bring him a coffee. When she returned, he claimed his coffee, asking how long she had been a secretary. She did not respond, but showed him into the meeting room where two senior members of the organization were already waiting. The woman walked around the table, sat down in the empty chair between the other two, and, to his great surprise, took the lead for the following forty-five minutes of the interview. I am pretty sure he regretted his misjudgment, but it was too late. This unfortunate candidate may have been suitably prepared in outward ways, but he was also substantially prejudiced. He had been standing alongside his lead interviewer, but she had been invisible to him. By failing to recognize her, he revealed his true colors. Sexism and ageism were not the qualities they were looking for in the vacancy. He had failed the interview before it even began.

This story contains a strong warning. I often recount it when friends and neighbors tell me they are applying for a new job. I would not like anyone to fall into the same trap because of whatever expectations and stereotypes are preprogrammed into our brains. I tell them to take care in the way they deal with strangers, because the strangers may not be who they appear to be. This was certainly true for Abraham, Jacob, and Gideon, as we have seen. Herod mistook God's identity too. He didn't realize he was trying to kill God himself as he set out to get rid of a baby he thought was a pretender to his throne. Being mistaken about God's identity is much more common than you might think. This theme comes to a head in a story in Matthew's Gospel, which contains perhaps the fiercest warning in the whole of Scripture. This passage is where Jesus teaches about a very frightening sort of stranger danger. It centers on the way an unrecognized stranger is treated and welcomed, and is such a revolutionary story that Professor Christine Pohl argues, "This has been the most important passage for the entire tradition on Christian hospitality."[1]

I need to offer a bit of a warning at this moment. There is some difficult language in this passage about fiery judgment and eternal death. Jesus really is turning up the heat here. For some of us this sort of language feels awkward at best, deeply offensive at worst. What are we to do with this kind of thing? Many Christians shy away from it totally, perhaps in reaction to those so-called "street evangelists" who provocatively declare it on street corners, or picket funerals with threats of hell and damnation. Perhaps they react to it because of the fire-and-brimstone caricatures of Christianity that lazy film directors use when they need a judgmental character. Too many people I know have been burned by eternal-fire-and-damnation Christianity. Those who preach it most strongly usually accompany their words with wagging fingers. They are often prohibition-focused pedants who have the gift of looking down on others and practice the non-virtue of inhospitality. They quickly manage to make any God they follow a decidedly unwanted stranger in the lives of those who meet them.

So how do we react to this language when it is there in black and white in our Bibles? It is difficult enough to deal with when we are studying the Old Testament, say when God sets up flashing swords barring humanity from Eden, or rains burning sulfur down on Sodom. But when we get to the New Testament, we expect better, don't we? So when we find the "red-letter" parts of the Bible—those parts that Jesus himself spoke, with language reminiscent of the type of Christians we usually disassociate ourselves from—we are going to have problems. Is God really threatening humanity with eternal damnation if we don't follow his rules? Is God so insecure and narcissistic that he has to turn up the heat to scare us into action?

The story we are going to focus on is the last of three back-to-back parables, just like the parable of the prodigal son we looked at briefly in chapter three. Both sets of parables culminate in the great final celebration. This one also warns of the great final judgment.

The first parable in this chapter takes place on the eve of a wedding, but half of the bridesmaids miss out on the whole event because they are out shopping for more lamp oil when the wedding march begins to play. They return to the wedding only to find that they have been locked out for good, while their better-prepared counterparts enjoy the party on the other side of the door (Matthew 25:10). The second parable also involves two groups with different outcomes. This time the people involved are stakeholders in a business. Two of them use all their energy to reinvest the capital entrusted to them by their manager, and see fantastic returns. The other one buries his shares in the sand, hoping his disdain for his boss and his lack of interest will not cost him his job—but it does. The wise investment of the first two not only pays off, but they get an additional bonus. The third man is laid off, and we see him left out in the darkness just like the late bridesmaids. Or, in Jesus' harsh-sounding words, "And throw that worthless servant outside, into the darkness, where there will be weeping and gnashing of teeth" (Matthew 25:30).

Both of these parables paint a picture of God's great hospitality for those who are ready and waiting to welcome him, while the rest not only miss out, but are left out, in a place of great danger. The warning is clear: if we are not busy preparing to welcome God, then we may find out that it is too late for God to welcome us. But these two stories are only warm-up acts ahead of the third and final terrifying parable about the sheep and the goats.

This story is the grand finale that will close the teaching ministry of Jesus in the Gospel of Matthew. It is a powerful and challenging story about welcoming strangers, true hospitality, knowing Jesus, and our eternal destiny.

> When the Son of Man comes in his glory, and all the angels with him, he will sit on his glorious throne. All the nations will be gathered before him, and he will separate the people one from another as a shepherd separates the sheep from the goats. He will put the sheep on his right and the goats on his left.
>
> Then the King will say to those on his right, "Come, you who are blessed by my Father; take your inheritance, the kingdom prepared for you since the creation of the world. For I was hungry and you gave me something to eat, I was thirsty and you gave me something to drink, I was a stranger and you invited me in, I needed clothes and you clothed me, I was sick and you looked after me, I was in prison and you came to visit me."
>
> Then the righteous will answer him, "Lord, when did we see you hungry and feed you, or thirsty and give you something to drink? When did we see you a stranger and invite you in, or needing clothes and clothe you? When did we see you sick or in prison and go to visit you?"
>
> The King will reply, "Truly I tell you, whatever you did for one of the least of these brothers and sisters of mine, you did for me."
>
> Then he will say to those on his left, "Depart from me, you who are cursed, into the eternal fire prepared for the devil and his angels. For I was hungry and you gave me nothing to eat, I was thirsty and you gave me nothing to

drink, I was a stranger and you did not invite me in, I needed clothes and you did not clothe me, I was sick and in prison and you did not look after me."

They also will answer, "Lord, when did we see you hungry or thirsty or a stranger or needing clothes or sick or in prison, and did not help you?"

He will reply, "Truly I tell you, whatever you did not do for one of the least of these, you did not do for me."

Then they will go away to eternal punishment, but the righteous to eternal life. (Matthew 25:31-46)

The scene is set at the end of time itself, with Jesus as the glorious King installed on his rightful throne and all the nations gathered before him. He calls everyone individually, placing them either on his left or on his right. This is not a recruitment drive at this point, but a reckoning. This is not a job opportunity, but the gateway to our eternal destiny. Just as in the previous two stories, the action divides its characters into two groups and shows us what Jesus requires of us in order for us to make the cut (Matthew 25:31-33).

First of all, Jesus identifies those who are blessed by his Father, who have an inheritance and kingdom waiting for them. This is no ordinary extension of hospitality—here the Lord of heaven is welcoming his people into a place that has been prepared for them since the creation of the whole world. This is Eden and more, as God's purposes are finally fulfilled and we get to see what life on earth was intended to be. Who gets to be in this group gathered together from all the nations? Those who have shown hospitality to Jesus. How have they shown hospitality to Jesus? In the way they have welcomed the stranger.

There are six types of welcome outlined by Jesus in this parable, and they all involve the compassionate and sacrificial meeting of the fundamental needs of others. The need of the hungry for food. The need of the thirsty for drink. The need of the stranger for welcome and accommodation. The need of the naked for clothes. The need of the sick for care. The need of the isolated for company (Matthew 25:35-36).

This parable diverts significantly from the pattern of the previous two parables in the chapter. The wise bridesmaids knew they were in the right place at the right time doing the right thing. So did the wise investors. They were looking forward to the groom's arrival and the manager's return respectively, to usher in the party and their reward. But the "sheep" in this parable are shocked and surprised. They do not have any recollection of earning this privilege, of welcoming Jesus like this. Like the interviewer in our opening story, it is time for Jesus to reveal that whatever they did for anyone, it was him all along. He replies, in the most serious and solemn terms the Greek language will allow, "Truly I tell you, whatever you did for one of the least of these . . . you did for me" (Matthew 25:40).

Before we take a detour through the controversy surrounding this verse, we must allow the clear challenge to sink in. There are three observations that we cannot ignore and must not forget. First, serving those in need is serving Christ. This is the distinguishing factor between those who will enter eternal life and those who will face eternal punishment. Just as Abraham offered hospitality to strangers and found himself welcoming God, so now the righteous are told that they have done the same. Just as Abraham only found out his guests' true identity afterward, so the righteous will only discover at the end of time whom it is they have been serving. God has turned up in their lives, and they will be surprised—and they will be rewarded. They were not showing compassion to seek to win points with God, or earn their way to heaven, or be "good Christians," or set themselves apart, or boast of their good deeds. No. Their actions came so naturally to them that they did not even consider it worth remembering. But Jesus remembers. He sees the passions and motivations of their hearts, and what flows out selflessly from a transforming relationship with him. We get a summary of the essence of this parable in the book of Proverbs: "Whoever is kind to the poor lends to the LORD, and he will reward them for what they have done" (Proverbs 19:17).

The second observation continues from what we discovered in the previous chapter. Just as Christ identified with poor and sinful humanity in his humble birth and his holy baptism, now even as the King on a throne he publicly expresses his solidarity with society's invisible people—the starving, the thirsty, the homeless, the outcast, the naked, the sick, and the imprisoned. This is not what we expect of royalty. Our picture of aristocracy is likely to involve palaces, fast cars, and showy weddings, but our King is more inclined toward the opposite end of the spectrum. God clearly shows special concern for the vulnerable, or, as some theologians describe it, he has a "preferential option for the poor"[2] that he expects us to join in with.

Jesus' identification with the poor here—not just putting himself alongside them or standing in their shoes, but suffering as they suffer—must rebut not only any idea of a distant, elusive God, but also any temptation to keep those in need at arm's length. Mother Teresa, the Albanian relief worker who spent most of her life working in Calcutta among some of the poorest people in the world, was inspired by the challenge of this parable. She explained, "Our work . . . calls us to see Jesus in everyone.

He has told us that he is the hungry one. He is the thirsty one. He is the naked one. He is the one who is suffering. These are our treasures. . . . They are Jesus. Each one is Jesus in a distressing disguise."[3] Again Christine Pohl argues, "This passage sets up a fundamental identification of Jesus with 'the least of these' and personally and powerfully connects hospitality toward human beings with care for Jesus."[4] On one hand, Jesus is the omnipotent King of heaven, fully God—he needs nothing. But he chooses to identify with the poor, suffering along with them, and receiving compassionate action toward the needy as worship directed toward him. Jesus is not made less by the comparison; but those in need are made more of—so much more. Jesus makes a very similar association of himself with those who suffer when Saul was on the Damascus road on his way to persecute, imprison, and, if he could, kill more Christians. Jesus stops him in his tracks and asks him, "Saul, Saul, why do you persecute me?" Saul replies, "Who are you, Lord?" (Acts 9:4-5). Saul did not recognize Jesus in the flash of light on the road, but most importantly he did not recognize Jesus in the lives of the Christians he was persecuting. Jesus suffers as his people suffer. He is persecuted as his people are persecuted. And he is welcomed as his people are welcomed.

Third, we see in this parable how the themes redolent throughout Scripture find a new level of fulfillment in Jesus' welcome of the righteous into eternal life. It is interesting that there is no mention of a doctrine test, no questions asked about how many church services have been attended, no examination of baptismal certificates or analysis of communion participation statistics. As we have been seeing again and again, welcoming the stranger proves true worship of God. Jesus highlights the connection between intimacy with God and hospitality to the vulnerable and shows it to be the litmus test of the Christian confession. James underlines it when he writes in his letter, "Religion that God our Father accepts as pure and faultless is this: to look after orphans and widows in their distress" (James 1:27).

In the parable of the sheep and the goats, there is a great reward for the righteous who welcome the invisible God by welcoming the stranger. However, the second group's response to Jesus gives us one of the direst warnings in all Scripture. If the righteous are surprised by God's judgment, so too are the rest, the "goats." They had no idea that they had rejected Christ by turning a blind eye to the needs of others. Yet they surely had no excuse. God's clear commands echo throughout the pages of the Bible—don't they? Time and again in the Old Testament God calls his people to show mercy to the displaced, the despised, and the dispossessed. God gives worked examples of his kind of hospitality through Naomi and Ruth, Elijah and Elisha, Jacob and Joseph. Not to mention the stories of Hagar and Esther, Jonathan and Mephibosheth, Samuel and Noah, and many, many others not included in this book. God includes care of the vulnerable in the Mosaic Law. He chastises his people through the prophets, calling them to stop their meaningless acts of worship and instead show mercy and act justly (Micah 6:8). God could not have been clearer when he said through the prophet Isaiah:

> Is not this the kind of fasting I have chosen: . . .
> Is it not to share your food with the hungry
>   and to provide the poor wanderer with shelter—
> when you see the naked, to clothe them,
>   and not to turn away from your own flesh and blood?
>   (Isaiah 58:6-7)

This list in Isaiah's prophecy has so much overlap with Jesus' parable of the sheep and the goats that no one familiar with the Scriptures should have been surprised by Jesus' words. In Isaiah's well-known prophecy, God tells his people in no uncertain terms that their worship was offensive to him because it did not involve loosing the chains of injustice, setting the oppressed free, sharing their food with the hungry, providing shelter for the stranger, and clothing the naked. Jesus is only reiterating what the prophets have been calling for all along. God's requirements have not changed.

Matthew has been building up to this crescendo of teaching on welcome and judgment through a series of five main blocks of teaching recorded in his Gospel. As a former tax collector welcomed into the elite friendship circle of Jesus, he knew firsthand the power of true hospitality shown toward those whom everybody else has written off. The first teaching block in his Gospel is the Sermon on the Mount, in Matthew 5–7. After issuing blessings to the least likely people and redefining the worship disciplines of fasting and prayer, the sermon similarly ends with a series of contrasting illustrations to demarcate true believers and those who are strangers to the Christian faith. Jesus speaks of two roads—a wide road that leads to destruction and a narrow road that leads to life. He describes two prophets— both teach the same doctrine, but the true prophets bear good fruit, and the false ones bear bad fruit. There are also two sorts of disciples—both call Jesus Lord, but the true believers are those who live out their confession through obedience.

This third comparison is surprisingly similar to the parable of the sheep and goats. Both illustrations show a surprised reaction in those who are excluded in the final judgment.

In the Sermon on the Mount Jesus declares, "Many will say to me on that day, 'Lord, Lord, did we not prophesy in your name and in your name drive out demons and in your name perform many miracles?' Then I will tell them plainly, 'I never knew you. Away from me, you evildoers!'" (Matthew 7:22-23). Charismatic gifts, exorcisms, and even miracles are not sufficient evidence of true discipleship. Even good theology is not good enough. They make the right confession, declaring Jesus as Lord, but there it ends. Again the litmus test of authentic discipleship is not one of doctrine but of obedience.

The frightening warning in both these illustrations is that apparently sincere disciples will find out at the final judgment that they have been strangers to God all this time. Whatever delusion of salvation they had conjured up, Jesus reveals it to be a sham, and declares that he never knew them. Whether their failing was to follow the letter of the law but miss its spirit, or whether they were willing to follow the outward rituals but not sacrificial obedience—either way, Jesus does not recognize them as his own.

The Sermon on the Mount ends with the parable of the wise and foolish builders. Both hear the word of God but only one puts it into practice. Both builders then face a storm, which destroys the house built on poor foundations but cannot touch the one built on rock. Many commentators understand the storm to be a picture of the judgment of God. In line with the witness of the Old Testament prophets and Jesus' own teaching throughout Matthew's Gospel, putting into practice the word of God and demonstrating the character of God is the indicator of what will happen at the final judgment.

Why would God use mercy as a test of faithfulness? What is it about engaging with the terrible reality of poverty and persecution that marks out his true disciples? Tim Keller, well-known author and lead pastor of Redeemer Presbyterian Church in Manhattan, helps us to grapple with this with an illustration.

> Imagine a wealthy older woman who has no heirs except a nephew who is always kind to her. Is his kindness just a facade? How can she know what his heart is really like? Imagine that she dresses up as a homeless street person and sits on the steps of her nephew's townhouse, and when he comes out he curses and threatens her. Now she knows his true character! So too, God is angry when we have one face for him and another for the needy.[5]

There can be no doubt that Christ is angry in this passage: "Depart from me, you who are cursed, into the eternal fire prepared for the devil and his angels" (Matthew 25:41). It might be easier to stomach this violent language if we knew he was talking about those responsible for genocide or abusing children. So why the harsh tone when he is talking privately to his friends and disciples about an error of omission? Imagine I find my young daughter playing with matches. I don't just remove them and ask her politely to leave them alone. I am scared myself, and I want her to be scared too. With a raised voice and a pointed finger, I leave her in no doubt that what she is doing is extremely dangerous. I spell out the worst-case scenario: fire could sweep through the room, burn the house down, and kill our entire family, maybe wipe out the whole neighborhood. If she bursts into tears and is frightened by my anger, I know that my message has hit home. Because I love her so much, I must ensure that she is sufficiently warned to avoid any chance of her making the same mistake again.

Jesus is not ashamed to talk about the fires of hell; in fact, he talks about eternal punishment more than any other person in Scripture. Yet perhaps we can see that he is doing so out of deep love. I am not convinced this is the motive driving the Christians I have met who seem to revel in talking about hell as an incentive to scare people into converting to Christianity. But this is never the context in which Jesus talks about hell. To those who consider themselves outsiders and sinners, Jesus speaks time and again about the grace and forgiveness of God. He saves his fire-and-brimstone messages for people who call themselves believers and disciples, but may actually be in danger of presuming on the grace of God. To those of us who are his declared followers, he wants his message to hit home hard: there are significant opportunities all around us to show worship to God through our hospitality to the needy, and there is hell to pay if we miss it.

Bearing Jesus' stern warnings in mind, we must confront the controversial elements of this parable. Sadly the church has often missed the main point, because we get sidetracked along two paths of error. On one side, some see in this parable a picture of salvation by works. They read the parable as saying that you get to heaven by serving the needy—you are saved in the next life by what you do in this life. But if salvation by works was possible, then all that is coming next in Matthew's Gospel is pointless. In the following chapters we will see Christ betrayed, arrested, convicted, abused, and then murdered. If human beings could have earned their way to eternal life through acts of kindness and compassion, there would be no need for Jesus to die on the cross. His death is redundant if good deeds are the qualifying requirements for entry to heaven. But Christ's betrayal and death were foreseen by Jesus and willingly submitted to in order to atone for the sins of the world, because this is the only way to be reconciled with God. Salvation cannot be earned. It is bought by Jesus.

That is not the end of the story. God did not rescue, forgive, redeem, and adopt us because we had performed sufficient good deeds. Yet he did have a purpose in mind when he did these things for us—he wants to involve us in his great plans to rescue, redeem, and restore the world. Paul explains these two positions quite clearly when he writes, "For it is by grace you have been saved, through faith—and this is not from yourselves, it is the gift of God—not by works, so that no one can boast. For we are God's handiwork, created in Christ Jesus to do good works, which God prepared in advance for us to do" (Ephesians 2:8-10).

Paul clearly explains that we are not saved by the works we have done. We are made acceptable to God by what Christ has done on our behalf through his life, death, and resurrection. And we honor his purposes for us by our involvement in his good works.

If the two go hand in hand, then why does the parable of the sheep and the goats not mention faith at all, and ask for actions instead? In his epistle James answers the critique:

> What good is it, my brothers and sisters, if someone claims to have faith but has no deeds? Can such faith save them? Suppose a brother or a sister is without clothes and daily food. If one of you says to them, "Go in peace; keep warm and well fed," but does nothing about their physical needs, what good is it? In the same way, faith by itself, if it is not accompanied by action, is dead. (James 2:14-17)

James, Jesus, and Paul are on the same page when it comes to showing that our faith is demonstrated through the way we treat vulnerable people. However, assuming that because we serve the poor we have earned the right to eternal life is just as foolish as assuming that the increasing number of candles on our birthday cake is making us older, or that standing on the bathroom scale is making us heavier. There may well be a correlation between positive pregnancy tests and gravidity, but babies do not come from blue lines, just as obesity does not come from bathroom scales, and maturity does not come from counting candles. The link is not causal but indicative. The same is true for good works and saving faith. There is a link, but the first does not cause the second. Rather, saving faith is indicated by good works. Just as we can know a true prophet by their fruit, and a wise builder by the longevity of their buildings, so we can know a true believer, says Jesus, by their response to the needy.

The second error is to get so sidetracked by debating the identity of the needy or the "least of these" that we become paralyzed by the parable. There are two main theories: one theory suggests that because Jesus says "the least of these *brothers*," and 'brothers" is a term only used in Matthew to refer to fellow Christians (see Matthew 12:48-49; 23:8; 28:10), so Jesus is therefore arguing that it is our response to fellow Christians in need that will be the defining factor of true Christian discipleship. The other theory is that in using the term "brothers" Jesus is identifying with humanity in general, recognizing all human beings as image-bearers of God, and that this parable therefore teaches that we must care for anyone who is in need, regardless of their faith. Some have become so embroiled in debating whether we are to help Christians or anyone, independent of faith, that they end up helping nobody.

The Bible elsewhere teaches various circles of responsibility for the Christian disciple. First, we are told to put God first, even if that means losing our family. Abraham, for example, leaves his wider family in Ur and is asked to sacrifice his own son. Jesus commends those who have lost families for his sake. But that does not remove the responsibility of Christians to provide for their own immediate and wider families. Paul writes, "Anyone who does not provide for their relatives, and especially for their own household, has denied the faith and is worse than an unbeliever" (1 Timothy 5:8). The Pharisees tried to weasel out of their responsibility to their family by invoking the idea of "corban," money set apart or consecrated for God, to prioritize supporting the temple community rather than their elderly parents (Mark 7:10-13). Jesus says they "nullify the word of God" (Mark 7:13). In other words, it is both-and, not either-or, when it comes to caring for both our biological family and our spiritual family. And our circles of care do not end here. Paul explains, "As we have opportunity, let us do good to all people, especially to those who belong to the family of believers" (Galatians 6:10). While upholding our responsibility to our church family, Paul encourages us to care for all people. Jesus' teaching is even stronger. He tells us to love God and love others, but he also teaches us to love strangers and even to love our enemies. Our compassion is not to be limited to one group or another, but is to overflow out to everyone. Nobody is excluded.

There was an Internet meme not long ago showing two books. The first book was called *What They Teach You on a Harvard MBA*. The second was called *What They Don't Teach You on a Harvard MBA*. The caption was: "These two books contain the sum total of all human knowledge." The commands of Scripture to love our neighbors and to love our enemies offer a truly comprehensive, all-inclusive mandate. No one is outside our responsibility of care.

I cannot accept the theory that Jesus' reference to the "least of these brothers" is supposed to restrict Christian care for the poor solely to fellow believers. But even those who do hold to this limited interpretation must hear the challenge of this parable. Around our nation and indeed around the world there are large numbers of Christian brothers and sisters who are in desperate need. There are many believers who are poverty stricken, homeless, persecuted, unjustly imprisoned, hungry, and naked. Jesus calls us to be on the lookout for opportunities in our church, in our nation, and in the world to personally get involved in their care. We are to invite them into our homes, to feed and clothe them, to spend time with them. If they cannot come, because, for example, they are in prison, then Jesus suggests we invite ourselves and visit them where they are.

I once met an amazing Kenyan believer in Nairobi. He had been born in the north of the country into a Muslim family, but when he came to faith in Jesus his family not only threw him out of his home but even attempted to kill him. Unwilling to renounce his faith, he went on the run and in the end was given refuge in a church. He was extremely grateful for the asylum the church gave him in the building and the food that the parishioners brought to him to eat each day. But he confided in me that Sunday mornings were the hardest part of his week. Following the service, and having been presented with a lovingly prepared picnic, he was left alone in the building while everyone else went home to their families and their Sunday lunches. Although, practically speaking, he had been given all he needed and more, he would gladly have exchanged his generous picnic for a lesser meal among a family. Jesus said, "Truly I tell you . . .

no one who has left home or brothers or sisters or mother or father or children or fields for me and the gospel will fail to receive a hundred times as much in this present age: homes, brothers, sisters, mothers, children and fields—along with persecutions—and in the age to come eternal life" (Mark 10:29-30). This promise contains a presumption: that the church will step up to be the replacement family for those who have lost theirs for the sake of their Savior.

I believe Christians have a fundamental responsibility to show just this sort of hospitality to our wider Christian family around the local and the global church. But I also believe the Bible is clear that we have a similar responsibility for neighbor, stranger, and enemy, in order to demonstrate the compassion of God. Anyone in need is to be considered our neighbor, no matter their ethnicity, gender, ability, or faith.[6] Jesus led by example. He fed the hungry crowds, clothed the naked demoniac, and healed the sick, whether Jew or Gentile. He did not check the doctrinal understanding of the ten lepers before he cleansed them, even though it seems that only one accepted God's grace along with his healing. Jesus did not offer an altar call at the feeding of the five thousand, only giving bread and fish to those who responded positively to the call to discipleship; he fed the crowd without distinction or discrimination. Jesus offered healing to the Syro-Phoenician woman even after he specifically pointed out that she was not from the chosen people of God. He healed the dismembered ear of the soldier who came to arrest him, and asked God to forgive his Roman executioners while hanging dying on a cross. In arguably the most famous parable of them all, Jesus challenges a Jewish leader to take seriously the command to love and practically care for even his hated neighboring Samaritans—in fact, the story he tells is so topsy-turvy that he even has the Samaritan showing the desperately needed generosity and hospitality, rather than receiving it. Jesus teaches all Christians to love their neighbors, and he practiced what he preached. Jesus tears down all possible boundaries that people use to discriminate between neighbors and strangers.

The early Christians certainly understood the parable in this way; for example, the great fourth-century bishop St. Basil of Caesarea alludes to the parable of the sheep and the goats when he writes,

> The bread which you hold back actually belongs to the hungry; the garment which you lock in your chest belongs to the naked; the shoes which rot in your store house belong to the bare-footed; and the money which you are hiding . . . belongs to the needy. Thus you do a great injustice to all those whom you could succour.[7]

This practical, compassionate care for the needy, whether friend, neighbor, enemy, or stranger, was always supposed to be an essential part of how the world was to understand the essence of the Christian faith. Jesus explained to his followers, "Let your light shine before others, that they may see your good deeds and glorify your Father in heaven" (Matthew 5:16). The way we live should astound the world. It is an irreplaceable apologetic for the truth of the Christian faith. Turning up at church services and hosting home group Bible studies is not going to draw praise from the watching world, however fresh the coffee or however delicious the cakes. Jesus said, "If you love those who love you, what reward will you get? Are not even the tax collectors doing that?" (Matthew 5:46). It is compassion to strangers and above-and-beyond hospitality to outcasts that demonstrates the love of God in an astounding way.

We have seen in the parable of the sheep and the goats the terrible warning given to those of us who call ourselves Christians. We have also heard the incredible challenge to engage in personal hospitality to brothers, neighbors, enemies, and strangers. But there is one more element to this passage—an amazing encouragement. For those of us left wondering if we have done enough, if we have indeed fed the hungry and visited the prisoners and welcomed Jesus in the guise of the stranger, then we have something in common with those Jesus placed on his right-hand side. They too could not recall showing such hospitality. Not because they hadn't, but because it was not a big deal. For them offering someone a drink, or sharing a meal, or giving away an item of clothing, or making people feel welcome in their homes was not a ministry they signed up for, a roster they joined, or a Friday-night challenge. It was part and parcel of everyday living.

Christine Pohl describes beautifully the encouragement of this difficult passage as a take-home message.

> As a way of life, an act of love, an expression of faith, our hospitality reflects and anticipates God's welcome. Simultaneously costly and wonderfully rewarding, hospitality often involves small deaths and little resurrections. By God's grace we can grow more willing, more eager, to open the door to a needy neighbor, a weary sister or brother, a stranger in distress. Perhaps as we open that door more regularly, we will grow increasingly sensitive to the quiet knock of angels. In the midst of a life-giving practice, we too might catch glimpses of Jesus who asks for our welcome and welcomes us home.[8]

I discovered during my studies in chemistry that because natural gas has no smell, the suppliers of gas to your home add a scent to it, so that if there is a leak, you can sense it. The trouble is, to keep our nervous systems from exhaustion through continued stimulation, our odor receptors adapt, and after just a few minutes they stop sending the brain messages about lingering smells. So if you don't respond quickly to a gas leak, you will forget it is there, and that can bring dire consequences. If you have experienced a pang of conscience as you read, I would encourage you to act on it, and quickly, before we get used once again to the way things are and the way things have always been, rather than the way Jesus wants us to be. Now we have been warned of the possibility of being deluded about our relationship with Jesus, we must do something to ensure that we don't get to the final judgment day only to find out that we didn't know who we thought we knew.

JESUS AND
THE STRANGER

The God who turns up as good as dead

In which a dying man makes a promise to a stranger,

and we steal a vital insight or two from thieves.

I barricaded my bedroom door that night. My mom had let yet another stranger into the house. This unexpected guest had knocked on our door late in the evening, and unlike all the other residents of Wellington Road, Brighton, my mother had fallen for his unlikely story. The young man who filled up the doorway hailed from Germany and was explaining in broken English that he had met a girl on a plane but it was only after he had passed through customs that he realized that he did have something to declare: his undying love for the stranger who had been on the seat next to his. He had searched the airport to no avail, but remembered she had told him she was heading for Brighton—so here he was, following the only lead he had and going house to house trying to find her. I am not sure how many other streets he had trawled so far on his search, but he steadfastly maintained that he was determined to try every one of Brighton's 120,000 homes until he found her.

My mom had arrived in Brighton from India aged sixteen to train to be a nurse. As an Anglo-Indian child growing up in an Indian orphanage, she had been treated as a pariah, and it was no better in the UK when she arrived in the 1950s. She knew what it meant not only to be on the receiving end of verbal and physical abuse, but also to be ignored, dismissed, and marginalized as an outsider. Because her grandmother had gone to such great lengths, following her son's death in the war, to rescue my mother and her sisters from various different orphanages and secure their education and careers, she also knew what it meant to be welcomed in by a family that had lost her and then found her again. Maybe that is why the German was not made to stay on our doorstep but was welcomed in and given tea and encouraged to share his story. Pretty soon she was turning our sofa into a bed for the stranger, and, because my bedroom was just opposite, I started to turn my furniture into a barricade.

Perhaps I had watched too many movies about con artists or home invasions, or heard too many dark fairy tales, or too vividly remembered my teacher's warnings about "stranger danger." I spent a disturbed night clutching my Swiss Army penknife and worrying far more about my own security than that of my gullible parents and defenseless younger sister, sleeping in their rooms with no barricades for protection. The next morning, after a hearty breakfast, this lovestruck loner resumed his crazy search. We never saw him again. I like to think that thanks to my mom's kindness, there is an Anglo-German couple living happily ever after and telling their children about an Indian woman who demonstrated through her hospitality to an unexpected guest that she too believed in love.

An unexpected guest going door to door through Bethlehem late at night is how the nativity story began. Eventually a kind innkeeper found a spare corner for the young man and his heavily pregnant wife, and then Jesus arrived. Jesus was an expert not only at being welcomed by the unexpected, but also at welcoming the unexpected, and calling his followers to welcome the unexpected, as we saw in the last chapter. All of this freely offered, open hospitality, though, is going to get Jesus into a lot of trouble. And instead of installing his defenses, he is tearing down the barricades.

Jesus' family had hosted uncouth shepherds and unclean foreigners at his birth, and his entire life was marked by this pattern of keeping inappropriate company. In Luke's Gospel in particular this is repeatedly noted, as part of the ongoing conflict between Jesus and the religious authorities. It is his association with the class of people that decent society wrote off as "sinners"[1] that enrages the Pharisees. He is criticized for eating with sinners (Luke 15:2), for letting sinners touch him (Luke 7:39), and for being a guest at a sinner's house (Luke 19:7). Decent society today would not like to use the word "sinners," but substitute the word "strangers" or one of the specific pejoratives we use for those we see as beneath our notice, and we might well come close to a similar outrage. That was why my mother, the next morning, faced the gathered disbelief of Wellington Road. "You let that stranger in your house?" "You believed that stranger's story?" "You gave a stranger tea—and breakfast—for nothing?" "Have you checked that the family silver isn't missing?" "What if he comes back again?" "You're not even going to change your locks?"

Jesus shrugged off the criticisms of the Pharisees; he recognized that his whole mission was wrapped up in the welfare of those whom society seeks to exclude. You might say that Jesus put the "hospital" in "hospitality" when he said, "It is not the healthy who need a doctor, but the sick. I have not come to call the righteous, but sinners to repentance" (Luke 5:31-32). This sentiment plays out repeatedly in Luke's Gospel. For example, Luke mentions two notorious tax collectors who find faith in Christ: Levi, who becomes a follower of Jesus (and is known to us as the disciple and Gospel writer Matthew), and Zacchaeus, the vertically challenged and unscrupulous embezzler. These two sinners find faith; the outcasts find healing and community, and their lives are turned upside down. There is an additional tax collector mentioned by Luke in Jesus' parable of the two men praying in the temple. Jesus reverses popular expectation when at the end it is the tax collector, not the Pharisee, whose prayers are welcomed and who goes home reconciled with God (Luke 18:9-14).

Jesus' enemies taunt him with the accusation that he is "a friend of tax collectors and sinners" (Luke 7:34). But what they mean as an insult Jesus is happy to own as a badge of honor. By way of contrast, the church in the Western world has a very different reputation. According to a Barna survey of sixteen- to thirty-year-olds who are not part of a church community,[2] the public reputation of the church is summarized by three words: "anti-homosexual, judgmental, and hypocritical."[3] What has happened to the church? We are supposed to be following in the footsteps of one who was criticized for being a friend of sinners, and yet we are known more for our faultfinding than our friendship. We are seen more for our exclusion than our embrace. More for our hypocrisy than our hospitality. It is no wonder that people look at us and think that God is as good as dead and thus live their lives without reference to him and without deference to the church. It was never meant to be like this.

As Lisa Cahill writes,

> The Christian family is not the nuclear family focused inward on the welfare of its own members but the socially transformative family that seeks to make the Christian moral ideal of love of neighbor part of the common good.[4]

It is vital that we as the church begin to rebuild our reputation, based on the actual principles that Jesus stood for. After all, what Jesus strongly urged in his teaching, and clearly illustrated in his lifestyle, he superbly and ultimately demonstrated in his death. The central moment in Christian history shows us God's all-embracing hospitality in action. The cross and hospitality hang inextricably together. As we look at Luke's account of Jesus' death, we will see how a stranger and an unexpected guest change the way we understand the power of the cross, and why the hospitality we have uncovered as an essential theme throughout Scripture is literally crucial to our faith.

The cross is one of the most recognizable symbols in the world, and yet the story of the crucifixion is one of the strangest moments in all of history. The brutality of the Roman regime is well known: they conducted thousands of crucifixions. Just like the barbaric beheading videos of ISIS, crucifixion was a way of spreading terror and fear. By making these executions both public and gruesome, the Roman Empire sought to prevent any kind of resistance to their rule. Yet the Christian faith has not just commiserated over the crucifixion of Jesus; it has positively celebrated it. It is the centerpiece of the majority of Christian art, architecture, and hymnody. It is difficult to imagine a loved one of someone murdered by the Islamic State choosing to have a loop of the YouTube video on display in their home. Yet is this not in effect what Christians do, continually remembering and celebrating the brutal murder of their beloved? This is a dramatic reversal of the Romans' intentions. However, it must be admitted that we perhaps sanitize the brutality, expurgating the horror of the execution in favor of focusing on the benefits it bought us. While celebrating the crucifixion as the rightful center of our faith, maybe we have become so overfamiliar with the story that we fail to see the stranger elements of this event. If we asked a stranger to study the story, all sorts of questions might arise. How can God die? Or is it only part of God that dies? Why did nobody stop them killing the Son of God? Then again, is it easy to die if you expect to be resurrected? And how can a death make anything right? How can one man's death carry the sins of the world? Equally, why would anyone die for strangers they had never met?

The crucifixion is not the God story that anyone would have expected. That God would die at the hands of his own creation is a bizarre twist that no one—not even Jesus' closest followers—could comprehend. Yet we are told that God planned this even before the creation of the world (Revelation 13:8). This gap between the grand scheme and the great surprise is reflected in the distance there is between the horror and the beauty of the cross. Between the terrible sin that caused the death, and the incredible forgiveness that brought us life. Between the grace that cost him so dearly, and the grace that we so easily take for granted. Between the events of two thousand years ago and our lives today. Between the facts of the Easter story and the festival as we now celebrate it with chicks and chocolate. I wonder if these gaps explain or express something of the distance between us and God? Are they perhaps the ultimate locus of the problem of thinking we know God, but discovering that we hardly know him at all? Might we find here the reason why we ignore his presence in the needy people all around us? Is this why we so often act as though God were as good as dead now too—the reason why we live our lives without much reference to him? Let us take a closer look at the crucifixion and try to narrow the gap in our understanding between the suffering and the salvation, between the brutality and the blessing, between the hostility and the hospitality—between the God we think we know, and the true God we can never fully know.

As Christians, we believe the crucifixion of Jesus marks the darkest moment of human history. Humanity conspires to kill the author of life. Jews and Romans collaborate against their common Creator. But even as it begins, we see the character of Christ shine through. Luke's Gospel records Jesus' first words from the cross as "Father, forgive them, for they do not know what they are doing" (Luke 23:34). Jesus is pleading for God's grace both for the Jews who are willfully rejecting him and for the Romans who are brutally executing him. Both for the soldiers who are hammering the nails in his wrists and for the crowds who are looking on in approval. It also has a greater resonance, far beyond those first-century executioners to their accomplices in sin from every century. This is the first of what many Christian traditions call the "Seven Last Words," Jesus' sayings on the cross. It is significant because Jesus' words are a prayer not for himself but for others. He does not use the last of his energy to call out for personal assistance from his heavenly Father, but to plead the case of men who were strangers and enemies to him. His prayer shows that he really meant his instruction to his disciples to "bless those who curse you, pray for those who mistreat you" (Luke 6:28). Indeed, his merciful words are a preemptive act of grace ahead of the obscene act that is to come.

Jesus' generous prayer for mercy for his enemies contrasts with what is recognized as his second saying of the cross. With the words "I am thirsty" (John 19:28), he now requests their mercy, in the form of a drink to give him relief. This seems ironic when we remember the stranger by the well who asks a Samaritan woman of many husbands for a drink, but then reveals that he is in fact himself the "water of life." This is the man who taught his disciples to quench the thirst of strangers as evidence of their love for God, now become that thirsty stranger in need of water. How ironic that the one who at the beginning of his ministry provided wine at the wedding party is now left, at the end of his ministry, with nothing to drink. Or perhaps it is not ironic but poignant that the one who could calm the storms and walk on water now restrains his own power and relies on others to bring him a drink. In his distress Jesus was offered wine vinegar on a sponge.[5] He received it, enabling and accepting an act of hospitality even at this darkest of all moments.

Luke paints the scene of Jesus' death in stark colors. The lack of relief, the thorns, the nails, and the physical hardship are exacerbated by the emotional torture he receives on all fronts. How could the most perfect person who ever lived find himself in this position? Jesus was put to death surrounded by opposition, degradation, mockery, and humiliation, because nobody, it seemed, recognized him as God's Son. They not only dismissed him; they collaborated in his death and intensified his suffering, because he did not match their predetermined expectations. How absolutely important it is to ensure that our own expectations of God are based on what he truly is, not on what we have imagined.

On one side, there was an unsympathetic crowd gathered to watch him die. It is more than possible that some of those present were among the people who a week earlier had laid down their coats and waved palm branches for him, chanting "Hosanna" as he entered Jerusalem on a donkey (Matthew 21:6-11). It is likely that some of this same crowd were there as Pilate offered the people a choice between the carpenter's son from Nazareth or Jerusalem's most wanted, Barabbas, and had chanted "Crucify him!"—pointing their fingers at Jesus (Luke 23:21). Inside a week Jesus had gone from fêted hero to failed Messiah. He would not live up to their expectations of a messiah to liberate them from Roman oppression, and adulation had turned to anger.

Alongside this hostile crowd, Jesus faced opposition from the religious leaders who were not there to administer the last rites or to offer him consolation, but to ridicule him for not being the savior they were expecting: "He saved others . . . but he can't save himself. . . . Let him come down now from the cross" (Matthew 27:42). What a cruel taunt—to ask a man who is nailed hands and feet to a cross to save himself! And yet the harshest irony is that he could, if he so chose. If they were not so ignorant of Jesus' true identity, they might have understood that Jesus was choosing not to save himself precisely so that he could save others. Jesus refuses to use the power that is at his disposal—the power he demonstrated by calming the storm, walking on water, raising the dead, and exorcising a legion of demons—in order that he might save humanity from the coming judgment of God. Against this backdrop of extreme animosity, we see the awesome generosity of God on display. Jesus used his power for the benefit of others and refused to use it for himself. Paul makes sure we hear this challenge of Jesus' extreme self-giving, his revolutionary hospitality. Alongside his poetic description of the humiliation of the cross in Philippians 2 stands this instruction: "In humility value others above yourselves, not looking to your own interests but each of you to the interests of the others" (Philippians 2:3-4).

Although absent from the scene at this point, the Roman procurator Pontius Pilate is present in spirit, using this execution to mock both Jesus and the Jews, by having a sign affixed to the cross. Pilate's intent seems to be to provide a punchline for the satirical cartoon created by the death scene of Jesus. Pilate's comment on the agony of Jesus is "This is the king of the Jews." Crucifixion was Rome's public address system, a grotesque demonstration of violence to strike fear into its subjects. The commentator J. Nolland describes it as "a form of execution by torture; it was about as cruel and barbaric as any deterrent dreamed up by humankind. The idea was to prolong the death agony for all to see and be warned."[6] Pilate wanted the world to know that this victim, bleeding and suffering and dying, could never live up to the title and expectations of "king"—and by extension that any "king" of the Jews was at Rome's mercy.

Then there are the Roman soldiers mocking Jesus. A man skewered on a cross makes for a very potent visual aid of the futility of challenging the might of imperial Rome. As if the humiliation of being stripped naked and nailed to a cross in the badlands on the wrong side of town was not degrading enough. As if the insults of the crowds and the rude sign and the Pharisees' rejection were not enough, the cruel soldiers, though they have no need of their weaponry, add their taunts (Luke 23:35-37). With no army and no weapons, Jesus was not the kind of leader they respected. Their offer of wine vinegar was a gesture of scorn and hostility[7]—cheap wine for a cheap king.

The brutality of the cross's physical torture, combined with the unrelenting verbal hostility, make this a deeply distressing scene. The cowardly cries of the crowd, the conspiracy of the religious leaders, the cruelty of the soldiers, and the callousness of Rome mark this out as a low point of human history—especially when set against Jesus' life. Jesus has lived his life in gentleness and compassion, feeding the hungry and healing the sick—and the world repays him by murdering him and mocking him as he dies. As if the scorn, shame, and rejection from all quarters was not enough, one last person adds his scoffing voice to the anarchy. Another convict being crucified next to Jesus chooses to spend his last gasps of air to spit abuse at his neighbor. Luke narrates: "One of the criminals who hung there hurled insults at him: 'Aren't you the Messiah? Save yourself and us!'" (Luke 23:39). Here is an ugly snapshot of the greater betrayal and rejection at play that day. This is an outworking of what was predicted of Jesus' life in the early verses in John's Gospel: "He came to that which was his own, but his own did not receive him" (John 1:11). God came to earth, not for a vacation or a reconnaissance trip, but to rescue humanity—and what kind of welcome and hospitality did we show him? We surrounded God's Son with scorn. We physically abused him. We unleashed arguably the world's most callously cruel and vindictive method of execution against him, and as he died to bring reconciliation to the world we scoffed at him. Not only those at a safe distance, but even one nearby, himself dangerously close to death.

Perhaps you know the pain of physical suffering. Perhaps you are familiar with social ostracism. Perhaps you are personally acquainted with injustice. Jesus' cross gives us a pattern of divine solidarity. Jesus can sympathize with our hurts: he is "a man of suffering, and familiar with pain" (Isaiah 53:3), as Isaiah promised

he would be. John Stott writes, "I could never myself believe in
God, if it were not for the cross. The only God I believe in is the
one Nietzsche ridiculed as 'God on the cross.' In the real world
of pain, how could one worship a God who was immune to it?"[8]
And so, for the sake of those of us who suffer or who know we
are sinners or feel like strangers, God the Father allows Christ
the Son to open the way of salvation for humanity by means of
the cruel cross, so that he might invite and welcome us to his
Father's house (John 14).

It is in the exchange of words between Jesus and the criminal
dying on the other side of him that we are given a second, and
significant, snapshot of the welcome God offers to us amid all
the trauma and tragedy. Speaking would have been extremely
difficult because of the macabre methodology of crucifixion, where
the weight of the body drags down and with exhaustion comes
a slow asphyxiation. Jesus chooses to use some of his last painful
breaths to speak words of comfort and compassion to a stranger.
The exchange shows us that the cross of Christ is a story of
incredible grace. At the heart of the atonement is divine hospitality, where God invites the undeserving and unexpected to
come home with him.

In reply to the criminal's challenge to Jesus, the second
criminal interjects, "Don't you fear God . . . since you are under
the same sentence? We are punished justly, for we are getting
what our deeds deserve. But this man has done nothing wrong"
(Luke 23:40-41). In the midst of the maelstrom of malevolence,
one voice offers a "minority report" intervention. The neighbor,
otherwise known as criminal number two, or the thief on the
cross, recognizes three important things.

First, he recognizes Jesus' solidarity with them: all three men
are in the same boat, facing the same fate. By challenging his

scoffing counterpart, the criminal challenges us too to recognize that right now is our opportunity to check whether we are in a right relationship with God.

Second, he recognizes Jesus' sanctity: there is a fundamental difference between Jesus and everyone else. While everyone else saw a would-be king, a powerless non-savior, a disappointing quasi-messiah, this criminal alone recognizes his own guilt and Jesus' innocence of all charges. Are we guilty of measuring Jesus up against our unilateral expectations, or are we rightly considering whether we in fact measure up to the standards set by Jesus?

The final thing the criminal recognizes is Jesus' sovereignty. There is no rescue party anywhere to be seen: the only thing on the agenda for Jesus and the two criminals with him was death. Yet this man still asks Jesus, "Remember me when you come into your kingdom" (Luke 23:42). His words reveal that he somehow recognizes that Jesus would enter his own kingdom on his death. Pilate had not grasped this, despite the caption he attached to the cross. The religious leaders had not grasped it, despite countless prophetic utterances that pointed to exactly this moment. Not even Jesus' disciples had grasped it, despite having spent three years listening to Jesus explain it. Looking back on this incident with the benefit of two thousand years of theological reflection on the death of Christ, it is hard for us to grasp the profound level of understanding this criminal demonstrates of the events he found himself unexpectedly caught up in. Apart from Jesus himself, not one person had understood that the crucifixion was not just a terrible miscarriage of justice, but was the very means by which Jesus was going to be crowned King. Jesus endorses his cross neighbor's take on events, graciously responding with the assurance that has become treasured as the third of Jesus' seven sayings from the cross: "Truly I tell you, today you will be with me in paradise" (Luke 23:43).

Jesus wants this self-confessed criminal guilty of a capital crime to be in no doubt that he will shortly be receiving the ultimate VIP welcome. He solemnly promises the thief the two key things he needs to know: he will be with Jesus, and he will be in paradise.

For Christians it is not just the final destination that is important but our final reconciliation. Ultimately, Christianity is not so much about going to heaven when you die as about being fully reconciled with God, his people, and ourselves. Jesus' words to the condemned criminal dying next to him emphasize the dimension of salvation that is centered on knowing intimacy with God. Amid the extreme pain he was suffering, these were words of comfort and privilege to cling on to. Just in case we have missed Jesus' preferential treatment of the outcast in his ministry, he makes sure we don't miss it here. Turning up for his inauguration as King of heaven, Jesus brings a convicted criminal as his plus-one.

As we have seen before in this book, location matters; geography and theology are intertwined. The word "paradise" used here is highly unusual in the New Testament, occurring only two other times—in 2 Corinthians and in Revelation. Both of those occurrences underline that paradise is to be understood primarily in relation to God's presence with his people. In 2 Corinthians Paul explains that he was caught up into paradise and given the opportunity to see and experience things of God that no one can express (2 Corinthians 12:2-4). In Revelation it is described as "the paradise of God" where human beings are given the opportunity to eat from the tree of life—exactly the tree humans were banned from accessing after the fall in Eden (Revelation 2:7). The word "paradise" is a Persian loanword meaning "garden," so we are clearly supposed to make the association with a renewed Garden of Eden.[9] The cross is where all the threads of the grand narrative, from creation to new creation, are tied together. Jesus' death is making a way possible for the lost to find a home, the sinful to find a place of forgiveness, and the outcast to be brought into God's presence.

As if to underline this welcome of welcomes, the curtain that separated the Holy of Holies from the rest of the temple is torn in two from top to bottom as Jesus dies, demonstrating symbolically that the inaccessible God has made a way for humanity to access his previously protected presence.[10] Just as it is now safe for unholy human beings to return to the newly restored Garden of Eden, so it is also safe for us to have unrestricted access to God himself.

We should not be surprised that it is a convicted criminal who sees in Jesus what no one else has noticed. Luke's Gospel has consistently highlighted Jesus' compassion and public recognition of those whom society had written off. But it has also highlighted the fact that it is often the marginalized and rejected who recognize Jesus first. It was not a Jewish religious leader about whom Jesus exclaimed, "I have not found such great faith in Israel," but a Roman centurion. It was not the learned Pharisees gathered at Simon's house whose hospitality was commended, but that of a shunned woman who lavished an extraordinary welcome on Jesus. It was not the religious types who were commended for their demonstration of justice, but a newly converted tax collector called Zacchaeus. It was not priests who came as honored guests following Jesus' birth, but poor farmhands and Gentile astrologers.

The learned, the wealthy, and the influential are often the voices we pay most attention to both in society and in the church, but it is precisely those people who are most disposed to miss Jesus. Through sharing God's hospitality, we have the opportunity to be brought into relationship with those who can help us understand most clearly who God really is: the poor, the marginalized, and the rejected. In his provocative book *Reading the Bible with the Damned*, Bob Eckblad argues, "The Bible is locked up by theologies we absorb from our subcultures . . . left unchallenged, these assumptions will cause us to consciously or unconsciously look for evidence in the Bible to support our ideas."[11] In other words, often it is just as we think we understand Scripture that we may lose sight of the truth, because we are reading the Bible to suit ourselves. Or, to put it another way, perhaps God becomes a stranger to us because we are not keeping company with the strangers who may recognize God in places we don't.

In Jesus' day it was not the educated and churched who recognized Jesus, but the strangers, sinners, and social outcasts. In our day, the more homogenous our churches are, the more closed our circle of friends, the less likely we are to see Jesus, the less likely we are to know the Father. On the other hand, the more diverse and welcoming our churches are, the more likely we are to see Jesus and know the Father. According to a study by the UK Social Integration Commission, it was found that churches "are more successful than any other social setting at bringing people of different backgrounds together, well ahead of gatherings such as parties, meetings, weddings or venues such as pubs and clubs."[12] This encouraging news shows there is great potential for the church not only to model the kind of community that welcomes the marginalized, but to allow their perspectives to help us better understand Scripture and thus bring us into greater intimacy with God.

That the death of Jesus demonstrates the welcome, the hospitality of God toward us, is seen not only in the ripping of the temple curtain, allowing everyone into God's presence, but also by his personal assurance to a convicted criminal that he is at the top of the guest list for paradise, by his prayer for forgiveness for his enemies, and, because he put himself on the receiving end of hospitality, even by his request for thirst-quenching water. But God's view of hospitality is in fact distinct in all seven of Jesus' sayings from the cross.

As Jesus hangs, John records his fourth saying. Jesus turns to his mother, Mary, standing by his friend John, and says, "Woman, here is your son," and to John he says, "Here is your mother" (John 19:26-27). As if dying for the sins of the world and securing our eternal home wasn't a big enough task, even as he dies Jesus secures temporal hospitality for those closest to him. The highly respected New Testament scholar D. A. Carson recognizes in these words the echo of "legal adoption formulae,"[13] and John himself tells us that "from that time on, this disciple took her into his home" (John 19:27). John adopted Mary as his own mother, to care for her needs and to console her in this time of great personal loss. What had happened to Jesus' other brothers at that time, the natural-born sons that Joseph and Mary had together, is uncertain. Perhaps they were still estranged from Jesus (John 7:5), or perhaps they were just not in Jerusalem at the time. Nevertheless, in this simple act we see Jesus promoting hospitality by enabling people to be reconciled to God and to one another.

Both Matthew and Mark record Jesus' cry of desolation from the cross in the fifth saying: "My God, my God, why have you forsaken me?" (Matthew 27:46; Mark 15:34). Here Jesus is quoting Psalm 22, where King David is facing serious troubles.

David's cry of desperation, his description of the ridicule and insults he received, his heart melting like wax, his thirst, and the gambling for his clothes seem to describe Jesus' crucifixion with uncanny accuracy. But Jesus' use of the words expresses a much greater despair at the isolation that he was experiencing as he, God the Son, was alienated from God, his own Father. In some profound and mysterious way, the Godhead, the one God who is in three persons, was disrupted by the cross. The consequence of Jesus carrying the crushing weight of the world's sins on his shoulders is that he and his Father are estranged. Somehow, mysteriously, Jesus had to be forsaken by his Father, so that we could be forgiven. He was rejected so that we could be accepted. He was excluded from the mercy of God so that we could be included. Here is the ultimate act of hospitality, that Jesus would be displaced from the presence of God so that we could be welcomed into it.

The final words of Jesus that Luke records come as darkness falls at noon. Jesus cries out, "Father, into your hands I commit my spirit" (Luke 23:46). These words demonstrate that despite the agony of his death, Jesus still has great trust and affection for his heavenly Father. The words on Jesus' lips are borrowed from Psalm 31, where King David writes:

> In you, LORD, I have taken refuge;
>> let me never be put to shame;
>> deliver me in your righteousness.
> Turn your ear to me,
>> come quickly to my rescue;
> be my rock of refuge,
>> a strong fortress to save me.
> Since you are my rock and my fortress,

for the sake of your name lead and guide me.
Keep me free from the trap that is set for me,
    for you are my refuge.
Into your hands I commit my spirit;
    deliver me, LORD, my faithful God. (Psalm 31:1-5)

By referencing the psalm, Jesus draws our attention to the whole
of this psalm, which is effectively a plea for asylum. In the middle
of great personal distress, David's cry expresses his trust in God's
protective care, in which he seeks refuge. Despite all appearances,
God is his safe place, his panic room, his fortress. Jesus now asks
for the same hospitality from God: for sanctuary from the turmoil
that he is in. It is a poignant moment, witnessed by one unexpected person—another outsider amid a crowd of insiders. A
Roman centurion declares his praise to God: "Surely he was the
Son of God!" (Matthew 27:54). Once again, it is an outsider who
suddenly sees the significance of what is going on. It is not a
member of the chosen people of God who sees that God has
turned up, but an enemy of God's people. It is not a religious
leader, a disciple, or a scholar, but a soldier and a stranger who
sees what no one else can. Once again, even in the very moment
of his death, Jesus is opening the way for those previously permanently excluded from the kingdom of God to be reconciled and
welcomed in.

These six sayings from the cross paint a beautiful, multifaceted
picture of Jesus as the great host of heaven. Strangely, each of
them remind us of stories we have considered in this book—
stories we thought were the lowlights of Scripture, but where
we found God right there in the center. When Jesus cries, "My
God, my God, why have you forsaken me?" he is caught up with
us in the fundamental fracture in our relationship with our

Creator, as we considered in our first chapter on Adam and Eve. When he declares, "I am thirsty," he is putting himself on the receiving end of others' hospitality, as we saw with Abraham in chapter two. When he says to Mary and to John, "Here is your son . . . here is your mother," we see him creating family bonds anew, as in chapter three when Jacob was reunited with his brother or in chapter five when Naomi was given a new family. When he says, "Today you will be with me in paradise," he is ensuring his criminal neighbor has a right relationship with God. Perhaps this is the way Gideon should have treated the retreating kings he murdered. Simultaneously Jesus makes clear that he is defeating death, the enemy that holds all of us captive. When he says, "Into your hands I commit my spirit," his witness is so astounding that even a stranger, a Roman centurion, confesses God. When Jesus says, "Father, forgive them, for they do not know what they are doing," his hospitality to his enemies shows another level of grace that reverses the sentiments of David's imprecatory psalm that we looked at in chapter six.

Now Jesus utters his final words: "It is finished" (John 19:30). There are so many different ways in which those words are true. Jesus' own suffering is finished—he has identified with the pain of humanity to the utmost extreme. The sacrificial system, that had sustained Jewish religious practice for so long, is finished and done with because the wrath of God is utterly satisfied with the sacrifice of his only Son. The captivity of humanity to sin is finished with the payment of the ransom necessary to liberate us from slavery to sin. The Passover is finished as Jesus, the Lamb of God who takes away the sins of the world, fulfills all that God's rescue of his people from Egypt symbolized. The decisive battle with evil is finished as Jesus the conquering King wins victory by dying in our place. Our exclusion from God's presence is finally over.

It is all finished, but just as there was a surprising time lag at the end of the Second World War between the decisive victory of D-day and the declaration of the end of hostilities on VE-day, so, while Jesus' work itself is finished, its implications are yet to be experienced by all of creation. We live now in light of Jesus' victory, knowing that the course of history has been set. Now is the time to call all people to come to God and recognize this stranger as Savior and Lord, Father and Friend, Rescuer and King, in their lives and receive the promise of God's company in paradise, before it is too late.

Although he was on the receiving end of the greatest hostility humanity could muster against him, Jesus turned the cross into the event that offers humanity the greatest hospitality. This intense irony inspired Dietrich Bonhoeffer to comment:

> Jesus Christ lived in the midst of his enemies. At the end all his disciples deserted him. On the Cross he was utterly alone, surrounded by evildoers and mockers. For this cause he had come, to bring peace to the enemies of God. So the Christian, too, belongs not in the seclusion of a cloistered life but in the thick of foes.[14]

These are challenging words, especially since we know that Bonhoeffer, when offered escape from Nazi Germany for the safety of an American seminary, decided to stay right where he was, in the midst of the enemies who would eventually kill him. Just as we cannot accept the free grace of God without reflecting that grace out to others, so too we cannot truly accept the costly hospitality of Jesus on the cross without reflecting that same costly hospitality out to others.

Throughout history Christians have put themselves in harm's way in order to offer refuge and shelter to others. Moravian missionaries sold themselves into slavery in order that they might be able to offer the gospel to those who were being kidnapped and trafficked from Africa to America. Christians at the heart of the Underground Railroad movement helped to free slaves from their captors in the American South. Corrie Ten Boom's family sheltered Jewish refugees in the Second World War, knowing that if they were ever discovered, it would lead to their own capture and imprisonment.

Corrie's story, as told in the book *The Hiding Place*, has moved millions around the world. She is reported to have remarked, "The measure of a life, after all, is not its duration, but its donation." That was certainly true of Jesus. Is it true of his followers today? Isn't it time for this same spirit of costly hospitality to infect our lives and begin a revolution around us? Can we stop building up selfish and fear-fed barricades for long enough to realize that, whatever the dangers, strangers can enhance opportunities to know God and make him known? Can we learn from the attitude of a guilty thief and the assurance of an innocent convict?

Victor Hugo beautifully wove some of these questions into his historical novel about redemption, *Les Misérables*. When Monseigneur Myriel is installed as the Bishop of Digne, he notices that next to his magnificent new palace is a low, narrow hospital building with a small garden, overcrowded and underfunded. Immediately the bishop calls the director of the hospital and suggests an exchange. The sick move into the ornate and spacious palace, and as for the bishop, his new home is, literally, a hospital. He does not have to wait long to show hospitality. There is a knock on the door, and the bishop opens it to find a stranger who has been going door to door asking for help. The telltale yellow color of his identity card makes it clear to everyone that he is an ex-convict. The stranger is a recently liberated galley slave who has spent almost two decades imprisoned for theft. He has no hope that anyone will give him refuge, but desperate men resort to desperate measures, and so he finds himself knocking on the door of an unassuming building that was once a hospital.

Victor Hugo has the bishop remain incognito as he answers the door and welcomes the man in. He sets an extra place at dinner and puts fresh sheets on the bed. The two strangers spend the evening eating and drinking together. This hospitality is over-whelming for a man who has not even seen a bed in nineteen years, let alone enjoyed a home-cooked meal. The bishop, his identity still secret, reaches out a hand to his unexpected visitor and says,

> This house is not mine but Christ's. It does not ask a man his name but whether he is in need. You are in trouble, you are hungry and thirsty, and so you are welcome. You need not thank me for receiving you in my house. No one is at home here except those seeking shelter. Let me assure you . . . that this is more your home than mine. Everything in it is yours.[15]

Later that night, after the bishop and his guest have gone to bed, there is another knock at the door. To the bishop's great surprise, it is the same stranger, this time accompanied by local gendarmes who apprehended him running off with the silver tableware. The man awoke in the night, and spent an hour wres-tling with his conscience before stealing from his generous host. To the prisoner's utmost amazement, the bishop welcomes him a second time with words that will change his life: "I'm delighted to see you. Had you forgotten that I gave you the candlesticks as well? They're silver like the rest, and worth a good two hundred francs. Did you forget to take them? . . . I have bought your soul to save it . . . and I give it to God."[16]

After being betrayed and robbed, the bishop repays the ungrateful stranger with yet more grace, mercy, and generosity, far beyond what he deserves. This bishop, found in a hospital, heaps so many burning coals of hospitality on the convict's head that his life cannot but be transformed. This opening encounter sets in motion a chain of grace that ripples throughout the whole of the novel, conveying this transforming power. Set in the time of the French Revolution, the West End show *Les Misérables* has also enthralled millions as the world's longest-running musical, famous for its setting on a revolving stage. Victor Hugo presents us with a revolutionary and moving version of the story of the thief on the cross: a thief who finds unexpected and revolutionary hospitality, redemption, and transformation. As Hugo rightly has it, this is just the beginning of the story.

My mother never read *Les Misérables*. She never had tickets to the West End musical. She didn't see the breathtaking staging of the street battles of Paris as young men died on the barricades. But she had read her Bible, and although she had experienced both hostility and hospitality, she chose to live by taking down barricades, welcoming the stranger, and letting love, not hate, define her relationship to outsiders.

CLEOPΛS ΛND
THE STRΛNGER

The God who turns up in the end

In which a hopeless traveler offers a stranger a meal,
and we are given serious food for thought.

I have written most of this book at my kitchen table. It is probably
the single most significant piece of furniture in our house. Its
value comes not from what it is made of, or how much we did
(or did not) pay for it, or the quality or quantity of food that
has been served on it. Its value comes from the relationships
that have been forged and sealed around it. I think of birthday
breakfasts with the table full of presents and young eyes full of
wonder. I recall the foster children who nervously wondered
where to sit for their first meal with this strange new family, just
as we nervously wondered whether they would eat the food we
had prepared for them. I remember lingering Christmas dinners—
including a particular one that would be my mother's last one

with us. She joined in as best she could, doing everything to disguise the pain she was in. Around this table tears have been shed, jokes have been told, arguments have been provoked and resolved, announcements have been made, and significant occasions have been celebrated. Around this table acquaintances have become friends and strangers have become family. It may hold a feast or just simple toast and butter, but three times a day without fail it serves to unite whoever happens to be in the house at the time and can squeeze around this fixed point of convergence. It is a faithful table, a precious place of shared sustenance and transformation, a symbol of God's hospitality to us.

The final chapter of Luke's Gospel offers a real twist in the tale of the story of the crucifixion as three people, who had been strangers to each other earlier in the day, gathered around a table to eat together. We began the book with three conspirators, Adam, Eve, and the snake, gathered around the tree to offer and eat fruit, and quickly moved on to the story of three divine visitors eating together at Abraham's table. Now three more hungry travelers are sitting down to eat, but before we get there, we need to take a journey of our own and catch up on where we left the story in the last chapter.

We left three strangers dying on wooden crosses with only a spongeful of vinegar to share between them. This is the greatest event in human history, but so far it seems only one criminal has understood its revolutionary significance. Jesus' disciples are in shock. They certainly did not expect the week to turn out this way when they entered Jerusalem to the adulation of the crowds just days earlier. But now their friend, master, and wished-for Messiah has been murdered. Some of them go into hiding, some of them run away, and some of them do what most of us do when bad things happen—reluctantly and dejectedly head for the safety and familiarity of the place we call home.

> Now that same day two of them were going to a village called Emmaus, about seven miles from Jerusalem. They were talking with each other about everything that had happened. As they talked and discussed these things with each other, Jesus himself came up and walked along with them; but they were kept from recognizing him.
>
> He asked them, "What are you discussing together as you walk along?"
>
> They stood still, their faces downcast. One of them, named Cleopas, asked him, "Are you the only one visiting Jerusalem who does not know the things that have happened there in these days?"
>
> "What things?" he asked. (Luke 24:13-19)

It is not hard to relate to these dispirited disciples as they trudge home. We have all known disappointment in our lives. How many times have we been sure that God was going to come through for us only to find, in the end, that he didn't? How often have we begged God to turn up and turn a situation around, desperately trying to drown out the pessimistic voices in our head, the voices that end up being the ones we should have listened to? How often have we been tempted to dream a bigger dream, but decided not to, so our dreams will never be shattered? Sometimes it is easier to believe in a God who never heals than to believe in one who does but won't. Sometimes it is easier to believe in a God who doesn't intervene than to believe in one who does but hasn't. Sometimes it is easier not to raise our expectations because there is less distance to fall when it all goes wrong. Sometimes it is just easier to go home, shut the door, and forget all about the God who has gone elusive on us, all the promises that evaporated.

Luke's account of the aftermath of the crucifixion focuses in on a duo of disappointed disciples walking back to their home in Emmaus. Physically, they have left Jerusalem—but their hearts and minds are still there. As they walk they share in a verbal postmortem of the events of the week, trying desperately to puzzle it all out. Who was Jesus, if not the Messiah? Who is the Messiah, if not Jesus? What sort of fools were they for believing he could save them? How could it happen that their best friend turned out to be a perfect stranger? As they wrestle with their fears and doubts and broken dreams, a lone stranger catches up with them, and they welcome his company. Just as in the story of Abraham entertaining God himself, we readers are let in on the secret that this is no stranger but Christ himself. Perhaps this is Luke's parallel to the parable of the sheep and the goats: those who unwittingly welcome strangers turn out to be welcoming Jesus. The two disciples, Cleopas and his unnamed companion, his wife or his brother or his friend, fail to recognize Jesus. Earlier in his ministry Jesus had very clearly spelled out to his disciples that he was going to be crucified and then resurrected from the dead. But even though Jesus couldn't have been clearer, Luke comments that the disciples still did not understand: "Its meaning was hidden from them, and they did not know what he was talking about" (Luke 18:34). So, now that the resurrected Jesus is there in the flesh, walking with these two despondent disciples, perhaps we shouldn't be surprised that God seems to be hiding from them in the same way he hid his identity when he appeared to Abraham, Lot, Jacob, and Gideon. Because it seems, when God turns up unannounced, uninvited, and unrecognized, that's when something revolutionary is about to kick off.

Throughout this book we have seen that when God is a stranger to us, there is good reason. It forces us to wrestle with the tough questions about who God really is. Jesus, the master of asking questions, once asked his disciples, early on in his ministry, "Who do people say I am?" and as a chaser, "But what about you?" (Mark 8:27-29). Of course, he knew the answer already, but his question helped Peter realize for himself and declare to the world that Jesus was the Messiah, the Son of the living God. Here on the Emmaus road Jesus asks a similarly foolish-sounding question. "What are you discussing together as you walk along?" Cleopas is incredulous. He simply cannot believe that anyone in Jerusalem would not have known what has just taken place. His flabbergasted reaction shows us just how public the events surrounding Jesus' death were: it was quite literally the talk of the town. And so with increasingly beautiful irony we see Cleopas explain to Jesus who he himself is:

> "About Jesus of Nazareth," they replied. "He was a prophet, powerful in word and deed before God and all the people. The chief priests and our rulers handed him over to be sentenced to death, and they crucified him; but we had hoped that he was the one who was going to redeem Israel. And what is more, it is the third day since all this took place. In addition, some of our women amazed us. They went to the tomb early this morning but didn't find his body. They came and told us that they had seen a vision of angels, who said he was alive. Then some of our companions went to the tomb and found it just as the women had said, but they did not see Jesus." (Luke 24:19-24)

It is at the words "they did not see Jesus" that the rich irony peaks and Jesus needs to interject. Just as an unseeing Mary had mistaken Jesus for the gardener earlier in the day, now these unseeing disciples are staring straight in the face of Jesus, and yet they do not see him, mistaking him for just another traveler. A few days earlier the crowds, rulers, soldiers, and even a fellow convict had mistaken Jesus for a blasphemer deserving of execution. The evening before that, the arresting soldiers were so worried about not recognizing Jesus in the dark that they arranged a secret signal with one of his disciples: the one he kissed would be the one on their hit list. Sometime before that, Jesus had warned that in the future many so-called disciples would mistake him for some hungry, thirsty, and under-dressed stranger whom they were free to ignore only at their eternal peril. In humility, God deliberately makes himself a stranger, so that humanity might make a genuine response to him. Could we too be so close to Christ and yet miss him entirely? May we have the divinely inspired humility not to consider ourselves above welcoming strangers.

> He said to them, "How foolish you are, and how slow to believe all that the prophets have spoken! Did not the Messiah have to suffer these things and then enter his glory?" And beginning with Moses and all the Prophets, he explained to them what was said in all the Scriptures concerning himself. (Luke 24:25-27)

The disciples remind me here of Naomi, heading for home, all out of hope, bitter and dejected. They remind me of David, angry and wondering why God had not saved them as they expected. This time Jesus does turn up, but not at first to comfort and cheer them up, but rather to chastise them for their foolishness and criticize them for their slowness to believe. This is strange. It doesn't fit my picture of Jesus. He is not being very pastorally sensitive. These poor disciples have been through a lot. They have witnessed the brutal murder of a personal friend. They have seen a living—and dying—example of what happens to those who put their trust in God and challenge the authority of the Jewish rulers of Jerusalem and the Roman imperial powers. They have witnessed the destruction of their dreams. So why isn't Jesus a bit nicer to them? Why does he critique their theology and disapprove of their interpretation of the Old Testament? Why does he give a negative evaluation of their faith? Were they really supposed to see what nobody else had seen in Scripture, including Jesus' twelve closest disciples? Were they really supposed to believe a bunch of women with not a shred of real evidence? Was their ignorance culpable? Was Jesus really disappointed in their disappointment?

No doubt there is some hyperbole here, but Jesus' rebuke is challenging. When I am disappointed in God, I often make excuses for my lack of faith. I attribute my inability to trust God to my circumstances, my tiredness, my church, my upbringing. These disciples have almost every conceivable excuse available to them for misunderstanding about the Messiah, and yet Jesus still holds them to account. Sometimes, rather than making excuses, I need to confess that I have failed to search the Scriptures. Sometimes I have heard the truth, but I have chosen to walk away. Sometimes we need to hear the challenge of Jesus' criticism to dig deeper into what the Bible really teaches.

Jesus' challenge to his disciples echoes his rebuke to the religious leaders: "You study the Scriptures diligently because you think that in them you have eternal life. These are the very Scriptures that testify about me, yet you refuse to come to me to have life" (John 5:39-40). Somehow it is possible to dig deep into the Bible and still miss Jesus. Sometimes we can be so fixed or focused on our ideas and assumptions that we fail to grasp what exactly it is saying to us. It is possible to love the Bible but miss its message. It is possible to know the Scriptures and miss the Savior. For both the disciples and the Pharisees, in different ways, the challenge was not that they were unaware of what Scripture said; it was that they were either too slow or too stubborn to see the implications. Having an exhaustive knowledge of the Bible does not always translate into a life of intimacy with God, or into obedience to him. Jesus never criticized anyone for studying Scripture too much, only for failing to allow it to transform their hearts, minds, and wills. Jesus points out to both disciples and Pharisees alike that taking the Bible seriously should help us recognize Jesus in the stranger.

I was brought to faith through a friend at school. I was mentored by staff at schools. I was trained in evangelism. I was tutored in apologetics. I was coached in leadership. I was prepared for marriage. I was commissioned as a missionary. I was enrolled in theological training. And not once in all those early years of spiritual formation did anyone explain to me God's concern for the poor. I was never taught how crucial it was to welcome the stranger, to care for the vulnerable, to feed the hungry, to clothe the naked. Not once. It took many true strangers to open my eyes to see in the Bible what I had been blind to for so long.

What a dreadful thing, to be challenged by Jesus himself that we have misunderstood his word. His criticism of the Emmaus disciples may have smarted briefly, but as Proverbs reminds us, the wounds of a friend are trustworthy (Proverbs 27:6). Jesus is merciful to his slow-to-believe followers, and he opens their eyes to show them what they have missed. There on the road they were given a crash course in biblical theology. They were given a personal tutorial in what must have been the best class on Old Testament theology ever. Jesus drew together the threads of Scripture and showed how it all pointed to him. I dearly wish we had the transcript of that Emmaus road conversation. As I say, we don't know all the ground Jesus covered, but let us pause briefly to review where we have come on our own journey through the Bible in this book and how it has pointed forward to Jesus. We began in Eden, where after the fall God estranged himself from his people, forcing them out as strangers into the wilderness. Humanity failed at the first hurdle, but God did not give up on us, repeatedly revealing himself down the ages to those willing to see him, and finally sending Jesus to bring us back into his presence. We moved on to Mamre, where Abraham was camping after he too had been moved on by God from his previous home. As he welcomed God by offering hospitality to strangers, we learned how God was willing to take on the role of a guest in his own universe, and how this would prefigure Jesus' explanation that when we welcome the needy stranger, we welcome him. We then moved on to Peniel, where Jacob's wrestling with the God he didn't recognize brought him into a new identity as Israel, wounded as a sign of his inward healing, blessed to be a blessing to others. Here we see a foreshadowing of the true Israel who will be wounded by God so that we can be healed, who wrestles with God in the darkness so that we can be welcomed. Moving on to Ophrah, Gideon met a stranger who called him into a new vocation leading Israel back to God again. His failure showed our need for a greater judge, to rescue God's people not just from enemy invasion but to bring personal renewal and transformation, so that all nations would worship him in Spirit and truth.

Around the same time in history, over in Moab, Naomi's bit-terness hindered her from seeing God at work until a stranger called Ruth came alongside her and journeyed with her back to Bethlehem, with the surprise conclusion of the two women later becoming included in the family of the Messiah himself. Later, in Jerusalem, we saw in David's anger disappointment in a God who didn't save the way he expected, not that dissimilar from the disciples on the Emmaus road. He called out to God not to be a stranger, but could not see the salvation that God had planned—although prophetically his words prefigured Jesus' own agony as he faced the anger of God on the cross. By the rivers of Babylon, we see a similar desperation as God's people had again become strangers after not heeding Isaiah's warning to engage in the worship God prioritized—the same worship that Jesus would teach about and live and die for: feeding the hungry, clothing the naked, and setting the oppressed free. And far away from Jerusalem, Ezekiel would meet the God who had become a stranger to his people because of their faithlessness. He would warn them about rejecting God and the violent end that would result. But God chose not to punish his people, instead allowing his own Son to be stripped, mobbed, torn apart, and killed outside Jerusalem while God turned his face away.

The Emmaus disciples cannot get enough of Jesus' whistle-stop tour of the Scriptures, which makes connections for them that they had never seen before. Suddenly God's history with his people is all tying in with all they had seen and heard of Jesus.

As they approached the village to which they were going, Jesus continued on as if he were going further. But they urged him strongly, "Stay with us, for it is nearly evening; the day is almost over." So he went in to stay with them.

When he was at the table with them, he took bread, gave thanks, broke it and began to give it to them. Then their eyes were opened and they recognized him. (Luke 24:28-31)

Naturally the travelers urge Jesus, though a stranger to them, to come into their home and stay with them. We hear echoes of Abraham urging his divine visitors to receive hospitality from him. Just like Abraham, these disciples will get far more than they bargained for. As they offer a stranger shelter, food, and drink, something remarkable happens.

Meals were so important to Jesus that theologian Tim Chester concludes, "In Luke's Gospel Jesus is either going to a meal, at a meal, or coming from a meal."[1] Bishop Tom Wright, the world-renowned New Testament scholar, remarks that "eating with 'sinners' was one of the most characteristic and striking marks of Jesus' regular activity."[2] In light of this, it seems entirely fitting that Jesus chooses to make himself known to these dejected disciples through shared food. Gathered around the table, the guest, unusually, takes the role of host. He takes the bread, gives thanks, and breaks it. It is at this moment that the two hosts, now made guests at their own table, recognize Jesus.

Perhaps they were at Levi the tax collector's house during his postconversion party where Jesus was the guest of honor for one of the most hated groups of people in ancient Israel (Luke 5:27-32). Or perhaps they were there at Simon the Pharisee's house when the host had neglected to show Jesus the most basic level of hospitality and an unsavory woman had honored Jesus instead (Luke 7:36-50). Perhaps these disciples were two of the five thousand whom Jesus had miraculously fed in one sitting (Luke 9:10-17). Perhaps they had been jockeying for the most important place at the dinner table when Jesus had taught a whole new mealtime etiquette that included inviting strangers, not friends, to dinner, blessing the poor, and being blessed by God at the resurrection of the righteous (Luke 14:12-14). Perhaps they had only just caught up with Jesus when he went to a party hosted by the newly converted tax cheat Zacchaeus (Luke 19:1-10). Or perhaps they had been at one of the many other meals where Jesus, ostensibly the guest, had taken on the role of host.

Or perhaps they had been privy to the last gathering Jesus had with his disciples—a reenactment of the Passover, the most important meal in the Jewish liturgy. It was a meal to celebrate God's liberation of the Hebrews from captivity in Egypt. Perhaps they had taken part in the Passover meal and remembered how Jesus had once said he was "the Lamb of God, who takes away the sin of the world!" (John 1:29). Perhaps they had taken the bread and wine at that meal, consumed it slowly and deliberately, remembering that salvation is from God—and God alone. Perhaps they had heard Jesus revolutionize the meal with his words, "Do this in remembrance of me" (Luke 22:19), declaring himself simultaneously the host and the object of the meal. This is what Jesus does again in the little home in Emmaus. Jesus has modeled the essence of revolutionary hospitality throughout his life, ministry, and teaching, and so it is fitting that he chooses to make himself known at just this point.

There is something significant about the way that food connects us. Our need for sustenance is a great leveler: whether we are posh or poor, heiress or homeless, all of us need to eat. But food is more than simply the satisfying of a physical appetite. The prestigious food writer Nigel Slater recounts how, on the night after his mother's funeral, only nine years old, he discovered two white marshmallows on his bedside table. In a school essay written shortly before his mother's death, Slater had described them as being the nearest food to a kiss:

> Soft, sweet, tender, pink. Each night for the next two years I found two, sometimes three, fluffy, sugary marshmallows waiting for me. It was my mother's goodnight kiss I missed more than anything, more than her hugs, her cuddles, her whispered "Night-night, sleep tight."[3]

Nigel understands that food is relational and spiritual as well as simply digestible. Food brings people together and that *speaks* to us as much as, if not more than, it sustains us.

Meals were not just the media of Jesus' ministry; they were the message too. Jesus' habit of associating with sinners was bad enough, but what really riled the Pharisees was that Jesus also ate with them (Luke 15:1-2). Sharing food with someone was a way of demonstrating social acceptance. What theologians describe as "table fellowship"[4] was a closely guarded privilege and not something that was offered lightly. Author and activist Tim Chester explains,

> Meals in Jesus' day were highly stratified. Roman meals expressed the social order. Jewish meals were similar . . . with the added twist that levitical food laws made it all but impossible for Jews to eat with Gentiles. So meals expressed who were the insiders and who were the outsiders. Jesus turns all of this . . . inside out. Outsiders become insiders around the table with Jesus.[5]

What Jesus was doing was socially disruptive. He was illustrating and initiating a social revolution through his hospitality, and the Pharisees knew it. They could not stand it. They could not comprehend why their carefully stratified society, divided along strict lines based on holiness, was being unpicked by Jesus—so Jesus used parables with a recurring theme of hospitality to help everyone understand the new social order that he called the kingdom of God.

The parable of the prodigal son was told in direct response to the criticism of Jesus' choice of dinner companions. The younger son asks for his share of his inheritance early, thus triggering a whole chain of events that ends up with the father refinancing his property, and the younger son squandering the wealth and ending up so hungry that his meals consist of pig swill. Hunger and deprivation bring him to his senses, and soon he is on his way home, prepared with a speech asking to be accepted as a slave in his father's household. But the father spots the son far away, runs to him, reconciles with him, reclothes him, and reinstates him as a son and heir. He then calls for a feast, with the prized fattened calf as the main course. The challenge to the Pharisees—and to us—comes with the story of the older brother. He hears the commotion, is outraged that his father is eating with such a lowlife, and refuses to join in the meal. The father who earlier went out to welcome the younger son then goes out to welcome the older son too. But the story is left after the father has remonstrated with the older son. Will the older-son Pharisees come in and join the celebration of lost people finding reconciliation with God, or not? Will they welcome the outsiders who have been turned into insiders, or will they stay outside the house, excluded from the meal and the party?

Once again our welcome of others is presented as the litmus test of our relationship with God. In the parable of the sheep and the goats we saw that the test was applied to how we respond to the stranger; in that of the prodigal son it is based on how we respond to the sinner. In the sheep and goats parable there is no question of blame for the stranger who is naked, hungry, thirsty, or even in prison. But through the parable of the prodigal son, Jesus asks how we will respond to those who have made choices we don't agree with. Will we sulk in the garden and bring shame to our Father, or will we put aside our prejudices and judgments and join in God's welcome feast?

The foster children who have come into our home have had all manner of descriptors attached to them. They have been described as biters, runners, damaged, hard-to-place, and high-risk. Some have definitely made bad choices, and some are so entrenched in antisocial behaviors that they are extremely difficult to care for. But at the end of the day, no matter what they have done or what has been done to them, they are all children, they are all vulnerable, and they are all victims. They all deserve a welcome, unconditional love and a family to belong to. We see our calling as offering unconditional love and open hospitality to all the children we possibly can. We cannot allow prejudice, snobbery, or indifference to blind us to the needs of others or to our own capacity to offer hospitality. Will we emulate the kindness of the father or the judgmentalism of the older brother? Will we join in God's great welcome feast?

A second parable that uses a great feast as its central image is told at a Sabbath dinner in a Pharisee's house. This time the event is no impromptu party, but a preplanned banquet (Luke 14:17). But when all is ready, one after another the guests all give lame excuses for not attending. Infuriated, the host will not let his hospitality go to waste. He sends his servant out to invite the least, the last, the lost, and the left out. "Go out quickly into the streets and alleys of the town and bring in the poor, the crippled, the blind and the lame" (Luke 14:21). Those people who never get invited anywhere are going to be made welcome by the host-in-waiting. When this is done, there is still space. The servant is sent out one last time, to those who don't even live in the town—to the outsiders. He is told to compel, urge, and persuade as many as possible to fill up the master's house (Luke 14:23-24). The backward hospitality of God is on display again. Rather than using a dinner party as a means of social climbing or personal preening, hospitality is a demonstration of compassion, inclusion, and acceptance.

Then their eyes were opened and they recognized him, and he disappeared from their sight. They asked each other, "Were not our hearts burning within us while he talked with us on the road and opened the Scriptures to us?"

They got up and returned at once to Jerusalem. There they found the Eleven and those with them, assembled together and saying, "It is true! The Lord has risen and has appeared to Simon." Then the two told what had happened on the way, and how Jesus was recognized by them when he broke the bread. (Luke 24:31-35)

At the end of the meal in Emmaus, Jesus does not linger long at the table. In fact, as soon as he is recognized, he disappears from their sight. Mind you, as soon as the disciples recognize him, they are off too. Back down the very road they had slumped along as dispirited disciples with hearts breaking, now their pace is quickened, their hearts burning, bursting to tell everyone the good news of the resurrection of Jesus.

It was as these disciples sought to bless a stranger that they were blessed. It was through offering spontaneous hospitality that they received hospitality and hope from Jesus himself. This turnaround moment for the disciples was also a turnaround moment for the early church. Jesus turned up and shared meals with various disciples over the course of forty days following the resurrection, after which the Holy Spirit was poured out. The disciples began to witness to the truth of the resurrection, but along with their spoken words came that spontaneous hospitality as recorded in chapter two of the book of Acts:

> They devoted themselves to the apostles' teaching and to fellowship, to the breaking of bread and to prayer. Everyone was filled with awe at the many wonders and signs performed by the apostles. All the believers were together and had everything in common. They sold property and possessions to give to anyone who had need. Every day they continued to meet together in the temple courts. They broke bread in their homes and ate together with glad and sincere hearts, praising God and enjoying the favor of all the people. And the Lord added to their number daily those who were being saved. (Acts 2:42-47)

This truly is revolutionary hospitality at work, and we see it not opposed to but hand in hand with evangelism, worship, and discipleship. This hospitality put the early church on the map. It transformed the people who were on the receiving end. It transformed the people who were on the welcoming end. It brought a foretaste of eternity into the present. It answered something of Jesus' prayer for his kingdom to come on earth. It showed a glimpse of a future worth longing for, where there will be no more strangers. Instead we will be welcomed together in God's perfect presence.

C. S. Lewis put it like this:

> The sense that in this universe we are treated as strangers, the longing to be acknowledged, to meet with some response, to bridge some chasm that yawns between us and reality,

is part of our inconsolable secret. And surely, from this point of view, the promise of glory, in the sense described, becomes highly relevant to our deep desire. For glory means good report with God, acceptance by God, response, acknowledgment, and welcome into the heart of things. The door on which we have been knocking all our lives will open at last.[6]

※※※※

The Bible describes the grand conclusion of history—the goodness that awaits behind that door—as a great feast (Revelation 19:6-9), indeed a wedding banquet. In other words, a banquet to celebrate the time when God shows himself in the end—at the marriage of Jesus to the church. This ties together the parables of the bridesmaids and the great banquet. Those of us who are well prepared, who have not refused the invitation or resented the other invitees, will find ourselves included in God's family. In the meantime, as servants of God we are commissioned to compel, urge, and persuade outsiders to fill up his house before they become eternally excluded. The hospitality we show now, sharing our lives with the needy, gives the world an enticing taste of what is to come.

As the church does this, together our world can be transformed. There have been important moments in the history of the church where this has been clearly demonstrated. Historian Rodney Stark argues in his popular book *The Rise of Christianity* that Christians through the ages have had a hugely significant impact on the social and moral fabric of their society through hospitality.[7] In the second century the church transformed from being "a tiny and obscure messianic movement from the edge of the Roman Empire" to "the dominant faith of Western civilization." By Stark's estimation this must have entailed growth of the order of 40 percent per decade, extended over three centuries. This growth was not due to any attempt to build or seize power in a human sense, but rather to a grassroots, transformative influence that demonstrated the compassion and grace of God in the middle of crisis. Specifically, the church's response to the great plagues of the second century was the tipping point for the explosive growth of Christianity. Stark argues that a key factor was the selfless acts of mercy and charity of Christians toward their neighbors, which made a huge impression on the population of the plague-ridden Empire in the second century.[8]

The Plague of Galen first struck in AD 165, and so many people died that cities and villages in Italy and in the provinces were abandoned and fell into ruin.[9] The second time the plague struck the Roman world it was even more severe, with up to five thousand people a day reported to have died in Rome alone.[10] Around AD 260, at the height of the plague, Dionysius, the bishop of Alexandria, wrote:

> Most of our brother Christians showed unbounded love and loyalty, never sparing themselves and thinking only of one another. Heedless of danger, they took charge of the sick, attending to their every need and ministering to them in Christ, and with them departed this life serenely happy; for they were infected by others with the disease, drawing on themselves the sickness of their neighbours and cheerfully accepting their pains. . . . The best of our brothers lost their lives in this manner . . . winning high commendation so that death in this form, the result of great piety and strong faith, seems in every way the equal of martyrdom.[11]

Stark's claim is that this reckless, revolutionary hospitality of love and care transformed the ancient world. Because the Christians lived differently to their pagan neighbors, caring for each other and their neighbors sacrificially, this meant that proportionally more of them lived, and those who benefited from Christian nursing survived and were converted to Christianity. In other words, their compassion won a hearing for the gospel.

In our increasingly divided world, I believe that the time is ripe for Christians to demonstrate to our world the truth of the gospel through the power of revolutionary hospitality. With our world increasingly fragmenting into tribes, with the gap between rich and poor increasing, with unprecedented numbers of people displaced from their homes, living in poverty, and considered outsiders, there is a great opportunity for us to demonstrate the compassion of God on a global scale. All of that starts with us as individual Christians choosing to obey God's call to neighborliness, hospitality, and welcome. If our passion to know God who is a stranger to us can be translated into passion to show God's love to the stranger, then it won't be God who is unrecognizable any longer, but the world we live in.

CONCLUSION

From an early age we warn our children not to talk to people they do not know. We read them stories at bedtime about a jealous relative disguised as a wizened crone offering apples laced with a super-sedative, or a child-eating monster stalking a girl on her way to her grandmother's house with provisions. We grow up thinking that the world is an unsafe place, filled with suspicious strangers with cruel intentions. When we have grown out of fairy tales about wicked witches and wolves in the woods, school briefings, news feeds, and feature films take over the task of reinforcing this fear into adulthood: that the greatest threat comes from those we don't know.

Fear of the stranger, otherwise known as xenophobia, is so ingrained into our psyche that it is hard to break the cycle of mistrust, suspicion, and hostility. It affects the way we relate to God, as we have seen through this book. It affects the way we relate to our neighbors. It affects the way we relate to everybody.

We plug in our headphones. We lock our doors. We build our walls. We install our security systems. We build panic rooms. We step up our border patrols and vote for greater immigration control. The stranger is too dangerous to allow anywhere near us or our loved ones. The faceless outsider needs to be kept as far away from our lives as possible.

Like many other phobias, xenophobia is not only debilitating but also irrational. Many of the newspaper headlines that feed our collective fear of the stranger are based on misrepresentative and misleading information. Crime statistics tell a very different story. Sadly, children are much more likely to be abused or attacked by someone they know and trust than by a stranger. Women are far more likely to be physically assaulted, raped, or murdered by a friend, a family member, or a spouse than by an anonymous stalker or intruder. Tragically, the vast majority of murder victims die in their own homes, at the hands of someone they know. If we based our fears on fact, rather than on fantasy, we should by rights be far more wary of those we know than those we do not.

Most of us experience the kindness of strangers much more often than the crimes of strangers. I could tell you about the stranger who went to surprisingly great lengths to return the wallet I dropped on the London Underground, or of another who pulled my son out of the deep end of the pool before I had even clocked that he had fallen in and was drowning, another whose kind words at the hospital made such a huge difference at a very difficult time. I am sure that you too could recount similar experiences of benevolent strangers reaching out when you most needed it and least expected it. Perhaps we need to tell more stories like these to counteract or subvert our deep-seated xenophobia.

There is a well-known urban legend (one that the author Jeffery Archer expanded into a gripping short story[1]) that feeds on and seems to fuel our xenophobia, but finally subverts it. The story centers on a terrified woman driving home at night, being followed by a man in a van. When she is eventually forced off the road, she is convinced the van driver is out to do her harm. But instead he reveals there is an attacker hiding in the back seat of her car. He had followed her to warn her and protect her. It is indeed a story about stranger danger, but the malicious stranger is discovered and defeated at the end. The stranger who dominates the story is in fact the woman's savior, intent only on rescue, although misunderstood for the majority of the tale.

The stranger who dominates Christianity is our Savior God, often misunderstood and overlooked, but intent on challenging our intrinsic xenophobia, rescuing us from our preconceived ideas and preconditioned fears, showing us who he really is, bringing us safely home, and showing us how to treat strangers properly. This Savior once told a story not that dissimilar to the urban legend above. We know it as the parable of the good Samaritan.

The parable is told in response to a question posed by an expert in the Old Testament law. He is confused about the strange kingdom of God that Jesus is talking about, but he wants in. He understands the heartbeat of the Bible—the inseparable mandate of loving God and loving the neighbor—but he doesn't know where to start (Luke 10:25). Perhaps that is where we find ourselves at the end of this book. We understand what the Bible says, but now it is time to put it into practice. As Jesus says, "Do this and you will live" (Luke 10:28).

Where should I start? Whom could I welcome? Who counts and who does not? Who are the worth-my-timers and who are the waste-of-timers? Who are the deserving poor and who are not? Are these legitimate questions, or is this, for the expert in the law at least, a stalling tactic? No doubt Jesus senses a reluctance, a repugnance even, in his question. That is when Jesus tells the story of the good stranger.

A man was going down from Jerusalem to Jericho, when he was attacked by robbers. They stripped him of his clothes,

beat him and went away, leaving him half dead. A priest
happened to be going down the same road, and when he
saw the man, he passed by on the other side. So too, a
Levite, when he came to the place and saw him, passed by
on the other side. But a Samaritan, as he traveled, came
where the man was; and when he saw him, he took pity on
him. He went to him and bandaged his wounds, pouring
on oil and wine. Then he put the man on his own donkey,
brought him to an inn and took care of him. The next day
he took out two denarii and gave them to the innkeeper.
"Look after him," he said, "and when I return, I will reimburse
you for any extra expense you may have." (Luke 10:30-35)

Jesus challenges the Bible scholar to recognize the God who
is stranger by reaching out to the strangers around him. First,
he affirms that there is no limit to our responsibility when it
comes to hospitality. Our neighbor is each and every stranger,
wherever they are from. In fact, you might say, the stranger they
are, the more they are our neighbor. Rabbi Jonathan Sacks writes,

> The Jewish sages noted that on only one occasion does the
> Hebrew Bible command us to love our neighbour, but in
> thirty-seven places it commands us to love the stranger.
> Our neighbour is one we love because he is like ourselves.
> The stranger is one we are taught to love precisely because
> he is not like ourselves.[2]

Second, there should be no limit to our respect for others
when it comes to hospitality. It would have been radical enough
for Jesus to tell the story of a wounded Samaritan who was
helped by a Jewish man, but Jesus turns the tables here: the
Samaritan was a savior to the Jew. Jesus makes the hero of the

story a foreigner, an outsider, an enemy. The stranger is given the position of providing the needed hospitality, and therefore commands our respect. Tim Keller comments on this story,

> By depicting a Samaritan helping a Jew, Jesus could not have found a more forceful way to say that anyone at all in need—regardless of race, politics, class, and religion—is your neighbor. Not everyone is your brother or sister in faith, but everyone is your neighbor, and you must love your neighbor.[3]

Third, there should be no limit to our level of response when it comes to hospitality. The parable of the good Samaritan is challenging, because he went above and beyond all expectations. He could have wished the injured man well from the other side of the road, prayed for him, or lit a candle as a symbol of solidarity. He could have called for help on his behalf, sent some money to the local shelter, or held a bake sale or run a marathon for other stranded victims. There is no end to the number of projects he could have undertaken. But this was no project—this was a person in need. The hospitality the stranger showed was immediate and intimate, above and beyond the call of his personal duty.

Finally, there is no amount of religious knowledge sufficient to replace hospitality. In this chapter it is revealed that the Bible expert was a mere novice when it came to mercy. He is not the only one with this fatal flaw, as we have seen in chapter six and chapter ten. Jesus sets out to challenge us. Our knowledge of the Bible, our church attendance, our standing within the Christian community, are no measure of spirituality, no evidence of relationship with God, and no guarantee of eternal life. Jesus consistently warns us and encourages us: mercy is what is required. Our natural prejudices and inbuilt xenophobia manufacture excuses for us; they procrastinate or seek to limit our duty of care, but Jesus insists on tearing down all boundaries. "Do this and you will live," as he says in Luke 10:28.

Why is this sort of hospitality so alien to most of us in practice? The atheist philosopher Peter Singer asks some poignant questions that are relevant here.[4] Imagine you are walking past a shallow pond. A child has fallen into it and is drowning. Would you wade in and pull the child out? What about your expensive clothes and new shoes? What about that meeting you will be late for? Why, in fact, should you feel obligation to rescue a child who is not yours? With each question he hears a unanimous sympathy that puts saving the poor child far above the inconvenience of spoiling our clothes or being late. So Singer presses in. What if there are other people who are also walking past the pond who could help but choose not to? Again everyone is adamant—that makes no difference, each one would still save the child without hesitation. What if the child were far away, in another country perhaps, but similarly in danger of death, and equally within your means to save, at no great cost—and absolutely no danger—to yourself? Still virtually all agree that distance and nationality make no moral difference to the situation. And yet at the same time, despite knowing the plight of children around the world, despite understanding the hospitality that is needed in this situation, we choose to do nothing.

An experiment took place in which students at the world-renowned Princeton Seminary were asked to prepare a talk on the parable of the good Samaritan and then present the talk for assessment. As they passed through an alley to get from the preparation room to the lecture room, they had to walk by a "victim" who was slumped in a doorway, groaning. The experiment discovered that despite having studied Jesus' teaching, the students were still unwilling to stop and help.

They passed him by, and some even stepped over the poor man, especially those who were running late. It is a sobering thought that this basic and well-known teaching of Jesus is still so hard to put into practice. Things take a long time to move from head to heart, from decision to action.[5]

Perhaps it is the fear of the stranger drummed into us from an early age that means we continue in our fear, suspicion, and avoidance of strangers even when we know the clear teaching of the Bible. Like the Bible scholar who challenged Jesus, we would rather stall, struggle, and stew over the questions, instead of finding the people who need us to love and welcome them. The Bible, through its plethora of stories, memoirs, historical accounts, poems, and parables, challenges our xenophobic prejudices at every turn. God's concern is focused on the last, the lost, the least, and the left out. And we should include ourselves on that list too. The Bible is realistic about the fact that each one of us is flawed, selfish, and broken. It is also consistent, insistent, and persistent that if we love God, we will make room for strangers, getting close enough to offer the hospitality that Jesus modeled for us by being a perfect stranger.

The Greek word for "hospitality" is *philoxenia*, virtually a mirror image of another word in their culture, *xenophilia*, which means "love of the stranger." Xenophilia and philoxenia together are the antidote to *xenophobia*, "fear of the stranger." Through a Christlike commitment to xenophilia, we can see hostility turned to hospitality, strangers turned into friends, despair transformed into hope, exclusion turned into inclusion, our stranger God become strangely present. Our deepest fear as a culture could actually be our greatest opportunity as Christians.

Rather than fearing the stranger, Christians are called to welcome strangers, for in so doing many have welcomed God without knowing it.

> Oh, the depth of the riches of the wisdom and knowledge of God!
>> How unsearchable his judgments,
>> and his paths beyond tracing out!
> "Who has known the mind of the Lord?
>> Or who has been his counselor?"
> "Who has ever given to God,
>> that God should repay them?"
> For from him and through him and for him are all things.
>> To him be the glory forever! Amen. (Romans 11:33-36)

ACKNOWLEDGMENTS

Thank you above all to strangers who read this book. I may not know you, but you have made the book worth writing.

Thank you also to the following colleagues, counselors, critics, cheerleaders, and coconspirators. Your support was invaluable.

Miriam Kandiah

Ian Metcalfe

Steve Holmes

Tim Davy

Dan Strange

Natalie Collins

Graham Twelftree

Cornerstone Church

And thank you to God, my family, and other strangers. You are my world.

NOTES

INTRODUCTION

[1]Dennis Covington, *Salvation on Sand Mountain* (Boston: Da Capo Press, 2009), 204.

1 ADAM AND THE STRANGER

[1]Bruce C. Birch et al., *A Theological Introduction to the Old Testament* (Nashville: Abingdon Press, 1999), 40.

[2]For an exploration of place and theology, see Graeme Goldsworthy, *Gospel and Kingdom* (Carlisle: Paternoster, 1994).

[3]Philip says, "Lord, show us the Father and that will be enough for us," to which Jesus replies, "Anyone who has seen me has seen the Father. How can you say, 'Show us the Father'?" (John 14:8-9).

[4]Francesco Femia, director of the Center for Climate and Security in Washington, DC, argues that climate change "can exacerbate those conditions that can make conflict more likely." Quoted in Hillary Mayell, "As Consumerism Spreads, Earth Suffers, Study Says," *National Geographic News*, January 12, 2004, news.nationalgeographic.com/news/2004/01/0111_040112_consumerism.html.

[5]"Rising consumption has helped meet basic needs and create jobs," said Christopher Flavin, president of Worldwatch Institute, in a statement to the press. "But as we enter a new century, this unprecedented consumer appetite is undermining the natural systems we all depend on, and making it even harder for the world's poor to meet their basic needs." Ibid.

2 ABRAHAM AND THE STRANGER

[1]See Lee Roy Martin, "Old Testament Foundations for Christian Hospitality," *Verbum et Ecclesia* 35, no. 1 (2014): article 752, www.ve.org.za/index.php/VE/article/view/752.

[2]From *havah*.

³Gordan J. Wenham, *Genesis 16–50*, Word Biblical Commentary 2 (Dallas: Word, 1998), 46.

⁴Ibid., 47.

⁵W. Robertson Smith, *Lectures on the Religion of the Semites: Fundamental Institutions* (London: A&C Black, 1927), 16.

⁶Waldemar Janzen, *Old Testament Ethics: A Paradigmatic Approach* (Louisville, KY: Westminster John Knox, 1994), 43.

⁷Christopher J. H. Wright, *The Mission of God* (Leicester: Inter-Varsity Press, 2006), 363.

⁸Ibid., 359.

⁹Wenham, *Genesis*, 50.

¹⁰Victor P. Hamilton, *Genesis 18–50*, New International Commentary on the Old Testament 2 (Grand Rapids: Eerdmans, 1995), 25.

¹¹In the book of Proverbs God is clear about his standards for human judges: "Acquitting the guilty and condemning the innocent—the LORD detests them both" (Proverbs 17:15).

¹²Hamilton, *Genesis*, 25.

¹³See James Davison Hunter, *To Change the World: The Irony, Tragedy, & Possibility of Christianity in the Late Modern World* (New York: Oxford University Press, 2010), 255ff.

¹⁴Walter Brueggemann, *Genesis*, Interpretation (Louisville, KY: Westminster John Knox, 2010), 171, 173.

¹⁵Many see homosexuality as the dominant sin of Sodom, hence homosexual practice historically was known as "sodomy." But the emphasis here is on gang rape of innocent, nonconsensual visitors, so it is not appropriate to label homosexuality as the sin of Sodom. See Wenham, *Genesis*, 55, who argues that "homosexual gang rape is being proposed, something completely at odds with the forms of all oriental hospitality."

¹⁶Judgment *is* precisely the Christian hope because the Judge is none other than the trinitarian God who calls us to share the feast. All human experience is brought into the fullness of God, through the Son who shares our humanity in every respect save sin. There can be no simplistic resolution of the horror of sin and judgment. There can only be transformation in the presence of God. Now we understand that we understand nothing. We see only the glory of divine mystery.

[17]Brueggemann, *Genesis*, 162.

[18]Mirjona Sadiku, "A Tradition of Honor, Hospitality and Blood Feuds: Exploring the Kanun Customary Law in Contemporary Albania," *Balkan Social Science Review* 3 (June 2014): 105.

[19]Lekë Dukagjini, Shtjefën Gjeçov, and Leonard Fox, *The Code of Lekë Dukagjini* (New York: Gjonlekaj, 1989), 132.

3 JACOB AND THE STRANGER

[1]C. S. Lewis, *The Horse and His Boy* (London: HarperCollins, 2009). First published by Geoffrey Bles, 1954.

[2]Ibid., 110.

[3]See Gordan J. Wenham, *Genesis 16–50*, Word Biblical Commentary 2 (Dallas: Word, 1998), 205.

[4]Three elements made this possible. First, in a Middle Eastern wedding it would be normal for the bride to be veiled. Second, it would not be unusual for wedding ceremonies to last up to a week and to proceed well into the darkness of the night. Third, alcohol was a constituent part of the celebrations.

[5]See, for example, A. Köstenberger and D. W. Jones, *God, Marriage, and Family: Rebuilding the Biblical Foundation* (Wheaton, IL: Crossway, 2004), 33: "While it is evident that some very important individuals (both reportedly godly and ungodly) in the history of Israel engaged in polygamy, the Old Testament clearly communicates that the practice of having multiple wives was a departure from God's plan for marriage. This is conveyed not only in Scripture verses that seem univocally to prohibit polygamy (cf. Deut. 17:17; Lev. 18:18), but also from the sin and general disorder that polygamy produced in the lives of those who engaged in the practice."

[6]See also Acts 10:34; Deuteronomy 10:17; James 2:1.

[7]Radiohead, "All I Need," *In Rainbows* (TBD Records, 2007). Music video: www.youtube.com/watch?v=DV1hQSt2hSE.

[8]Joyce G. Baldwin, *Haggai, Zechariah and Malachi: An Introduction and Commentary*, Tyndale Old Testament Commentaries 28 (Nottingham: Inter-Varsity Press, 1972), 241.

[9]Derek Kidner, *Genesis: An Introduction and Commentary*, vol. 1 (Nottingham: Inter-Varsity Press, 1967), 179.

[10]C. S. Lewis, *The Problem of Pain* (New York: HarperCollins, 1996), 91.

[11]Iain W. Provan, *Discovering Genesis: Content, Interpretation, Reception* (London: SPCK, 2015), 167.

[12]Wenham, *Genesis*, 292. There is some serious wordplay going on as Jacob (*Ya'aqov*) is in the Jabbok (*Yabbok*) and he gets wrestled (*wayye'aveq*).

[13]Ibid.

[14]Walter Brueggemann, *Genesis*, Interpretation (Louisville, KY: Westminster John Knox, 2010), 270, cited in Provan, *Discovering Genesis*, 168.

[15]John H. Walton, *Genesis*, NIVAC (Grand Rapids: Zondervan, 2001), 606-7, cited in Provan, *Discovering Genesis*, 167.

[16]The authorship of this poem is disputed, with many different people claiming to have penned it. Some attribute the poem to Mary Stevenson, others to the inspiration of a sermon by Charles Spurgeon, while others claim that a hymn by Mary B. Slade is the origin of the verse.

[17]Miguel D'Escota, quoted in Charles Ringma, *Cry Freedom* (Albatross Books), July 27, 1998.

4 GIDEON AND THE STRANGER

[1]William Shakespeare, *The Merry Wives of Windsor*, act 2, scene 2, line 295.

[2]G. T. Manley and D. J. Wiseman, "Judges," in *New Bible Dictionary*, ed. D. R. Wood, I. Howard Marshall, A. R. Millard, J. I. Packer, and D. J. Wiseman (Nottingham: Inter-Varsity Press, 1996).

[3]Barry G. Webb, *The Book of Judges*, New International Commentary on the Old Testament (Grand Rapids: Eerdmans, 2013), 227.

[4]"Internally Displaced People Figures" (2015), UNHCR accessed April 28, 2016, www.unhcr.org/pages/49c3646c23.html.

[5]See "The Job Paradox" in Krish Kandiah, *Paradoxology* (Downers Grove, IL: InterVarsity, 2017).

[6]Christine D. Pohl, *Making Room: Recovering Hospitality as a Christian Tradition* (Grand Rapids: Eerdmans, 1999), 11.

[7]King Zebah and King Zalmunna, whose respective names meant "sacrifice" and ironically "withheld its hospitality." See Arthur E. Cundall and Leon Morris, *Judges and Ruth: An Introduction and Commentary*, Tyndale Old Testament Commentaries 7 (Nottingham: Inter-Varsity Press, 1968), 115.

[8]Cundall and Morris, *Judges and Ruth*, 119.

5 NAOMI AND THE STRANGER

[1]Walter White, "Pilot," *Breaking Bad*, Season 1 (AMC, 2008), episode 1.

[2]The Hebrew Bible has several terms that recognize different kinds of "alien." See Nick Spencer, *Asylum and Immigration: A Christian Perspective on a Polarised Debate* (Carlisle: Paternoster, 2004), 85.

[3]"The book opens by clearing the stage of all male characters—not to establish notions of female superiority as some might wish, but to give us a clear view of the women and underscore the fact that the story centers on them and on their relationships with God." See Carolyn Custis James, *The Gospel of Ruth: Loving God Enough to Break the Rules* (Grand Rapids: Zondervan, Kindle Edition, 2009), location 158.

[4]Wesley J. Fuerst, *The Books of Ruth, Esther, Ecclesiastes, The Song of Songs, Lamentations,* Cambridge Bible Commentary (Cambridge: Cambridge University Press, 1975), 13.

[5]Custis James, *Gospel of Ruth*, location 397.

[6]Steve Corbett and Brian Fikkert, *When Helping Hurts: How to Alleviate Poverty Without Hurting the Poor and Yourself* (Chicago: Moody Press, 2015).

[7]Frederic William Bush, *Ruth, Esther,* Word Biblical Commentary 9 (Dallas: Word, 1998), 156: "What . . . happens at the threshing floor is as essential to the story-teller's purpose as what happened on the Moabite highway between Ruth and Naomi, or what happened in the harvest scene when Boaz praised an impoverished widow who was gleaning, or what will happen in the solemn civil hearing at the city gate. At each of these points in the story, a moment of choice is presented to both actors and audience, and at each of these points the choice is made in favor of what righteous living calls for."

[8]Arthur E. Cundall and Leon Morris, *Judges and Ruth: An Introduction and Commentary,* Tyndale Old Testament Commentaries 7 (Nottingham: Inter-Varsity Press, 1968), 288.

[9]Henri J. M. Nouwen, *Reaching Out: The Three Movements of the Spiritual Life* (New York: Image, 1975), 71-72.

6 DAVID AND THE STRANGER

[1]This quote is attributed to a monologue recorded by Rich Mullins featured on the *Here in America Bonus DVD*, cited at www.crosswalk.com/11617790/.

[2]"Instead of brokenness and contrition, holy adoration and prolonged petition, there is noisy commerce." D. A. Carson, *The Gospel According to John,* The Pillar Commentary Series (Nottingham: Inter-Varsity Press, 1991), 179.

[3]Ibid.

[4]John R. W. Stott, *The Message of Romans: God's Good News for the World* (Nottingham: Inter-Varsity Press, 2001), 370.

[5]Samuel E. Balentine, *The Hidden God* (New York: Oxford University Press, 1983), 58, cited in M. E. Tate, *Psalms 51–100*, Word Biblical Commentary 20 (Dallas: Word, 1998), 198.

[6]R. T. France, *Matthew: An Introduction and Commentary*, Tyndale New Testament Commentaries 1 (Nottingham: Inter-Varsity Press, 1985), 401.

[7]J. Carl Laney, "A Fresh Look at the Imprecatory Psalms," *Bibliotheca Sacra* 138 (1981): 35.

[8]"The proposed revision of the BCP in 1928 provided for the omission from public recitation of such portions of the Psalter as were considered incompatible with the spirit of Christianity. In some modern Anglican Prayer Books such passages are printed in brackets and are commonly omitted." See F. L. Cross and E. A. Livingstone, eds., *The Oxford Dictionary of the Christian Church*, 3rd ed. rev. (Oxford: Oxford University Press, 2005), 829.

[9]Laney, "Fresh Look at the Imprecatory Psalms," 35.

[10]These insights appear in a video series of lectures: Walter Brueggemann, *The Psalms: The Hard Road from Obedience to Praise* (Miko Productions, 2009).

[11]Walter Brueggemann, *The Psalms and the Life of Faith* (Minneapolis: Fortress Press, 1995), 71.

[12]Viktor E. Frankl, *The Harvard Lectures* (Vienna: Viktor Frankl Archives, 1961), 122, cited in V. E. Bruner and P. Woll, "The Battle Within: Understanding the Physiology of War-Zone Stress Exposure," *Social Work in Health Care* 50, no. 1 (2011).

[13]Aristotle, *Nicomachean Ethics* (Hertfordshire: Wordsworth Editions, 1996), 46.

[14]Walter Brueggemann, *Praying the Psalms: Engaging Scripture and the Life of the Spirit* (Carlisle: Paternoster, 2007), 67.

[15]Stott, *Message of Romans*, 336.

[16]Brueggemann, *Praying the Psalms*, 75.

7 ISAIAH AND THE STRANGER

[1]See William J. Dumbrell, *The Faith of Israel: A Theological Survey of the Old Testament*, 2nd ed. (Grand Rapids: Baker Academic, 2002), 109.

[2]Alec Motyer, *Isaiah: An Introduction and Commentary* (Nottingham: Inter-Varsity Press, 1999), 82.

[3]Motyer, *Isaiah*, 82.

[4]Walter Brueggemann, *Isaiah 40–66* (Louisville, KY: Westminster John Knox, 1998), 188.

[5]Josh McDowell and Bob Hostetler, *Josh McDowell's Youth Ministry Handbook: Making the Connection* (Nashville: Thomas Nelson, 200), chap. 32.

[6]Motyer, *Isaiah*, 21.

[7]Brevard S. Childs, *Isaiah: A Commentary* (Louisville, KY: Westminster John Knox, 2001), 478.

[8]John Coffey, *Exodus and Liberation: Deliverance Politics from John Calvin to Martin Luther King* (New York: Oxford University Press, 2014), 105.

[9]Brueggemann, *Isaiah*, 189.

[10]Personal interview available at www.christiantoday.com/article/meet .the.christian.woman.who.adopted.eight.children.from.a.russian .orphanage/84243.htm.

[11]Speaking at the 2006 National Prayer Breakfast, Washington, DC, cited in Greg Garrett, *We Get to Carry Each Other: The Gospel According to U2* (Louisville, KY: Westminster John Knox, 2009), 86.

[12]Henri J. M. Nouwen, *Reaching Out: The Three Movements of the Spiritual Life* (New York: Image, 1975), 65.

8 EZEKIEL AND THE STRANGER

[1]Apple Computer, Inc.

[2]Walter Isaacson, *Steve Jobs* (New York: Simon and Schuster, 2011), 112.

[3]Ezekiel 1 describes the call of Ezekiel which takes place approximately five years after his exile to Babylon. See H. L. Ellison, "Ezekiel," in *New Bible Dictionary*, ed. D. R. Wood, I. Howard Marshall, A. R. Millard, J. I. Packer, and D. J. Wiseman (Nottingham: Inter-Varsity Press, 1996), 354.

[4]Cited in Anthony Imbimbo, *Steve Jobs: The Brilliant Mind Behind Apple* (New York: Gareth Stevens, 2009), 96.

[5]Walter Isaacson, *Steve Jobs* (New York: Simon and Schuster, 2011), 457.

[6]Elaine Storkey, *Scars Across Humanity: Understanding and Overcoming Violence Against Women* (London: SPCK, 2015), 18.

[7]Ibid.

[8]Ibid., 19.

[9]In 1990, the economist Amartya Sen estimated that 100 million girls had "disappeared." That figure is much higher today. See "They Call It Gendercide," *The Economist*, March 12, 2010.

[10]Joel M. LeMon and Kent Harold Richards, eds., *Method Matters: Essays on the Interpretation of the Hebrew Bible in Honor of David L. Peterson* (Atlanta: Society of Biblical Literature, 2009).

[11]One girl under the age of fifteen is married every seven seconds, according to a new analysis by Save the Children, which reveals the scale of the threat posed by child marriage. Each year, 15 million girls are married before the age of eighteen. In developing countries one in three girls is married before the age of eighteen, and one in nine before the age of fifteen. See A. Lenhardt et al. "Every Last Girl: Free to Live, Free to Learn, Free from Harm," Save the Children (2016), 5, www.savethechildren.org.uk/sites/default/files/images/Every_Last_Girl.pdf.

[12]See Storkey, *Scars Across Humanity*.

[13]Ibid., 4.

[14]Cheryl Exum describes the way that some have read this passage as more evidence of sexism where the women are blamed for the violence against them. "It is the woman's fault that she is sexually abused because she asked for it by deliberately flaunting her husband's will (control) and thereby antagonizing him. Sexual sin is punished sexually in the most degrading way." Cited in L. Juliana and M. Claassens, "Transforming God-Language: The Metaphor of God as Abusive Spouse in Ezekiel 16 in Conversation with the Portrayal of God in *The Color Purple*," *Scriptura* 113 (2014): 1.

[15]See for example Geerhardus Vos, *Reformed Dogmatics: Theology Proper* (Bellingham, WA: Lexham Press, 2014).

[16]Louis Berkhof, *Systematic Theology,* rev. ed. (Grand Rapids: Eerdmans, 1953), 55.

[17]John Calvin, *Inst.* I.xvii.13, 227.

[18]Steve Jobs, 1994, quoted in P. Weiss, *HyperThinking: Creating a New Mindset for the Age of Networks* (Farnham: Gower, 2012), 125.

9 MARY AND THE STRANGER

[1]John Fieldsend, *A Wondering Jew* (Thame: Radec Press, 2014), 178.

[2]Stephen R. Holmes, *The Politics of Christmas* (London: Theos, 2011), 33.

[3]Luke 2:24. "Use of pigeons in sacrifice as an alternative to the usual sacrificial animals was a special concession to the poor." See John Nolland, *Luke 1:1–9:20*, Word Biblical Commentary 35A (Dallas: Word, 2002), 118.

[4]For more see Holmes, *Politics of Christmas*.

[5]Charles Wesley, "Hark the Herald Angels Sing."

[6]D. A. Carson, "Matthew," *Expositor's Bible Commentary*, vol. 8 (Grand Rapids: Zondervan, 1984), 89.

[7]E. E. Ellis, "Magi," in *New Bible Dictionary*, ed. D. R. Wood, I. Howard Marshall, A. R. Millard, J. I. Packer, and D. J. Wiseman (Nottingham: Inter-Varsity Press, 1996), 713.

[8]Tamar, Rahab, and Ruth.

[9]Carson, "Matthew," 84.

[10]Patrick Kingsley, "Top 10 Refugees' Stories," *Guardian*, May 18, 2016, www.theguardian.com/books/2016/may/18/top-10-refugees-stories.

[11]"Theologically, the baptism of Jesus identifies Jesus as the messianic servant who stands in solidarity with his people." See D. S. Dockery, "Baptism," in *Dictionary of Jesus and the Gospels*, ed. Joel B. Green, Scot McKnight, and I. Howard Marshall (Nottingham: Inter-Varsity Press, 1992), 57.

[12]Corrie Ten Boom, *The Hiding Place* (London: Hodder & Stoughton, 2012), 99.

10 YOU AND THE STRANGER

[1]Christine D. Pohl, *Making Room: Recovering Hospitality as a Christian Tradition* (Grand Rapids: Eerdmans, 1999), 22.

[2]This term forms the basis of much Catholic social teaching and is prevalent in the liberation theology of Gutierrez. Though there are many flaws in liberation theology, the insight that God shows special concern for the needy and marginalized is an important lens to apply to our reading of Scripture. See M. Higueros, "Preferential Option for the Poor," in *Global Dictionary of Theology*, ed. William A. Dyrness and Veli-Matti Kärkkäinen (Nottingham: Inter-Varsity Press, 2009), 708.

[3]Cited in Eileen Egans, *Peace Be with You: Justified Warfare or the Way of Nonviolence* (Eugene, OR: Wipf & Stock, 2004), 149.

[4]Pohl, *Making Room*, 22.

[5]Timothy J. Keller, *Ministries of Mercy: The Call of the Jericho Road*, 2nd ed. (Phillipsburg, NJ: P&R, 1997), 39-40.

[6]See the parable of the good Samaritan, as explored in the conclusion to this book.

[7]St. Basil the Great, *Homilia in illum dictum evangelii secundum Lucam: Destrueram horrea mea 7*, in *Patrologia Graeca* 31.275-78, cited in Ryan C. McIlhenny, *Render Unto God: Christianity and Capitalism in Crisis* (Cambridge: Cambridge Scholars, 2015), 13.

[8]Pohl, *Making Room*, 187.

11 JESUS AND THE STRANGER

[1]Luke uses the term *sinners* eighteen times compared to Matthew's four.

[2]David Kinnaman and Gabe Lyons, *UnChristian: What a New Generation Really Thinks About Christianity . . . and Why It Matters* (Grand Rapids: Baker Books, 2007), 28.

[3]Based on a survey sample of 867 young people. From that total, researchers recorded responses from 440 non-Christians and 305 churchgoers. From those outside the church, their perceptions of the church were as follows: anti-homosexual (91 percent), judgmental (87 percent), and hypocritical (85 percent).

[4]Lisa Sowle Cahill, *Family: A Christian Social Perspective* (Minneapolis: Fortress Press, 2000), xii.

[5]All four Gospels record the offer of wine vinegar, though it is unclear who offered it to Jesus. The wine mixed with gall, which seems to be a sedative to ease the pain, offered at the beginning of the crucifixion and which Jesus refused should not be confused with the wine vinegar, which is just the cheap wine soldiers drank that would have sustained Jesus and actually prolonged his pain. See D. A. Carson, *The Pillar Commentary Series: The Gospel According to John* (Nottingham: Inter-Varsity Press, 1991), 620.

[6]John Nolland, *Luke*, Word Biblical Commentary on the New Testament 35C (Dallas: Word, 1998), 1148.

[7]Ibid., 1147.

[8]John R. W. Stott, *The Cross of Christ* (Nottingham: Inter-Varsity Press, 1987), 335.

[9]David E. Aune, *Revelation 1–5*, Word Biblical Commentary on the New Testament 52A (Dallas: Word, 1998), 152.

[10]This is how Hebrews 10:20 seems to interpret the events.

[11]Bob Ekblad, *Reading the Bible with the Damned* (Louisville, KY: Westminster /John Knox Press, 2005), 2.

[12]John Bingham, "Churches Are Best Social Melting Pots in Modern Britain," *Telegraph*, December 7, 2014, www.telegraph.co.uk/news/religion /11276878/Churches-are-best-social-melting-pots-in-modern-Britain .html.

[13]Carson, *Gospel According to John*, 616.

[14]Dietrich Bonhoeffer, *Life Together: The Classic Explorations of Faith in Community* (San Francisco: HarperSanFrancisco, 1993), 1.

[15]Victor Hugo, *Les Misérables*, translated with an introduction by Norman Denny (London: Penguin, 1982), 87.

[16]Ibid., 111.

12 CLEOPAS AND THE STRANGER

[1]Tim Chester, *A Meal with Jesus: Discovering Grace, Community and Mission Around the Table* (Nottingham: Inter-Varsity Press, 2011), 13.

[2]N. T. Wright, *Jesus and the Victory of God* (London: SPCK, 1996), 431, cited in Luke Bretherton, *Hospitality as Holiness: Christian Witness amid Moral Diversity* (Farnham: Ashgate, 2010), 129.

[3]Nigel Slater, "The adored mother whose meals I hated. The evil stepmum who cooked like a dream. And the food that shaped my bittersweet childhood," *Daily Mail*, December 30, 2010, www.dailymail.co.uk/femail /food/article-1341290.

[4]"Being welcomed at a table for the purpose of eating food with another person had become a ceremony richly symbolic of friendship, intimacy and unity." See S. S. Bartchy, "Table Fellowship," in *Dictionary of Jesus and the Gospels*, ed. Joel B. Green, Scot McKnight, and I. Howard Marshall (Nottingham: Inter-Varsity Press, 1992), 796.

[5]Chester, *Meal with Jesus*, 9.

[6]C. S. Lewis, "The Weight of Glory," in *Transposition and Other Addresses* (London: Geoffrey Bles, 1949), 29-30.

[7]Rodney Stark, *The Rise of Christianity: How the Obscure, Marginal Jesus Movement Became the Dominant Religious Force in the Western World in a Few Centuries* (San Francisco: HarperSanFrancisco, 1997), 3.

[8]Ibid., 87-88.

[9]Ibid., 76.

[10]Ibid., 77.

[11]Ibid., 82.

CONCLUSION

[1]Jeffrey Archer, *Twelve Red Herrings* (London: HarperCollins, 1994), 240ff.

[2]Jonathan Sacks, *Faith in the Future* (London: Darton, Longman & Todd, 1995), 78.

[3]Timothy Keller, *Generous Justice: How God's Grace Makes Us Just* (New York: Riverhead Books, 2010), 67-68.

[4]Peter Singer, "The Drowning Child and the Expanding Circle," *New Internationalist*, April 5, 1997.

[5]J. M. Darley and C. D. Batson, "'From Jerusalem to Jericho': A Study of Situational and Dispositional Variables in Helping Behavior," *Journal of Personality and Social Psychology* 27, no. 1 (1973): 107, doi: 10.1037/h0034449.

ALSO AVAILABLE

Missio Alliance

Missio Alliance has arisen in response to the shared voice of pastors and ministry leaders from across the landscape of North American Christianity for a new "space" of togetherness and reflection amid the issues and challenges facing the church in our day. We are united by a desire for a fresh expression of evangelical faith, one significantly informed by the global evangelical family. Lausanne's Cape Town Commitment, "A Confession of Faith and a Call to Action," provides an excellent guidepost for our ethos and aims.

Through partnerships with schools, denominational bodies, ministry organizations, and networks of churches and leaders, Missio Alliance addresses the most vital theological and cultural issues facing the North American Church in God's mission today. We do this primarily by convening gatherings, curating resources, and catalyzing innovation in leadership formation.

Rooted in the core convictions of evangelical orthodoxy, the ministry of Missio Alliance is animated by a strong and distinctive theological identity that emphasizes

Comprehensive Mutuality: Advancing the partnered voice and leadership of women and men among the beautiful diversity of the body of Christ across the lines of race, culture, and theological heritage.

Hopeful Witness: Advancing a way of being the people of God in the world that reflects an unwavering and joyful hope in the lordship of Christ in the church and over all things.

Church in Mission: Advancing a vision of the local church in which our identity and the power of our testimony is found and expressed through our active participation in God's mission in the world.

In partnership with InterVarsity Press, we are pleased to offer a line of resources authored by a diverse range of theological practitioners. The resources in this series are selected based on the important way in which they address and embody these values, and thus, the unique contribution they offer in equipping Christian leaders for fuller and more faithful participation in God's mission.

missioalliance.org | twitter.com/missioalliance | facebook.com/missioalliance